A Son of the Game

To Patrick —
A true son of the game.
(Sandy and I save His
fan in Myrtle Beach!)

April 2005

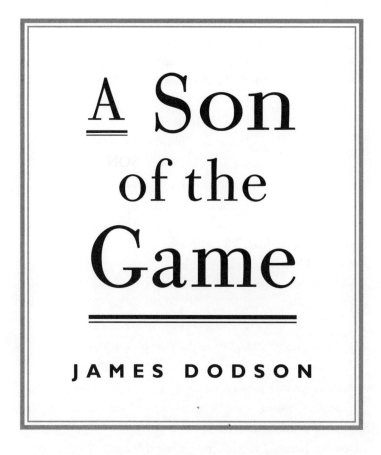

A Son
of the
Game

JAMES DODSON

Algonquin Books of Chapel Hill 2009

Published by
Algonquin Books of Chapel Hill
Post Office Box 2225
Chapel Hill, North Carolina 27515-2225

a division of
Workman Publishing
225 Varick Street
New York, New York 10014

Published simultaneously in Canada by Thomas Allen & Son Limited.
Design by Anne Winslow.

Library of Congress Cataloging-in-Publication Data
Dodson, James.
    A son of the game / James Dodson.
       p. cm.
    ISBN-13: 978-1-56512-506-3
    1. Dodson, James.   2. Golfers—United States—Biography.
    3. Fathers and sons—United States.   4. Pinehurst Resort &
    Country Club (Pinehurst, N.C.)   I. Title.
    GV964.D63D64 2009
    796.352092—dc22
    [B]   2008052219

10 9 8 7 6 5 4 3 2 1
First Edition

To my friends Max, Myrtis, and Jean;
To Tom, Ilana, and Bryan;
For opening your hearts and doors.
But most of all—to Jack, my best golf pal of all.

Every man is the son of his own works.

—MIGUEL DE CERVANTES SAAVEDRA

Tell your story of hard luck shots,
Of each shot straight and true;
But when you are done, remember, Son—
That nobody cares but you!

—EPITAPH OF JOE KIRKWOOD,
GOLF GREAT AND TRICK SHOT ARTIST

You, yesterday's boy,
To whom confusion came:
Listen, lest you forget who you are.
It was not pleasure you fell into,
It was joy.

—RAINER MARIA RILKE

A Son of the Game

The Last Amateur

Toward the end of a clear winter afternoon, I reached the front porch of the Pine Crest Inn and put down my travel bag. A small orange cat got up from a final patch of sunlight and walked over to greet me.

"Hello, Marmalade," I said, stooping to scratch her behind the ears. "Long time no see. Looks like you've put on some weight, old girl. That makes two of us."

"You two must be old friends," a woman said pleasantly.

She was sitting in a white rocking chair a few yards away, dressed for dinner and enjoying a glass of white wine. A group of other well-dressed guests sat by the outdoor bar at the far end of the hotel's porch, laughing and talking about their day's golf adventures.

"We are," I confirmed, "though she probably doesn't know me from Greg Norman's house cat."

Marmalade's unique talent, I explained, was an ability to recognize anyone who loves golf and keeps returning to Pinehurst year after year, which could pretty much describe every person who arrives on the porch of the Pine Crest.

Set on a graceful curve of Dogwood Road, just off the square of one of America's most picturesque village centers, the homey Pine Crest Inn, the world's most charming and eccentric golf hostelry, has been welcoming discriminating golf travelers to Pinehurst — the self-described "Home of American Golf" — for almost a hundred years. In this golf traveler's case, it has been his home away from home since he was a young boy trailing after his old man's game.

"What a nice evening it is going to be," the woman observed, looking at the fading winter light. "Are you here for the golf tournament, too?"

This was a natural assumption for her to make. With more than forty golf clubs scattered across the region, called the Sandhills of Central North Carolina, it's a safe bet there is always some kind of golf tournament going on somewhere in either the Village of Pinehurst or its larger neighboring town, Southern Pines.

"No, ma'am. I'm just here to finish some work and say good-bye to a friend."

She smiled and swirled the last of her wine. "I can't imagine why anyone would want to leave *this* place. My husband is ready to sell everything and move here tomorrow."

"I know the feeling," I said. "Unfortunately, my friend doesn't have any choice. He's dying."

The words slipped out, perhaps because she was the first person I'd spoken more than ten words to in almost as many days. During that time, I'd been driving slowly south from my longtime home in Maine to my old Carolina stomping ground, allowing myself a little space and time to reflect on several recent upheavals in my life.

The woman in the rocker blushed with embarrassment. "Oh, I'm so *sorry*. Now I *have* gone too far. Please forgive me."

"That's okay," I assured her, scratching Marmalade behind the ears. The queen of the Pine Crest was purring faintly, eyes squeezed shut. "Marmalade's just happy to still be here. I am, too."

TRUMAN CAPOTE ONCE observed that every son of the South eventually comes home again — if only in a box.

Perhaps fear of this fate explains why, for better or worse, during the quarter century I'd lived in northern New England, I'd returned on a fairly regular basis to my boyhood haunts of Pinehurst and Southern Pines, coming back whenever my spirits needed a lift or my ailing golf game required a jump start. This is where I played my first full eighteen holes of golf — as a hotheaded, club-tossing teenager — and where I eventually learned to calm down, grow up, play by the rules, and as my late father once put it, appreciate the "higher game." The simple truth is, after laying eyes on the splendors of Pinehurst and Southern Pines, I never threw another club in anger again — at least not when my dad was anywhere in sight. And though it took me some years to realize it, I never felt more at home anyplace else.

"If it's true a writer's world is shaped by the experiences of childhood and adolescence," Mississippian Willie Morris wrote after he abandoned the literary salons of Manhattan for his native Yazoo, "then returning at long last to the scenes of those experiences, remembering them anew, and living among their changing heartbeats gives him the primary pulses and shocks he cannot afford to lose."

Perhaps, in my case, the perpetual attraction was as simple as that: As my life changed and moved in new and unexpected directions, as my children grew up and middle age came on, there were heartbeats I simply couldn't afford to miss back here in the ancient Carolina Sandhills, a place where so many of my fondest and happiest and most uncomplicated memories lay as unchanged and welcoming as the front porch of the Pine Crest. Both my parents were devoted patrons of this funky and beloved hotel. The first night I ever spent here in 1969 was in an upstairs corner room beneath the rafters, and it was here the Barrett family, the Pine Crest's longtime owners, always stashed me when I came calling.

In this instance, duty summoned in the form of the galley proof of a forthcoming book, waiting for me at the front desk of the hotel, a comprehensive biography of golf legend Ben Hogan that was supposed to have taken two years to research and write but in fact required almost four years of diligent work.

A bittersweet happiness comes with finishing a book. Suffice it to say, keeping in mind Arnold Toynbee's famous admonition that a faithful biographer must "live" his subject's life if he hopes to capture the person's essence, I was deeply relieved to have the Hawk, perhaps the most mythic yet misunderstood sports figure in American history, safely translated to the page and easing his way out of my life—to say nothing of my wife Wendy's feelings on the subject. In many ways, "living" Ben Hogan's dark but ultimately redeeming life had turned my own inside out and, unexpectedly, drained away my zest for playing the game. This was one of several mysteries I had come to Pinehurst to try and decipher. Was this a condition of age or circumstance, the result of too much work and too little play? Or maybe something else entirely?

I felt real pleasure in the prospect of reading over the final proof pages and officially signing off on the project, yet it was mitigated by the other solemn reason I'd circled around to Pinehurst again, which was to say goodbye to my friend, Harvie Ward.

During the early 1950s, ironically just as Hogan's star began to fade, Edward Harvie Ward rose out of the green-gold vastness of rural eastern North Carolina to become the most admired and thrilling player in the game of golf.

During the spring of 1948, cheered on by his rowdy fraternity brothers from Chapel Hill and wielding a wooden-shafted putter he'd found as a kid on a bench in the locker room of his father's nine-hole golf club in tiny Tarboro, Ward came out of nowhere to win the coveted North and South Amateur Championship at Pinehurst, making himself a star overnight. After college, while working as a stockbroker in Atlanta, Ward captured the 1952 British Amateur Championship at Prestwick, then beat out his longtime college rival Arnold Palmer and a host of other supremely talented amateur players to win the U.S. Amateur Championship in both 1955 and 1956. With his movie-star good looks, witty frat-boy charisma, and a playing temperament that never lost its cool, Ward became the darling of the national sports media and the toast of American golf. Wherever he went, sportswriters exhausted themselves finding superlatives to describe his playing abilities, while adoring college girls trailed dreamily in his wake.

No less a golf legend than Byron Nelson proclaimed Harvie

to be "the next Ben Hogan," and most observers believed the affable son of a small-town pharmacist was on track to win an unprecedented third National Amateur title—until unimagined disaster struck.

Following a wave of scandals that emerged from IRS investigations into huge illegal payouts given to amateur players at amateur golf tournaments held at several prominent private clubs, Ward became the scapegoat of the darkest episode in USGA history, alleged to have been financially subsidized—essentially paid to play golf as an amateur. In a sweeping sanction that shook golf to its core, the governing body of golf in America suspended Ward's amateur status and prevented him from going after an unprecedented third consecutive National Amateur Championship, a fall from grace that effectively ended the age of the golden amateur.

Harvie Ward disappeared quietly into a whiskey bottle and effectively stayed there for the next thirty years, bitterly drinking away the most promising game, many felt, since Bobby Jones.

One morning not long after the 1999 U.S. Open at Pinehurst, Harvie and I met for the first time for breakfast at the Pine Crest, a meeting arranged by our mutual pal Tom Stewart. After four failed marriages and a failed attempt to jump-start a professional career, Ward had finally sobered up and returned to Pinehurst to establish himself as one of the premier teachers in the game.

"That turned out to be the smartest decision I ever made—*we* ever made," Harvie told me emphatically in his soft Carolina drawl. "Without Joanne, see, none of this would have ever happened. I would probably have been dead years ago."

The next morning, I met Harvie and Joanne Ward in the

cheerful lobby of the Carolina Hotel, and the three of us had coffee and a long chat about the possibility of finally telling Harvie's amazing story in detail—the rise and fall and unlikely rebirth of the greatest player who once, briefly, ruled the game.

We agreed to get under way the moment I finished work on Hogan's biography, which I had only recently begun researching. Coming off successful bypass surgery, Harvie assured me there was no rush, that his long-range prospects were excellent.

He said he felt like a man with a new lease on life. "You go take care of Ben," he cheerfully put to me, offering his hand. "I'll be waiting for you when you're ready to get going on our little thing."

We decided to call it "The Last Amateur."

"You'll have to excuse my appearance," Harvie said wryly as he led me back to his sunny den where some pointless end-of-the-season golf event was flickering on a large plasma TV screen. "I've spent all night partying with a bunch of crazy Chi Omegas and did a quick eighteen before breakfast this morning."

Not long after that handshake at the Pinehurst Resort, a routine checkup showed spots on Harvie's liver which turned out to be cancer. He had more surgery and for a while seemed to be recovering nicely. But not long after my fiftieth birthday, the phone rang and it was Harvie calling from Pinehurst.

"If we're gonna talk, Old Champ," he drawled in his inimitable Harvie way, "you'd better get on down to Tobacco Road. I can just about see the clubhouse from here."

I knew from Harvie's physician, a young Pinehurst doctor and golf nut named Walt Morris, that he'd recently completed a last-ditch round of chemotherapy up in Chapel Hill, attempting to reverse the aggressive progress of the disease. Several new experimental therapies had been attempted. None had worked.

Harvie looked exhausted but grinned at me impishly. The Chi Omega joke was a running gag between us. "There was a day, you see, when my eyes were blue and *both* my pecker and my putter were red hot," he added right on cue. "Now, unfortunately, in both cases, it's the other way around."

We both laughed. The laughter helped ease the painful awareness that, owing to my delays in the Hogan book and his rampaging cancer, we'd probably run out of time to collaborate. So we sat and talked about other things for more than an hour, carefully avoiding the topic of "The Last Amateur."

He asked me how my son Jack's game was progressing, and I explained that Jack, who was thirteen, exactly the age I'd been when my dad brought me down a winding road to Pinehurst, had recently attempted to organize a golf team at his middle school in Maine.

"Does he love the game the way you did at his age?"

"He says he does." I told Harvie how after I took him with me on a Hogan research trip to Fort Worth and left him for the week out at Hank Haney's Golf Ranch in Lewisville, Jack came away with a fine golf swing and declaring he would soon be the best schoolboy golfer in the state of Maine—maybe even go to college on a golf scholarship.

"We'll see how it works out," I said. "You know how kids are. He seems to have a dozen other interests at the moment."

"Give it time. Something will light the fire in his belly,"

Harvie said quietly, nodding. "I'd sure looked forward to getting him out to Forest Creek."

A year or so previously, while on our way to play a round of golf with Tom Stewart and his son Bryan at the Mid South Club, Jack had briefly met Harvie on the range at Forest Creek, the outstanding new private club north of town where Harvie was teaching a host of promising young players, including the current North Carolina schoolboy champ. The two seemed to have good chemistry. Harvie promised to give Jack his first putting lesson the next time he came back to the Sandhills. In his prime, Harvie Ward was possibly the finest putter in the game.

I nodded and smiled. "That would have been great."

Golf, as journalist Henry Longhurst once observed, is the Esperanto of sports — the finest game on earth for making enduring friendships and passing along something of value to others. In my case, like golfing dads and moms everywhere — like my own father before me — I simply hoped my son might develop a genuine interest in playing a marvelous old game that teaches timeless lessons while remaining new and different every time you play it.

Moreover, the chance for my son to be exposed to the wit and brilliance of one of the finest teachers, and nicest fellows, in the game was a major bonus of helping Harvie put his story on paper. If golf brought Jack only half the pleasure and friendships it had brought both Harvie and me, this would be a father's gift for a lifetime. And for my part, I looked forward to the day I had a ready golf partner and reliable opponent to carry me into my golfing dotage, just as I had done for my dad.

After sitting and talking for an hour about his hopes to go

to Merion Golf Club in Philadelphia for the fiftieth anniversary celebration of his U.S. Amateur Championship and maybe "take a spin out West to see old friends in California and putter around Cypress Point a little," meaning the famous Monterey course where Ward, Hogan, Byron Nelson, and Ken Venturi once played perhaps the most dramatic golf match ever, Harvie walked me to his front door. Joanne had warned me that his strength might suddenly give out.

Two large golf bags stood on either side of the entry. Harvie pulled a putter out of one and casually handed it to me. "Do me a favor and give this to Jack," he said quietly. "Tell him it's from ol' Harv. I wish I could have given him that putting lesson."

This act, so graceful and unexpected and fraught with avuncular tenderness, was more than a little symbolic. The putter was an ordinary Odyssey White Hot No. 2, but it looked well used and loved. I held the putter in my hands, feeling my throat constrict. When I looked back at my host, Harvie's blue eyes bored straight into my head as though reading my anxious thoughts.

"I forgot to ask how things are with you these days," he said. "Everything ever get straightened out at the magazine?"

I nodded faintly, groping to find the right words. It didn't seem the moment to air my work troubles.

In fact, my seemingly rock-steady life had begun to unravel in ways I'd never seen coming. First my mom passed away shortly after I took her out of her home of fifty years in Greensboro and moved her eight hundred miles north to an assisted-living facility on the coast of Maine. Then two of my longtime golf partners died unexpectedly, essentially dissolving my regular golf group of nearly twenty years. Not long after this, the golf publication that had been my happy professional home for nigh on twenty years got purchased by a media colossus that promptly fired its legendary editor and began systematically cleaning out the staff—putting my best friends and colleagues on the street and gutting one of the top golf magazines in the business. The new editor had invited me to stay on the masthead, but to do so felt totally disloyal and a complete betrayal of the values I believed in. I was still wrestling with what to do about this matter, though in my heart I knew my magazine days were over.

That's when Harvie called to tell me his liver cancer had returned—devastating news, the final blow to a reeling psyche. I'd been as excited as a kid at the prospect of beginning work on "The Last Amateur," which meant spending time in my favorite place in the world, playing golf with Tom Stewart and his son, Bryan, and watching Harvie Ward light the flame beneath Jack.

"Everything's fine," I calmly lied, hoping he believed this at least half as much as I needed to myself.

Harvie cleared his throat. "Here's what I think, Old Champ. You ought to come back to the U.S. Open in 2005 and bring Jack with you. That would do you both a world of good."

"If Jack wants to come, I'll probably come," I said.

"No," he said a little more forcefully, as if I'd missed his point. "I'm thinking you should come back for the Open and then stick around."

"You mean to live?"

Harvie nodded. "You know what they say, don't you? You can take the boy out of Carolina but not the other way around. Maybe you should give some thought to coming back here the way I did."

I smiled, but said nothing. This thought had long been lodged in the back of my brain, I confess—probably at least since I was a teenager banging around Southern Pines on a borrowed bicycle—but at this stage of my full and complicated life, I couldn't imagine how that could ever happen.

Harvie reached over and took hold of my arm. "Let me tell you something," he said quietly. "This place saved my life and gave me a happiness I never found anyplace else."

"I know that," I said respectfully. "It seems to have that effect on a lot of people."

Harvie glanced out at his yard. It was a perfect mild winter afternoon in the home American golf. A yardman was raking up distinctive longleaf pine cones into a pile near the curb. A number of seconds passed. Harvie eventually looked at me again.

"Maybe you ought to come back and find out why this place seems to cure people of their problems. That's why old man Tufts founded the place, you know. Golf had nothing to do with it originally. There was something magical here in these old pines—nobody has ever figured out what exactly. You'd think, as a son of the place, you'd want to come back and find out what it is."

He gave me a peculiar smile, as if he knew something I didn't.

"You know, Hogan always said this place saved his life and playing career. He called it the Pinehurst *cure*. But I guess you know that better than anyone."

I nodded again. The story was very familiar to me, though the phrase wasn't. It made perfect sense, however, given what happened to the Hawk in Pinehurst. It was nothing shy of a personal epiphany, a lifesaving transformation.

"So what next for you?" Harvie asked. He was still holding my arm.

For a moment, I wasn't sure what he meant. For me the future seemed to lie like heavy fog on an Angus fairway.

"Tom and I are going to play golf tomorrow," I explained lightly. "Then I might have lunch with some guy named David Woronoff on Monday. He says he wants to talk with me about the upcoming Open. After that, I guess, I'll head up the road to Maine."

Harvie smiled. "I know David. Nice young fellow. He owns *The Pilot* newspaper. He bought the house I lived in over in Southern Pines when I first came back to North Carolina. He probably wants to offer you a job."

I shrugged and smiled. I didn't have the heart to tell Harvie that during the long drive south, I'd decided to take a much-needed sabbatical from the world of golf writing in order to research and write a book about the competitive world of horticulture.

I thanked Harvie for his friendly advice and said goodbye, aware that I probably would never see him again.

As I walked along Blue Road, slowly swinging the putter Harvie was sending to Jack, I vaguely wondered what kind of player my son might have become under his tutelage. In the near distance, I heard the hourly carillon serenely drifting from the bell tower of the historic Village Chapel, its steeple rising through the longleaf pines.

I knew this stately hymn, I realized, "Blessed Be the Tie That Binds," a bittersweet anthem from my vanished boyhood. But for the life of me, having been away too long, I couldn't recall the words.

CHAPTER ONE

Pants That Just Say Pinehurst

A T THE END OF Spring 2005, on my way to cover the 105th United States Open Championship at Pinehurst, I stopped off to buy a new pair of pants.

I realize how unexciting this sounds, but buying new pants is a rare event for me, something I do about as frequently as Americans go to the polls to elect a new president, which may explain why my pants, always tan cotton khakis, look as if they've seen better days.

In this instance, it was a perfect Sunday afternoon, twelve days before the start of our national golfing championship, and I'd just rolled into Pinehurst following a long drive from Maine.

Actually, when I arrived, I had no intention of buying pants. I was mostly worrying about locating the small log cottage in the middle of Southern Pines that I'd rented sight unseen via telephone from a local realtor named Ed Rhodes, who casually informed me the key would be waiting beneath a stone angel by the back door. I was also vaguely wondering if I'd made the dumbest career move of my life by agreeing to go to work for the Southern Pines *Pilot,* the award-winning community newspaper of the Carolina Sandhills.

Some guys, when facing a midlife crisis, roguishly splurge on a red sports car, or get hair plugs, or maybe even buy a secret condo in Cancún. Fresh from a year in which I'd traveled to Africa with exotic plant hunters and loitered at the elbows of some of the world's top horticulture experts, I'd merely yielded to the persuasive charms of *The Pilot*'s enthusiastic young publisher, David Woronoff, scion of a distinguished Old North State newspaper clan. Almost on a whim, I'd agreed to write a daily golf column for the paper's ambitious *Open Daily* tabloid during U.S. Open week. There was also a friendly conversation about the possibility of my staying on to write a Sunday essay after the Open circus left town, though nothing had been formally proposed, much less agreed upon. That wasn't by accident.

Truthfully, I feared that I had little in the way of wit or current insight to offer *The Pilot* and its Open readers because, factoring in the four long years my brain had been focused upon the distant, well-ordered world of Ben Hogan and another kind of America, and adding two years for my absorbing romp through the garden world, I'd been out of the current game for a small eternity. Since the death of Harvie Ward and the dissolution of my longtime golf group back in Maine, in fact, I'd scarcely touched my own clubs or watched a golf tournament on television or even felt much desire to read about who was doing what in a game I'd loved, it seemed, forever.

Like some sad, burned-out bureaucrat from a Graham Greene novel, I'd even begun to consider the once-unthinkable possibility that my hiatus from golf and the golf world, rather than rekindling my desire to play and restoring interest in the professional game as well, had radically cooled my passion and turned my game to sawdust.

This realization had come during the drive, when I'd stopped off to compete with a friend named Howdy Giles in his one-day member-guest event at Pine Valley Golf Club in New Jersey. Though Pine Valley is justly famous for its strategic brilliance and difficulty, I often play the course surprisingly well for a casual player, typically managing to achieve my five- or six-stroke handicap. In this instance, I thought my lengthy time away from the game might even serve to boost my prospects of making a decent score—partly because I tend to play better golf on a difficult course and partly because some of my best rounds of golf have come following the long winter layoffs every New Englander comes to know.

Well, the golf gods must have needed a good belly laugh that day. By the fourth hole, I was six over par, and by the end of the first nine, I'd jotted a big fat fifty on the card—probably my worst competitive nine holes in forty years. The anger and embarrassment I felt made me want to grab my clubs and bolt.

"Don't worry about it," my genial host assured me at the halfway house, as I licked my wounds, guzzled Arnold Palmer iced tea, and wondered if perhaps I was through with golf or, more likely, if golf was through with me. "You'll put it together on the back nine," Howdy confidently said. I wasn't so sure.

Fortunately, Howdy was right. I shot a not-quite-so-horrific forty-five. As I left the grounds of the world's number-one-ranked golf course, my cell phone rang. It was my son Jack calling, curious to know how the old man had fared that afternoon.

Originally Jack had planned to accompany me to Pinehurst to work as a standard-bearer with his friend Bryan Stewart at the U.S. Open. But late spring snows in Maine had extended his freshman-year high school classes all the way to the start of Open week. There was still an outside chance he might fly down on Tuesday of that week, however, and find a spot working in the National Open. This was my great hope, anyway. I wanted the time with my son, and I also felt the experience would be invaluable for him.

"Let's just say I left the course record more or less intact." I attempted to shrug off the disaster, fessing up to my woeful ninety-five.

"Gosh, what *happened*?" Jack sounded genuinely astounded and also a little disappointed. After all, one of the carrots I'd long held out to him was a promise to play shrines like Pine Valley, Pebble Beach, and Pinehurst No. 2 if and when his game reached a level those courses demanded. "Pine Valley must be *really* hard," he said.

"It is hard, Nibs. Make no mistake. But truthfully I was just awful today. I hit every kind of bad shot you can—hooks, shanks, even a whiff. I five-putted a hole from twenty feet."

"Maybe you should have played a little more before you went there," he said, politely stating the obvious.

"You're right. I should have," I agreed, wondering if the lengthy hiatus had done more serious damage to my game than I realized.

DESPITE MY MISGIVINGS, David seemed to have no doubts about why he wanted me to work for *The Pilot*.

"Between you and me," David had confided at lunch in a crowded café overlooking Southern Pines' picturesque main street the morning after I said goodbye to Harvie, "we're eager to show the national media that Pinehurst is *our* golf turf, not theirs. We'd like *you* to help us do that."

David explained that during the 1999 Open at Pinehurst, *The Pilot* had broken new ground by being the first to publish a comprehensive, full-color daily tabloid newspaper, fifty-six pages in length, for the two hundred thousand spectators who attended the Open, a publishing feat for which Woronoff and his staff had collected a pile of industry awards. Now, he said, for the 2005 Open, they were out to reprise their effort and in the process double the output in pages and increase market penetration.

"This is where you come in," he said, sipping his iced tea. "I took a poll, phoned everybody I could think of in the golf world, and asked the same question: If I could get one nationally known golf writer to come write exclusively for us for the Open, who should I try to get? Your name kept coming up. I know we can't possibly pay you what the national media guys do. But on the other hand, I've read your books and know from Tom Stewart and others how connected you are to the Sandhills."

"This is where I learned to play the game—or at least to re-spect it," I admitted, thinking of the venerable Mid Pines Golf Club where I learned to quit throwing my clubs.

David smiled. "*Exactly.* That's why I'm hoping you might agree to come do this—on a lark, I don't know, for the pure fun of it. We can't pay you much, but I can promise you all the barbecue and sweet tea you want."

I tried to remember the last time I did anything purely for the fun of it. I believe Jerry Ford was in office then. Double knit slacks and Day-Glo orange golf balls were all the rage.

As it happened, being a son of both the Old North State and the newspaper business, I knew a little about *The Pilot*'s illustrious past. The paper had once been owned by Sam Ragan, the poet laureate of North Carolina, and its unlikely literary roots reached all the way to New York's famed Algonquin Round Table, owing to James Boyd, a Southern Pines horseman and adventure writer whose best-selling books about the Revolutionary War, one of them illustrated by N. C. Wyeth, had sat on a bookshelf in my own boyhood bedroom. Boyd, who had run with a crowd that included Thomas Wolfe and Scott Fitzgerald, had owned *The Pilot* sometime in the 1940s and 1950s. That, however, was pretty much all I knew about the newspaper.

Then I casually mentioned something that sealed my fate.

"Here's a strange coincidence," I said to David. "My dad was a small-town newspaperman, like you. He once owned—and, through no failure of his own, lost—a weekly newspaper called the Gulfport *Pilot and Breeze* down in Mississippi. My first memories of life come from that little newspaper. Maybe I'll tell you about it sometime. It's quite a story."

"I'd love to hear it." David replied thoughtfully. He paused a respectful beat, then added, "Well, *The Pilot* is *my* dream. Remind me to tell you what I went through just to get this newspaper. Basically, I stalked the dying owner for two years and almost had to name my second daughter after him before he would agree to sell it to me. Imagine having to tell your pregnant wife that your infant daughter is going to be named Sam Ragan."

David Woronoff's congenial friendliness and small-town optimism struck a familiar chord. Then it hit me who he reminded
me of: my own dad. The resemblance was, in fact, uncanny, and
not a little disarming.

David smiled. "So, I guess we've *both* got printer's ink in the
blood, huh? Sounds to me like you're almost *destined* to come
write for *The Pilot*. In fact, if you want to, you can stay on and
write for us after the Open leaves town. I'll bet your dad would
like that."

For a moment I considered this unforeseen development,
coming essentially out of nowhere, in the midst of my midlife
career crisis. On paper, at this stage of my busy life, going to
work for *The Pilot* didn't make sense. To begin with, the money
he would offer was undoubtedly a fraction of my regular pay for
magazine work, and it would mean somehow having to create
two homes and be in two places at once, because I was fairly
certain no one in my immediate family was eager to pull up
stakes and on a lark move to North Carolina simply so I could
reconnect with my redneck roots. My wife, Wendy, was im-
mersed in teaching at-risk kids in the public schools and was active in community affairs. My children, Maggie and Jack, were
enjoying high school. For a decade, their mom and I had shared
legal custody of them, an agreeable arrangement that had them
spending equal time at both their homes.

As if these factors weren't deterrent enough, I'd recently
agreed to serve as writer-in-residence at Hollins University in
Virginia for the spring 2006 term, a distinguished teaching ap-
pointment I was thrilled to have been offered but still had logis-
tically to work out.

"Well congratulations," David said, not appearing to think that any of these obligations presented a roadblock to his ultimate aims. "If Hollins doesn't happen till next year, why, you could stick around and keep writing for *The Pilot*. We could make you *our* writer-in-residence, too!"

"I've never heard of a newspaper having a writer-in-residence," I pointed out.

"Neither have I. So we'll be the first," he said pleasantly. "We're famous for our firsts at *The Pilot*."

"I still have to figure out how I'm going to alternate two-week intervals between Virginia and Maine. I've developed a serious aversion to airports," I countered. "I can't imagine adding the Sandhills to the scenario. Then I'd have to be three places at once, or at least once a month."

"You could figure it out," he said mildly. "I can tell you really want to do it. Enthusiasm makes most things possible."

I studied David Woronoff. He looked scarcely old enough to attend an R-rated movie on his own. One thing was for sure, the boy publisher of the Sandhills didn't throw in the towel easily. But then, neither had my father, a man whose sunny persistence never failed him. "Our best days," he liked to say, "are ahead of us." In time I would learn that this was one of David's guiding beliefs as well.

Thinking all this over, trying to weigh the upsides against the downs, I glanced out the window of the restaurant just as a kid in a striped T-shirt pedaled by on an old-fashioned bike. I suddenly remembered being that kid.

In its own way, Southern Pines was even prettier than nearby Pinehurst, more of a working town, with a railroad bisecting its thriving Main Street area into two neat halves. With its handsome old houses, towering magnolias, and sensible grid of streets named for New England and Midwestern states, Southern Pines—which an enterprising Southerner created to lure wealthy Yankees south and disencumber them from their money—was like a New England town set smack in the middle of the sleepy South. As towns go, it felt like a place that combined the best of both worlds: small town Southern life and Yankee village ingenuity.

"You know," I said, suddenly embarking on a foolish trip down memory lane, "when I was a kid my parents had some friends named Howie and Brenda Butz. I think Howie worked with my dad at the *Washington Post*. They lived in a big old house on Massachusetts Avenue and had three or four kids, all girls—prissy, *bossy*, red-haired girls. We once went to visit them after playing golf at Mid Pines and stayed for supper. I was twelve or thirteen at the time. It was complete torture, till I found an old bicycle in their garage and escaped by pedaling all over Southern Pines. I decided this was the coolest town I'd ever seen and began to secretly wish we could live here instead of Greensboro, even if it meant I had to go to school with the ugly Butz sisters."

David smiled. "Man, did you ever *blow* it. I think they all grew up to be supermodels. We had a piece on the Butz girls."

I liked this guy. And I sensed I might enjoy working for him. I couldn't help wondering if he possessed a decent golf swing.

"Truthfully, I always had this crazy fantasy about someday living here," I confessed, "playing golf on weekends, writing about whatever passed in front of my nose. Kind of like Charlie Kuralt and E. B. White and Russell Baker rolled into one. That would be the life."

David smiled. "Well, I'm the guy who can make *that* kind of fantasy happen. We may be small town but we're not small time." He explained that *The Pilot* was full of refugees and talented bail-outs from wider spots on the information highway. This included the editor of *The Pilot*, the paper's ad director, even the circulation manager. "They either burned out or got sick of the bureaucracy and jumped at the chance to come live in a place where life is more sane and civilized—and the golf is great. They'll tell you that coming here has given them a new lease on life. Ask 'em."

"Maybe I will," I said, thinking I could use a new lease on life—or at least a fresh start of some kind.

"If you do come," David chipped in, "you could even play in our majors."

"You have *majors?*"

"A guy named John Dempsey and I ranked all the charity golf tournaments in town. Dempsey is the president of the local community college—a total golf nut. Your kind of guy. There's a charity golf event just about every week starting in October."

"I'm taking a sabbatical from all things golf," I felt obliged to inform him. "I'm not sure when—or if—I'll ever be back. Between you and me, I'm pretty fed up with the professional game right now. I can only bear to watch the majors these days. Haven't yet figured out whether that's because I'm such an old fogey or because the Tour has grown so colorless I can't tell one player from the next save for Phil and Tiger. I'm hoping a long break from the game will recharge my batteries."

"Not a problem. Everyone needs a break. I'll bet you'll come back raring to go—to *play* and write golf."

"I hope you're right," I said, thinking how few things in life had given me more enjoyable moments, or better friends, than this funny old game.

So here I was, still smarting from the beating I'd taken from Pine Valley but oddly relieved to be rolling into the Sandhills to take possession of a log cottage I'd never laid eyes on and to report to work at my first deadline newspaper job in more than thirty-five years.

My reverie was interrupted when my mobile phone rang out. The caller turned out to be my wife, simply checking to see if I'd survived my all-night drive from Pine Valley. She undoubtedly felt some responsibility for my being here, because it was she who had pushed me out the door to go say goodbye to Harvie Ward, which in turn led me to the lunch with David Woronoff and this unexpected new job. At this point, I hoped my revived golf writing would turn out to be considerably better than my revived golf playing.

"I'm safely here," I told her, "just passing good old Belk department store. That's where I used to buy my scout stuff about half a million years ago."

"Oh, good," she responded. "Why don't you stop in there and get some nice new pants. Not scout pants, honey—golf pants."

"But I don't need new golf pants," I argued pointlessly. "My old golf pants are only three years old. They haven't even been through a full presidential election cycle yet."

"They look like you've worn them every day since the first Bush administration. I know you really love the old fart look, sweetie, but you're going to represent the newspaper at the Open. You should get something smart to wear for the tournament."

"It's a major championship," I corrected her, a little cranky from being up all night as well as from the thought of having to shell out fifty bucks for new pants. "Not a tournament."

"Whatever," she said.

A few minutes later, inside Belk, I found a clerk standing by his cash register, examining his well-buffed cuticles.

"I need some new pants for the Open," I said to him.

"Excellent," he said, perking right up. "Anything particular in mind?"

"Pants for golf. I like cotton, preferably khaki. Reasonably priced or, better yet, dirt cheap."

"I take it you're a golfer?"

"Isn't everyone who shops in here except for maybe the Boy Scouts?"

He sniffed. "Your timing is perfect. I have just the pants for you. These are absolutely *flying* out of the store. All the golfers are buying them. *Tres* retro."

With visible reluctance, I followed him down several aisles to a table display where three different colors of cotton pants were neatly stacked. One stack was a faded lobster pink in hue. Another was the washed blue of a Carolina summer sky. The third was an electric shade of green.

I casually fingered the green duds. They did feel pretty good, and the clerk was right about retro. Point of fact, I hadn't seen anybody wear outrageous green golf pants like these since I was a kid watching Arnold Palmer blow the Greater Greensboro Open.

I could still see the scene in my mind. There stood my hero, the King of Golf, in the muddy creek bed by the sixteenth green, clinging to a slim two-shot margin with three holes left to play in the tournament, wearing perhaps the brightest green pants anyone had ever seen.

I was on the sandy creek bank a few feet away as he hitched up his electric green pants and daringly attempted to blast his ball from the sand at the water's edge, just missing the shot. Palmer's army groaned in collective agony as his ball trickled down the bank and rolled into the water.

Hitching up his green duds a second time, Palmer blasted even harder and flew his ball twenty feet over the putting surface, after which he chipped back and untidily three-putted for a horrendous triple bogey that dropped him two strokes behind the new leader in the clubhouse, George Archer.

"The silence was deafening as he left the green," I said, attempting to recapture the drama of the moment for the benefit of the Belk clerk, who was once again examining his cuticles. "Everyone was stunned, speechless. The King of Golf had *blown* the GGO, a tournament he always vowed to win. Years later, he personally told me that was one of the most painful moments of his professional life. Arnold never managed to win Greensboro, you see."

"How tragic," the clerk said sympathetically, then quickly returned to extolling the charms of the retro green pants. "Aren't they simply fab-*u*-lous? In my opinion, these pants just *say* Pinehurst. Don't you agree?"

I nodded, too tired to argue the point.

Before I realized it, the clerk had whipped out my exact size and was personally escorting me to the dressing room.

"You should wear them for Arnold Palmer at the Open golf tournament. He'll love seeing you in them!" the clerk declared, hovering outside the dressing room door.

"It's the U.S. Open *championship*," I said testily, and then pointed out that Arnold Palmer was seventy-six years old and living quietly at home in Latrobe, Pennsylvania. He hadn't played in a U.S. Open in nearly a decade.

"Oh well," the clerk said with a sigh. "If you do see him again, be sure to wear these beautiful green slacks. They'll take you both back to a *much* happier place."

CHAPTER TWO

Sacred Ground

SHORTLY AFTER SUNRISE on Monday of Open week, I sauntered up to the media center of the 2005 Championship and presented my shiny new *Pilot* press credentials to a volunteer named Doris who was staffing the security checkpoint and X-ray machine. She took one glance at my badge, checked out my new electric green pants, and burst out laughing.

"My God," she said, "I thought you were making it up about your ugly green pants. But, I guess not. Whoa, hon, are those britches ever *green*."

In my second official Sunday *Pilot* column that had appeared the previous morning, I'd revealed to the paper's readers that I'd bought the world's ugliest green pants on my way into America's golf capital, pants that supposedly "just said Pinehurst" but might as clearly have proclaimed I'd lost all sense of professional self-respect. For what it's worth, this was the first time I'd had the nerve to wear them out in public. It was also the last time.

Doris punched me playfully on the arm as if we were old chums. She was your classic U.S. Open volunteer: tanned, fit, a beaming golf retiree from somewhere up North or maybe in the Midwest. "And before I forget, I *loved* that column you wrote about taking your mother's old dog's ashes back to Greensboro, dear. That was so sweet I clipped it and sent it to my son Lionel. He lives in Poughkeepsie. We used to have a pug named Mister Snuffy."

"Thanks," I said.

"And the one you wrote today in the *Open Daily*, dear—oh, my *goodness*." Here she made a sweet gesture, feigning motherly speechlessness, touching her bosom with a flattened palm. "That Mr. Wind must have been something *truly* special."

This remark stopped me in my tracks. The woman had read not only my first two Sunday columns in *The Pilot* but also today's back-page column in the *Open Daily*. This meant she either had far too much free time on her hands or was possibly that rarest of things—a regular reader.

"Herb was a great guy," I agreed, pointing out how fortunate I'd been to get to know the dean of America's golf writers during the last years of his life. Wind, who suffered from Alzheimer's, had passed away the week before I arrived back in the Sandhills. Among other things, our annual spring lunch at his favorite restaurant north of Boston had yielded several deeply revealing stories about Ben Hogan for my biography, which had just received the USGA International Book Award for 2005, mere days after Wind's death. There was talk among the bluecoats of the USGA about renaming the award the Herb Wind Award, a move I wholeheartedly endorsed.

"I can't believe you've read both my Sunday columns," I said to Doris gratefully. She grinned at me and patted my hand.

"Are you kidding? You crack me up, cupcake. Can't wait to see what you write about next. Herb loves 'em, too. Aren't I right, Herb?"

For an instant I was confused, then realized the Herb she meant was a skinny volunteer standing a few yards away, chatting with some other guy also decked out in the Open's official volunteer regalia. Evidently *this* Herb was her husband. He was drinking coffee and sneaking a cigarette before the flood of spectators began.

"Right, Doris," he responded with deadpan stare, leaking smoke from both nostrils.

"So what's up for next Sunday, hon?"

"Whatever passes in front of my nose," I said, shamelessly stealing a line from Russell Baker. I mentioned that someone in my neighborhood over in Weymouth Heights had a rooster that went off like a state-fair champion every morning at four a.m. sharp, my usual rising time, and I said I might write about him. I asked Doris if she had any suggestions. Gas pump gossips and championship gatekeepers are the lifeblood of small town newspaper hacks everywhere.

Doris nodded vigorously. "Maybe you can write about my Herbert. He snores like a backfiring truck. Don't you, dear? Nobody over at Pinehurst Manor can even sleep!"

Herb glanced back at his wife. He had a face like a sack of old range balls.

"*You're* crazy as any rooster, Doris," he grumbled.

Doris cackled and I then turned to get on with my business,

eager to make my noon deadline. By then I had to conceive, write, and file eight hundred reasonably intelligent, moderately insightful words about the first-day doings at the 105th United States Open. At this point, however, I had no clue who was doing what, or what those words might be about. But then, professional panic is my middle name.

"By the way, Mr. Funny Pants," Doris called after me, her tone pleasant, "remember you're *only* permitted to use your cell phone *inside* the media center—not on the golf course! Don't make me come hunt you down, dear! Also, you might want to have the newspaper people take a new picture of you. The one they're using, I have to tell you, is pretty *dreadful*. Makes you look like my *husband*!"

"Don't mind her," Herb muttered as I passed him. "Doris likes to run everybody's life. She's just sore because the USGA wouldn't let her run the U.S. Open, too."

WITH MY NEW PRESS pass dangling around my neck, I hiked along the first fairway of famed Pinehurst No. 2, enjoying the peaceful early slant of sunlight through the longleaf pines, inhaling the sweet perfume of freshly mown summer grass, hoping something interesting developed quickly.

It was simply impossible to walk here without thinking about all the greats of the game who had preceded me along this hallowed patch of turf, this sacred ground of the American game. It was also impossible to walk here without thinking about all the fine afternoons my dad and I had played good old No. 2 together, through good times and bad, fine weather and foul, mostly back in the days when you could just show up, slap down twenty-five bucks, shoulder your bag or hire a caddie, and take off on a golf adventure that would leave you bruised but happy.

Those simpler days were long gone, of course. Since the first Open was played there in 1999, Pinehurst No.2 has become even more of a public golf shrine, and now charged non–hotel guests at least four hundred dollars (counting the caddie and official souvenir golf towel) to play the course widely considered to be designer Donald Ross's masterpiece. Furthermore, rumors perpetually circulated around the area that ClubCorp, the Dallas-based company that had owned the Pinehurst Resort since 1981, was about to jack the greens fees another hundred bucks the moment this latest Open road show packed up and left town. If that was true, on my humble new *Pilot* wages, it was doubtful I would ever play No. 2 again, at least anytime soon.

Still, there were few places I could think of that evoked such pleasant and even life-altering memories. One afternoon in the spring of 1983, for example, my dad and I hooked up for a casual round of golf on No. 2, a round that ended up changing the direction of my career. I arrived there on a brief break, a bit of a psychological wreck after having spent seven years working as a journalist in Atlanta—where I basically sacrificed my love of golf for career prospects—and now was headed for a long-anticipated job interview at the *Washington Post,* my dad's old newspaper. After a fairly dismal round of golf on my part, while sitting together on the Donald Ross porch, I admitted to my dad that I was, in truth, fed up with writing about politicians and crime bosses in the New South—and wasn't even sure I wanted to go work at the *Post.*

"I feel like I'm trafficking in other people's sorrows, building a career on other people's problems," is how I put it to him.

Looking back on that critical bend in the road, which I eventually described in a book called *Final Rounds,* it perhaps wasn't the major career crisis I imagined it to be at the time, but my dad's simple, commonsense advice had a transformative and healing effect. "In that case, Bo, why don't you write about things you love?" he said. "Things you care about or that simply interest you, and everything may fall into place. Things we love tend to take us where we need to go."

A father's simple advice. And a short time later, against the good advice of every colleague in the business, I turned down a job from an editor at the *Post* and went to work instead for *Yankee Magazine* in rural New Hampshire, trading my big-time newspaper ambitions for a fly rod and golden retriever pup, vowing to write only about things that either made someone laugh or pause to think, a career shift that opened a whole new world of possibilities and perhaps, looking back, may have even saved my life.

ANOTHER FELLOW WHO REACHED a turning point at Pinehurst was Ben Hogan. In 1940 he was nearly thirty years old and had yet to win on the professional golfing circuit. Twice during the previous decade he had failed to make the Tour and was forced to retreat to his hometown of Fort Worth and work a succession of menial jobs just to pay the rent and keep himself and his young wife in something to eat.

During the forty-eight months prior to coming to Pinehurst, though, the fanatically hardworking "Bantam Ben" had finished second no less than six times in tournament play, yet never managed to close the deal. With each near miss, rumors amplified that the chilly, workaholic Hogan planned to ditch the circuit if he didn't break through and finally win a tournament—any tournament—soon.

In those days, the North and South Open at Pinehurst was one of the most popular stops in the game, regarded by some as the classiest tournament this side of a National Open. Two weeks prior to the start of the North and South, as always haunted by his missing father and driven by fear that he might never measure up to the field, Hogan did something he'd never done before. Following a tournament in Thomasville, Georgia, he skipped a pair of lucrative exhibition matches and drove his aging Buick straight to Pinehurst in order to practice and prepare by memorizing every feature of No. 2.

On opening morning, dressed in gray slacks, blue sweater, and a white flat cap that would soon become his sporting trademark, Hogan split the opening fairway of No. 2 with a new driver, carved a seven-iron shot to within twelve feet of the cup, and rapped home the putt for birdie. He birdied the second hole, too—three of the tournament's opening four holes, in fact.

Clearly, he was a man on a mission, a man on fire. Two days later, Hogan finished the tournament thirteen strokes under par, three strokes ahead of his nearest rival, Sam Snead, and in the process nipped two strokes off the existing North and South record. "I was beginning to think I was an also-ran," a visibly drained but elated Hogan told reporters as he accepted the trophy and first-place check from the celebrated course designer himself.

Four days after his stunning Pinehurst breakthrough, Hogan romped over the field at Greensboro and moved on to the Land o' Sky Open at the Biltmore Forest Country Club in Asheville where, seventy-two hours later, he won again.

In ten days, Ben Hogan had won the first three professional golf tournaments of his life, something no player had ever done so quickly before, possibly the most sensational stretch of tournament golf ever played, a fact borne out by the impressive statistics of his accomplishment. Over 217 holes of competition, Hogan missed only three fairways, and he three-putted only twice. Pinehurst had worked its magic.

"I spent that crazy three-week period writing Ben's name over and over," John Derr remembered, when I called on him at his home in Pinehurst to talk about his longtime friendship with the Hawk. Derr had been the assistant sports editor at the *Greensboro Daily News* during Hogan's big breakthrough. "There's no question in my mind that he always felt coming to Pinehurst had saved his neck. There was something about this place that elevated his game and his spirit and opened a brand new world of possibilities to him. After coming to Pinehurst, he once admitted to me, he was never the same man again."

My dad had also been a spectator in the North and South gallery that cool March afternoon at No. 2 and had come home inspired by what he'd witnessed. It was the only time my father ever saw Ben Hogan in real life. He, too, worked at the *Greensboro Daily News,* as an aviation writer and part-time ad salesman.

Within six months, my father would move on to a larger job in Maryland and soon would join the Eighth Army Air Force to train as a glider pilot. John Derr would move on, too—becoming first a military correspondent in the Far East and eventually a legendary broadcaster for CBS Radio, anchoring the tower at the sixteenth hole at Augusta for more than five decades. The parallel between these two upbeat sons of the Old North State was, I would come in time to realize, nothing shy of remarkable. They were exactly the same age, genial sons of small-town working men (a rural postman in Derr's case, a carpenter in my dad's) who'd dropped out of college to chase a life in newspapering.

During the war, they both became Golden Gloves boxers of some renown. John Derr boxed under the moniker Dirty Derr. My dad, briefly bantamweight champ of the Eighth Army Air Force, boxed as "Battling Brax." They even resembled each other enough to have been mistaken for brothers. They both adored golf.

"I remember your dad," Derr told me one afternoon after I'd revealed our *other* connections to the game and each other via Pinehurst, mentioning my dad and the *Greensboro Daily News,* where I'd started my own career in 1977. "What a small and marvelous world this is, don't you agree? So, in effect, there were four of us sons of the game who got our starts here in the St. Andrews of America—Ben, your father, myself and *you!*"

I WAS THINKING about all of this, marveling at the sweet symmetry of golf and life, as I approached the green where the first practice group of Open hopefuls was dropping extra balls and putting them to try and get a handle on Donald Ross's murderous putting surfaces.

I immediately spotted a player who I thought might be fun to follow for a while. I had a warm spot for him because he once kindly posed for a photograph with Jack at a Golf Writers Association dinner at Augusta and later agreed to sign the photograph, which now hung in Jack's bedroom. The player was Tiger Woods.

Not far away, arms folded and watchful, stood Tiger's new

swing coach, Hank Haney. I knew Hank, too, though I wasn't sure if he would remember me.

Tiger was putting a second ball from one of the green's infamously firm and mounded edges. He was still grappling with the recent decline of his father, Earl Woods, and appeared to be deep in a cocoon of concentration that recalled Ben Hogan at his best.

While I was researching my Hogan book in Texas, Jack had spent a delightful week out at Hank's golf ranch north of Dallas. He'd come away from the experience with a promising golf swing and a stated desire to become the next Tiger Woods. That was then, though, and this was now. What a difference two years and a foot of growth made.

As we all stood there on the dewy threshold of U.S. Open week, with our footsteps still visible in the tenacious Bermuda rough, Haney glanced over at me and smiled. I could see him flipping through his mental Rolodex, trying to put a name to a face.

I knew from a brief conversation with Paul Jett, No. 2's head superintendent, that almost an acre of new sod had been planted around some of the course's infamous putting greens, replacing grass that had failed to come back after a winter that was too warm and a spring that was too cold. A week ago, however, Carolina summer arrived in the nick of time, pushing daytime temperatures into the upper nineties and liberally watering the course with heavy evening thundershowers. You could almost see the grass growing and feel Jett's relief. No. 2 had never looked more beautiful—or more intimidating.

After Tiger rapped another putt, Hank Haney casually strolled over.

I offered him my hand and reintroduced myself, reminding him of the lovely week Jack had enjoyed at his ranch.

Hank smiled broadly. "That's *right*. Congratulations on the Hogan book, by the way. So how's young Jack doing?"

I in turn congratulated him on his new association with Tiger Woods and said my son was doing well, explaining that he'd been selected to work as a group standard-bearer for Open week but was unable to get free of his school in time to do so. The truth was more complicated than this and, for me, disappointing. A few days before, after I'd gone to some length to secure a four-day spectator ticket so he could at least see the Open if not work in it, Jack had phoned to say he'd decided not to fly down as we'd agreed. His reason for not coming, as far as I was concerned, was pretty thin. "I want to hang out with my friends before they all go away for the summer," he said. "I won't get to see them again until the fall."

Part of me could fully understood—even admire—his devotion to his pals. Another part of me couldn't fathom his decision. Hard as I tried to convince myself it wasn't so, I couldn't help but take it as a personal rebuff.

"That's too bad," Hank commiserated, shaking his head. "He must be really disappointed."

"I'm probably more disappointed than he is," I admitted.

Three years after Jack's productive interlude at Hank's ranch in Texas, he was a rising sophomore in high school who seemed content to plug along on the junior varsity golf squad, equipped with a swing that resembled that of a young Tiger Woods, but rarely practicing between matches. His scores fluctuated between moments of brilliance and screwball comedy. Near as I could tell, for Jack, golf now ranked somewhere above playing ice hockey but definitely below watching independent movies, wooing girls, and composing songs on his guitar.

"I remember what a promising swing he has," Hank remarked.

"Nice golf swings are wasted on the young," I said. "I'm afraid the swing you gave him is more advanced than his desire to actually use it at the moment."

In retrospect, this was probably more than I should have said, but I was deeply disappointed not to have my son with me at Pinehurst that week—and more than a little worried that his interest in the game might be trailing off.

Hank smiled understandingly, shifting his gaze back to his famous client. "Well, just give it time. Maybe you should bring Jack down here anyway after the Open leaves. This place can light a fire in any kid's belly."

"I hope to do that," I said, remembering my own volatile teenage epiphany in the Sandhills. I later realized Hank's words were eerily similar to Harvie Ward's.

"Tell him I said hello—and to keep at the game." Hank moved along as Tiger strode past us toward the second tee.

"Will do. Good luck to you and Tiger. I know Jack will be rooting for him."

Just then, my cell phone rang. Heads swiveled, one of which belonged to Tiger Woods. Glancing neutrally in my direction, he shook his head and then smiled as if to say it was only Monday and everything was cool.

NONETHELESS, KNOWING I was in violation of the rules, I ducked quickly out of sight behind a small set of spectator bleachers and hurried for the relative isolation of an empty concession stand.

The imperious voice that greeted my whispered "hello" belonged to an elderly woman who held very firm views about golf, life, and everything else of human or spiritual consequence.

"I just read the nicest thing about you in the Boston newspaper," declared Mary Pat Robinson. "Your lovely wife tells me you have gone home to the hills—or in your case, dear, the Sandhills."

Dame Pat was eighty-four, a formidable bookseller I'd known for fifteen years who had once managed the Dartmouth College Bookstore and been a leading literary rep for a major New York publisher. She'd known Dylan Thomas and Robert Frost on a first-name basis, corresponded with reclusive William Saroyan, once lunched at the Plaza with M. F. K. Fisher, and was presented a bouquet of spring jonquils by an admiring Virginia Woolf. Most interesting of all to me, besides being my surrogate mom and de facto literary advisor, Dame Pat had once taken an impromptu golf lesson from none other than Ben Hogan. While stationed in England as a navy wife, she'd also helped organize volunteers for the 1953 Ryder Cup matches at Wentworth—the one that came on the heels of Hogan's greatest year of golf, and for which he failed to show up to play for the Americans, setting off a firestorm of criticism on both sides of the Atlantic.

Unfortunately, Pat had recently suffered a heart attack and been forced to give up both golf and her post at the bookstore. She was recuperating at her daughter Jane's cottage by the sea in South Harpswell, Maine.

"I see in the paper this morning that your Hogan biography has won the USGA's top award. Bravo and kudos to you, young man. A well-deserved honor. I know how hard you worked on that book. Mr. Hogan would be very pleased, I think."

"Thanks," I said. "So how are you feeling?"

"Not terribly inclined to get up and go dancing, if that's what you're asking. On the other hand, I'm seated here in Jane's garden this morning looking across the water at Orr's Island. So there's no reason to moue about my plight. Where have I found you, dear?"

"Hiding in a dark concession booth at the Open," I explained. "The bad news, madam, is that I'm not supposed to have this cell phone on. The good news is, you just disturbed Tiger Woods."

"Oh, *really?*" Pat gave a snort, followed by a girlish giggle. "Perhaps you should have a word with him about his most *un*becoming behavior. He just might listen to *you.*"

I loved pushing Dame Pat's buttons and had to smile at the notion that Tiger might listen to anything I had to say.

"I'm going to have to call you back, Pat. I'm in violation of the rules."

"Very well," she said with a sigh. "Just remember one thing."

"Yes ma'am?"

"At this moment in time, dear boy, you are exactly where you are meant to be. I believe that with my whole heart and you must, too. Promise you won't forget that."

"Promise," I said, wondering vaguely what she was getting at.

Tiger Woods was one subject about which Dame Pat and I agreed to respectfully disagree. The proper schoolgirl in her couldn't abide Tiger's emotional outbursts, his violent fist pumps, and occasional expletives. The very things that attracted Jack and a generation of impressionable young golfers like him to

Tiger Woods deeply offended the old-fashioned values of Dame Pat, who believed Ben Hogan's cool and regal demeanor established the gold standard for behavior on the course.

Given the blandness of modern players and corporate dominance of current professional golf, on the other hand, I believed fans everywhere should have thanked their lucky stars for the likes of Tiger Woods, Phil Mickelson, John Daly, Sergio Garcia, and a handful of other throwbacks to a time when players revealed their personalities and passion on the golf course. Ironically, Ben Hogan's chilly gray personality—underscored by his heroic comeback and success—helped bring about a transformation of the Tour's personalities from colorful characters to emotionally constipated automatons, overcoached protégés of swing gurus and sports psychologists who mistook Hogan's fabled reserve for a genius that could be emulated in order to create a champion. In fact, the source of Hogan's forbiddingly remote persona had nothing to do with "playing within himself," as a certain TV commentator forever droned on about, but rather with a shattering boyhood experience—his father's suicide when Hogan was ten, an event that happened probably directly in front of him—that sent young Bennie Hogan on a lifelong quest to feel both accomplished and loved. As no less an authority than sportswriter Dirty Derr and several of Hogan's closest lunch pals confirmed, the powerful desire to feel as if he belonged in the world of successful men was really the motivating factor that drove Ben Hogan to conquer his demons and the world of professional golf. This was really Hogan's famous "secret."

What Dame Pat and I *did* wholeheartedly agree upon, in any case, was that modern professional golf was in danger of finally doing something that the Augusta National Golf Club founder Clifford Roberts had once warned Masters champion Arnold Palmer about in 1960, the year Palmer captured his second Masters.

"Cliff told me the one thing that could kill professional golf was if we ever reached a point where *too* much money was flowing around the game," Palmer told me during an early morning chat in his Latrobe workshop, as we discussed the directions the modern game was taking. "He felt that if the sponsors ever came to mean more to a tournament's life than the fans who turned out to support it, why, that just might be the beginning of the end of pro golf's popular appeal. The players would play for money rather than the love of playing, and you'd eventually get one big business rather than a game."

This explained why, the King added, the Masters had always remained *the Masters*, unadorned by any named corporate patron, with its financial sponsorship significantly downplayed out of simple respect for the championship's difficulty and importance to fans of the game.

I thought of Roberts's prophetic warning every time I saw another tournament being taken over by some corporate behemoth that wanted its name and logo plastered on every possible freestanding space at a tournament venue. In 2004 the venerable Western Open, once considered on par with the National Open in stature, had been officially rechristened the Cialis Western Open, giving a whole new spin to the timeless golfing maxim "Never up, never in."

Moreover, at a moment when the PGA Tour, drunk with sponsorship and advertising dollars, seemed to stretch numbingly from New Year's Day to Christmas Eve, taking only brief timeouts for either the odd-year Ryder Cup and Presidents Cup plus a handful of meaningless made-for-TV golf matches staged in exotic locales, professional golf seemed, at least from my perspective, not only more colorless and unappealing with each passing year, but further removed from its fan base. Corporate skyboxes, premium seating, restricted interview areas—all were relatively new to the tournament scene.

Factor in players who traveled with royal entourages that typically included a personal swing coach, physical fitness trainer, psychologist, caddie, agent, and personal financial advisor, and you had a formula for a slow death by corporate prosperity—or, as King Arnold once said, "forgetting what the game means and how you got here."

Admittedly, I'd been spoiled by coming of age during professional golf's most colorful and entertaining years—beginning with Arnold Palmer and Jack Nicklaus and lasting a few years beyond Greg Norman and Nick Faldo—an era that embraced everything from Calvin Peete's wonderful four-part golf swing to Ben Crenshaw's stylish mastery of the greens, from Lee Trevino's "Merry Mex" routine to Fuzzy Zoeller's towel-waving antics. We all understood that Nicklaus was the best there had ever been, but when Tom Watson captured his five Claret Jugs in the cold links wind of the British Open, we had to blink back tears, too. We died a small death watching the Great White Shark blow all those major championships, and marveled at Seve Ballesteros's Moorish magician skills from field and stream. We loved watching Johnny Miller drive a golf ball down the stretch, or classy Nick Price pull off a murderous up and down in the clutch. We even developed a sideways affection for the flinty charm of Nick Faldo. Ditto Curtis Strange, Hale

Irwin, Raymond Floyd—they weren't easy characters to fall in love with, but they all instinctively understood Walter Hagen's maxim that golf is a showman's game and they all put on one *hell* of a show.

Watching Payne Stewart win his first National Open at Hazeltine in 1991 was anything but dull—he was a passionate young man on fire with the idea of conquering the world. Eight years later, his emotional, come-back triumph at Pinehurst No. 2 was simply the exclamation point on one of the game's most colorful careers—and, in many respects, the close of pro golf's most colorful period.

Luckily for all of golf, a Stanford college boy named Tiger Woods—the Harvie Ward of his day, one might dare to say—began making headlines about that time and soon claimed an unprecedented three U.S. Amateur Championships on his way into the professional ranks. A generation of kids like my son began to take notice.

Since that time, though, according to the National Golf Foundation, participation of Americans in the game of golf had not only leveled off but had even begun to decline for the first time since the days of Arnold Palmer. Old-line clubs were withering on the vine, desperate to find new members. Hotshot upscale public courses built in the blush of golf's booming years in the late 1990s were now declaring bankruptcy and even being sold off for house lots. Many blamed the horror of 9/11 for the big chill that fell over the hospitality industry in general and the golf world in particular.

Whatever the cause, as an aging patron of the game myself now, I happened to believe the real source of the problem was that pro golf had become, in a word, too *boring* to watch. More skilled and athletic than ever before, the players' passion was rarely if ever on display.

Johnny Miller's genius, like Faldo's, now shone from the broadcast booth, and not even the greatest stage of all, the United States Open Championship, was immune to employee review.

Not long after I said goodbye to Harvie Ward, the newest editor in chief of my old magazine tracked me down to see if I would be willing to write a monthly essay "defending," as he put it, "the traditional values of the game."

"I wasn't aware the traditional values of golf needed to be defended," I said to him, a bit mystified by his premise.

"Specifically," he argued, "a growing number of people are beginning to think the U.S. Open might have outlived its usefulness and ought to be either radically revamped or maybe scrapped all together. The players say it's too hard, and some sponsors feel it could be, well, a *lot* more exciting."

I had never met this man before. He seemed a nice enough chap—the second or possibly third editor my old magazine had employed since the new corporate bosses fired the man who'd spent twenty-five years turning it into the game's top golf publication.

"So, exactly what do you want me to do?" I was at least curious to hear him out. We seemed to agree, after all, that pro golf had grown a trifle dull. We just seemed to have a different cure for the problem.

"We see you doing an essay explaining why the U.S. Open shouldn't be scrapped or significantly altered. You'd become our voice of tradition. There will be other debates down the road, of course. We're going for something edgier, and we think golf should, too."

When I had casually mentioned this to Pat Robinson one day at lunch, she gave one of her mare-like snorts of disbelief.

"If *that's* their attitude," said Pat, "I'm surprised you would wish to have your name on their silly masthead. If the Open is outdated, dear boy, so are *you.*"

She was right, of course. Unfortunately, I'd already written the essay and fired it off to the new editor, pointing out how, even with its dull cookie-cutter players and sports shrinks and whatnot, the U.S. Open was *still* the National Open and *still* the hardest golf championship on earth to win. The next day I e-mailed this same young editor and politely requested that my name be removed from his masthead. A short time later, the new corporate owners fired the edgy young editor.

FOLLOWING MY ILLICIT cell phone conversation with Dame Pat, I roamed happily over the grounds of my favorite *unchanging* golf championship, chatting up fans and elderly volunteers, making field notes on young players whose names I didn't even recognize, eavesdropping on player-caddy conversations, watching ground crews go through their last-minute preparations, and generally soaking up the relaxed ambiance of Open Monday in the pines.

Along the way I met a couple from Kentucky who drove all night in order to watch a youngster from their town who snagged the final qualifying spot in the championship, and I met as well a pair of newlyweds who planned their honeymoon at the Pinehurst Resort to coincide with the Open championship so they could make a provocative wager of a highly creative nature on the outcome.

By the putting green I watched my old friend Davis Love III put on his game face, and I strolled over to say hello. At this point I also saw my good friend Eddie Merrins from the Bel-Air Country Club waving me over to the practice tee.

"I want you to meet a really special young man — your kind of guy," said the famous Little Pro, leading me along the back of the range to a large, sweating teddy bear of a fellow hitting balls into the pale blue sky. His name was Jason Gore, a new father just up from the nationwide Tour who grabbed one of the National Open's final qualifying spots. He'd driven from Tennessee with his wife and infant daughter, having his car burglarized along the way.

"I don't know if I have any chance of winning," Gore informed me after a friendly twenty-minute chat about his late father and his difficult road to Pinehurst, "but it thrills me beyond belief to be here. I dreamed of this as a kid. I just wish my dad was still around to see this. If I could finish in the top twenty . . . wow."

"How about if you won? I'll bet that would make your dad happy," I said to him, thinking of my own father somewhere in the golf afterlife — and even more of Jack, wishing he was here to meet Jason Gore.

Gore grinned like an overgrown kid. "Oh man. He'd be totally thrilled — beside himself."

A LITTLE WHILE LATER, with my noon deadline looming, I slipped through the media center to say goodbye to my colleagues from *The Pilot* and head back to write my Tuesday column in the relative quiet of the paper's offices.

Inside the center, I bumped into my former colleagues Mike Purkey, John Feinstein, and Peter Kessler, chatting with a guy from the media colossus that had recently acquired my former magazine. I congratulated Purkey on helping Eddie Merrins craft his delightful memoirs. I also congratulated Peter on his recently syndicated golf show on XM Radio, and John on his latest terrific sports book.

Mike congratulated me on venturing back to my journalism roots to work for *The Pilot.* "I always had a hunch you might wind up back where you started," he said pleasantly.

"You sound like Harvie Ward," I told him.

"Once a Carolina boy . . ." Mike said with a knowing shrug.

"What's this about you going to work for a *weekly* newspaper?" asked the executive, whose parent company had bought our magazine and put us both on the street. "I mean, are things really that *bad*?" He gave what some might have interpreted as a sympathetic smile.

The collar of his polo shirt was artfully turned up. Personally, I've never cared for guys who artfully turn up their collars. Or maybe it was his cologne.

"On the contrary," I told him as pleasantly as possible, "I'm having a great time. I'm just going back now to try and become the new Dick Taylor or Charlie Price. Or maybe just do a Derr and Drum."

He stared blankly, obviously having never heard of Taylor and Price. Dick Taylor was a legendary editor of *Golf World* magazine, a publication started by former Tour public relations man Bob Harlow in Pinehurst during the late 1940s. Charles Price, who literally wrote the book on the Masters, began his career covering pony races and putting contests for the tiny *Pine-hurst Outlook,* the area's first newspaper. John Derr gave up his CBS broadcast booth to retire to Pinehurst in the 1970s, while Pittsburgh sports reporter Bob Drum—who covered young Arnie Palmer's ascent and popularized the phrase "modern Grand Slam"—moved to the Sandhills to work for the Diamondhead Corporation in the 1980s and do his delightful, curmudgeonly *Drummer's Beat* segments for the aforementioned CBS.

In my opinion, these guys not only distinguished our chosen profession but defined the grace and charm of old Pinehurst, creating a golf fraternity that made the likes of me yearn to somehow join their ranks.

"So what will you be writing about?" Artful Polo asked. "Who won the ladies club final or painted the naughty words on the town water tower?"

"You know," I admitted, "those are things I'd *love* to know and write about."

"Me, too," Mike said, winking.

I was tempted to launch into a speech about what a publishing dynamo *The Pilot* really was. At a time when daily newspapers everywhere were hemorrhaging vast amounts of red ink, closing bureaus, and laying off news staffs, the community newspaper of the Sandhills was thriving under David Woronoff's creative leadership and possibly reinventing the industry from the grass-roots level. At least four times during the twelve years Woronoff and his partners had owned it, *The Pilot* had been named the top general-interest newspaper in North Carolina. At least twice it had been picked top community newspaper in America.

Another part of me, however, realized that the effort to ex-plain any of this to this corporate hipstser would be pointless.

So I simply wished them all best of British luck and started for the door, pointing out I had a deadline to make for my Tuesday *Open Daily* column. But then I stopped and walked back to the group.

"By the way," I calmly said to Artful Polo, "*The Pilot* is not a weekly newspaper. It comes out three times a week."

Purkey laughed, and Feinstein and Kessler smiled. They seemed to have no difficulty grasping why I'd come back to get in touch with my roots.

"We know the truth," Peter quipped. "You're really here for the same reason any golfer comes to live in Pinehurst. You want to work on your game. That'll just be *our* little secret."

"It's called the Pinehurst cure," I said in agreement. "Harvie Ward told me about it. Don't tell my boss that's what I'm really after."

As it happened, my new boss was standing a few feet away and had overheard this entire exchange.

"Nice pants," David Woronoff commented dryly as I walked past him toward the media center exit.

"Glad you like 'em!" I barked the way Bob Drum might have as he headed somewhere to meet a looming deadline. "I'll wear them to my first Sandhills major."

"Can't wait," David shot back with a laugh. "Those pants just *say* Pinehurst."

CHAPTER THREE

Open Hooky

O<small>N</small> S<small>UNDAY</small> <small>MORNING</small>, the last day of the 2005 U.S. Open, I put on a red-striped bow tie like the one my grandfather used to wear and walked around the corner and four blocks down Massachusetts Avenue to Emmanuel Episcopal Church. It was a pretty stone building with a cheerful red door. I'm partial to churches with red doors. I'm partial to red-striped bow ties, too.

As I settled into a pew, breathing the lovely perfume of beeswax and wood polish, I thought of Francis Bacon's famous remark about parenthood — how a father's joys and disappointments are all alike: he can't speak of one; he won't speak of the other. This was the first Father's Day I'd ever spent without my children. It was also my only official day off from my *Pilot* duties. I'd planned to spend it following new papa Jason Gore around Pinehurst No. 2, hoping to watch this refreshing young man make Open history. I'd also hoped to have my own son with me. But that wasn't going to happen.

As the organ prelude began, a large orange cat wearing a noisy bell collar hopped up on my lap and began purring loudly and rubbing against my elbow. Around me people politely stifled smiles.

"That's Sam, the church cat," explained a nicely dressed older woman seated a few feet away. As she whispered, she inched over, flicking fingers at the cat. "Throw that silly nuisance on the floor if he becomes too much trouble. Sam loves to pester newcomers and Baptists. So which are you, dear?"

I nudged the cat to the floor. He sprang back as if attached to a bungee cord, bell jingling.

"I'm . . . a newcomer."

"I see. And where do you *live,* dear?"

As I put Sam down a second time, I mentioned the small log cabin around the corner on Highland Road owned by Lloyd Cutler, a Boston widow.

"I know *exactly* the one you mean. The haunted cabin. It once belonged to the caretaker of the Highland Pines Inn. Lots of people in town have lived there."

"I'm sorry," I whispered, tilting politely in her direction. "Did you say it's *haunted?*"

She gave me a coy smile. "Oh, yes. Didn't anyone tell you about the ghost? I think it's probably a friendly ghost—a mother who lost her child or a lonely father. Something like that. Haven't you met Lloyd yet? She'd know for sure about the ghost."

I admitted that I had not, explaining that I'd merely lucked into her cottage via a desperate phone call to a friend who knew everybody in town. Mine had been a last-minute transaction, mainly because I'd suddenly had strong misgivings about going to work for *The Pilot,* which delayed making proper arrangements until the last possible moment. The reason I had cold feet had a lot to do with my tendency to lead with my heart rather than listen to my head.

Since I was a kid, Pinehurst and Southern Pines had always been comforting places for my heart. That much was indisputably true. Being here never failed to make me almost ridiculously happy. But now that I'd actually put this complicated midlife scenario into motion, perhaps subconsciously believing there might be something to Harvie Ward's Pinehurst cure, it suddenly struck me that as soon as the excitement of being a part-time resident of the Sandhills lost its novelty, and the reality of commuting eight hundred miles every fortnight between one busy life and another settled in, I might quickly come to regret the open-ended commitment I'd made to David Woronoff. I had, after all, plenty of other work to do — my African horticulture adventure to finish writing, plus a history of Seminole Golf Club I'd promised to research and write for the members of that distinguished club. Though the week had gone even better than I'd hoped for, who was I kidding? I hadn't worked for a daily newspaper in more than thirty years. That couldn't be discounted.

Jack's decision to hang with his school pals in Maine instead of joining his old man at the U.S. Open seemed to contain a message of some kind. Maybe he was suggesting that I was shirking my paternal duties in favor of trying to rediscover my own lost golf child, although on the surface his life would be marginally affected by the move. Jack and Maggie, a rising high school junior, had long ago become comfortable with spending half the month at their two separate homes, which were only a few miles apart. Even after we both remarried, Alison and I worked to foster a sense of family continuity, talking almost every day by phone about whatever issues or concerns had arisen, reviewing schedules, and sharing stories about our spirited children, generally staying in touch and being responsive, responsible co-parents. We'd had our ups and downs, to be sure, but other parents in town remarked upon the apparent success of our cooperative extended families.

For her part, Maggie, the family romantic and adventurer, appeared to accept my Pinehurst gig in the spirit I'd hoped she might, keeping an open mind about where it might lead. Her kid brother, on the other hand, was eerily silent on the subject. Maybe his Open no-show was Jack's way of saying I'd upset a good family working system. All these considerations had brought on doubts, and had led me to this charming stone church I'd long been curious about, perhaps in hopes I might find some answers and insights.

"You'll like Lloyd. She's quite educated and perfectly delightful—for a Yankee," my pew buddy said without a trace of concern that I might be one, too. "Of course, half the people in this town are Yankees. They came here before most of the Southerners. But we all get along just fine. Must have something to do with the kind of people who like horses or golf. Those are the only types who seemed to find this little patch of wilderness all that appealing."

She appraised me again. "So which are you?"

"Golfing Southerner. But I've lived in the North for twenty

years. You should see the night sky on my snowy hilltop. I have a garden, too."

"Do you have a wife and children?" She gave me the faintest wink. "Don't mind me, I'm old enough to be a nosey parker."

I smiled back. "Yes, ma'am, I do. Girl and boy. Both in high school. They're coming down here week after next to explore their Southern roots."

She smiled, opening her Book of Common Prayer. "In that case, dear, you ought to fit in fine around here."

After the service, she walked me out to the sidewalk.

"So how do you find our lady rector?" she demanded.

"Not bad," I replied. "A trifle on the dull side at times. I hail from a long and . . . checkered line of pinewood Carolina preachers, so I know good preaching when I hear it.

To be fair, I honestly couldn't recall a word of the sermon because I had been pondering Jack's silence and wondering about the ghost that haunted my cabin. Maybe that was why a stone angel stood guard by the back door—to look out for the hearts of worried fathers and mothers who were missing their children. I was certainly missing mine this beautiful, sun-splashed Father's Day. As for Lloyd Cutler's cute log cabin, with its simple rooms, cheerful robin's-egg-blue kitchen, deep-set windows, and garden in a grove of towering oaks and hickories, I'd rarely slept in a place so downright tranquil. If indeed there happened to be a resident ghost, it must have been sympathetic, perhaps even a gardening golfer in his or her former life.

"Well, I thought it was *dreadful*," my pew buddy said, drawing me back to the moment. "She's a fill-in, poor thing. Emmanuel Church is still in mourning, you see. Our regular pastor,

Father Hank, had a heart attack and died. He was cross-country skiing when he collapsed. Such a lovely man, about your age. Fit as a fiddle to look at him."

She sighed and glanced at me. "Never put off for tomorrow what you should do today—*that's* the moral. You remember that. Hope you'll come back to church," she added brightly. "This is the oldest church in town, you know. I'll make sure Sam behaves himself next time."

I promised I would and started back up Massachusetts, loosening my bow tie, suddenly embarrassed to realize I'd forgotten to introduce myself or even ask my pew buddy's name, eager as I was to get on to the U.S. Open action and clear my head of all these complicated family thoughts.

A block from Highland Road, near the curving driveway that once belonged to the Highland Pines Inn, I came upon a large mottled toad stretched out on the warm asphalt. He appeared to have been struck by a car just one good hop shy of freedom.

Mr. Toad, who'd died as unexpectedly as Father Hank, deserved a proper burial and someone to note his passing, so I buried him beneath the loamy mulch of someone's daylily bed a few feet from the curb, in front of a house aptly called Heaven on Earth Cottage, according to a hand-painted sign at the end of the driveway. Many of the handsome manor houses and small bungalows in my new Weymouth Heights neighborhood had colorful names, reminding me of the neighborhood where I'd grown up in Greensboro.

I marked Mr. Toad's grave with a small gray stone I would recognize in the event I walked this way to services again, a Sunday-morning column already beginning to take shape in my head.

A STRANGE THING HAPPENED on my way to see if young Jason Gore could somehow win the 105th U.S. Open. He began the day only two strokes off the lead, and I sensed perhaps the greatest story since Payne Stewart's comeback at Pinehurst about to happen. The only problem was, I failed to get there.

I took the media bus, as planned, to the championship just in time to wiggle through the immense crowds and watch the last pairing, Gore and Retief Goosen, tee off and begin their final trek. As I stood there watching, however, I suddenly realized I'd had enough pro golf for one week, at which point I took the media bus back to the Holiday Inn where my aging Volvo was parked, climbed in, and headed north out of town, taking a back road through the country.

I slipped a CD that Maggie had made of Bonnie Raitt and James Taylor into the player, switched off the air-conditioning, and cranked down the car windows to smell the fields of Carolina rushing past. It was a smell I'd known since I was a boy.

I had no firm idea where I was headed. Drawn by some invisible gravity, I suddenly had a desire to have a better look around at my old hometown. A few days before the start of the Open, I'd driven up to Greensboro to meet the middle-aged woman who'd purchased my mother's house on Dogwood Drive, ostensibly to spread my mother's old dog's ashes through the lily of the valley beds out back where Molly once guarded the premises. The new owner's name was Nancy. She'd made me a lovely brunch, and we'd sat in the back garden of my childhood home talking about the unexpected way she'd come to own the house. Not long before I'd moved my mom to Maine, my brother, Dick, had persuaded her to give the house and most of her financial assets to his wife of only a few weeks—a woman who turned out to have been married multiple times before and soon put the house on the market and tossed my brother out onto the street. Before I could seek any kind of legal remedy, the property had been sold and family assets meant to take care of our ailing mother were gone.

My brother, simply put, had been duped by love. In time, I'd gotten over the shock and anger prompted by his inconceivable actions, but our relationship had never been the same again. Somewhere in the back of my mind, I was half convinced one reason I felt a powerful tug back to the Old North State was because I meant somehow to make peace with him and begin anew. Whatever else was true, I loved my brother and missed the camaraderie we'd always had. Our family burrowed back ten generations into North Carolina soil, and curiously enough, he and I were the last of the line on our particular branch of our impressive family tree.

As I rolled toward Greensboro, however, I realized I wasn't ready to track down my big brother, at least not today. I needed to figure out what my real reasons were for coming back here after being away for so long, and then to decide how long I might stay. Besides, for all I knew, Dick was attending the very National Open from which I was playing hooky. He was a terrible golfer but a huge fan.

Another possibility occurred to me. I could phone up my oldest friend and longtime golf nemesis, Patrick McDaid, to see if I could lure him out for an afternoon round at his club in Eden, an Ellis Maples layout north of Greensboro. But then I remembered Pat was off fly-fishing at his trout club in the mountains. Pat was family—Uncle Pat, my children called him

Thus, with no firm Father's Day objective in mind, officially off the lease and whereabouts unknown, remembering what my guardian muse Pat Robinson had said about wherever I happened to find myself being exactly where I was supposed to be, I stopped at a roadside farm stand and bought a basket of fresh Sandhills peaches and, on impulse, a pot of magenta banded geraniums.

An hour or so later, I placed the pot in the grass between my parents' graves at Westminster Gardens near the Guilford Courthouse battleground in Greensboro. Then I sat down in the shade of a nearby elm and began eating a juicy peach, soaking up the serenity of a Father's Day Sunday, wondering what kind of afternoon both Jason Gore and my son were having. Gore winning the Open, I decided, would be a much-needed tonic for pro golf—a classic Cinderella story in a game that has become far too predictable. As for Jack, I hoped . . .

Just then my cell phone rang. It was none other than the lad himself.

"Hey, Dad," he said in his familiar, low-key way. "Where are you?"

"Eating a peach and sitting on top of your grandparents," I said. Noting the confused silence on his end, I explained: "I decided to come up to Greensboro and bring some flowers for your grandparents' grave."

"Oh. Aren't you supposed to be at the Open?" He sounded surprised.

"I've been there all week, Nibs. Frankly, I needed a break from the action. So I hopped in the car to take a Sunday drive and wound up here. I'm playing hooky from the Open. I plan to catch the end of it on TV anyway."

"Is everything okay?" Jack, like his old man, is a natural worrier. The peach doesn't fall far from the tree.

"It's fine, buddy. Today was my only day off, and I decided to come up and snoop around Greensboro. Needed to think a few things over. That's all."

"What kinds of things?" Worry turned to suspicion. Normally the first question out of his mouth would have been about Tiger Woods.

For an instant I debated how much to share. I decided the truth, or at least some version of it, wouldn't hurt, though I didn't want him to know how disappointed I was that he had not come to the Open—nor did I want him to feel guilty. He had to live his own life, not mine.

"Well, I'm wondering whether this plan to work at *The Pilot* after the Open really makes sense for all of us—including you, your sister and mom, and Wendy too. As fun as it's been, I think I may have overestimated my abilities to make it all work out the way I hoped. I've got too much going on back there for it to be feasible."

I explained that I'd pretty much decided to thank David Woronoff for his generous hospitality and a nice two-week interlude in the Sandhills, then head back home tomorrow.

Jack's reaction to this decision surprised me. He sounded incredulous and put out.

"You mean you're not going to work for *The Pilot* after all?"

"If this opportunity had come along in a year or two, Jack, it would have been great. But the timing isn't right. I gave it a good shot. That's all you can do in life."

"What about teaching in Virginia next year?"

"I'll cross that bridge when we get to it. Right now, Ace, I'm just eager to come home and see you guys. I'm a little homesick, if you want to know the truth. That's why I came up to visit with your grandparents."

"But aren't we coming back there next week?"

"I suppose we could. If you and Maggie still want to come. It'll be hot down here, and Pinehurst will be a ghost town," I pointed out. "Everybody is heading straight for the beach and the mountains the instant the Open ends."

There was thoughtful silence at his end. "I kind of wish I'd come down to the Open after all," he allowed, a touch dolefully, as if in retrospect that might have made a difference. And, in retrospect, it might have. "Did Bryan carry a standard?"

"He did. I think he's working today, but I can't tell you which player he has. Tom says he's had a blast collecting a lot of autographs, though." I finished my peach and started on a new one. "So what are you up to this lovely afternoon, Junior?"

There was a pause.

He sighed. "Not much. Andy and I were talking about going over to Highland Green to play golf, but I'm just hanging around, playing my guitar, working on a song. Want to hear it?"

"Love nothing better." A Father's Day serenade, I thought.

I leaned back against the elm, holding the phone to my ear. At Jack's age I'd played the classical guitar and even entertained silly notions of striking off for Nashville after high school. But Jack was a genuine talent, a much finer guitarist than I'd ever been, far more instinctual a player than his old man. His golf swing seemed to fall into the same category.

What I heard over the telephone was predictably wonderful— a complex yet infectious melody that recalled the Taylor and Raitt I'd been listening to earlier. Not for the first time, the thought went through my head that when Jack figured out what passion he wished to pursue in life, the kid was truly going to be something. In this way, his guitar playing rivaled his abilities with a golf club.

"Sorry. It's still kind of rough."

"That sounded fantastic, Rocket."

Rocket was one of half a dozen affectionate nicknames I had for my son. I also called him J.B., Ace, Amigo, Boss, and Nibs, from the character Nibs the Lost Boy in *Peter Pan,* one of Jack's favorite childhood books, and mine. Whenever, like his wise older sister, Jack made fun of his father's rural Southern heritage, I put on my best *Hee Haw* accent and called him Junior.

"Thanks," he said. "Justin Simpson wants me to join his band, but I haven't decided whether I want to do it or not."

"Know the feeling," I said.

"So who do you want to win?" He meant, of course, the Open.

"I'm rooting for a kid named Jason Gore. Nice young fella, unspoiled by success as far as I can tell. But when I root for them, that's usually the kiss of death. Your man Tiger is six back."

"I don't think he can win."

"Sure he can." I reminded him that Arnold Palmer once came from nine back to win his only U.S. Open.

"Dad . . ." He paused again, once more sounding emphatic. "I'd *really* like to come down there and play some golf with you and Bryan and Mr. Stewart. You said the four of us could play No. 2 this summer."

"Fair enough. I'll head home tomorrow, and we'll discuss it. Would you play me another song?"

"Sure." He put down the receiver and I heard him tune a

few strings. Then he picked up the receiver again. He sounded happier.

"I really called just to tell you happy Father's Day. Mom reminded me it was today."

"I appreciate that, Jack," I said.

"Here it goes," he said. "It needs work, but I think it's pretty good."

"I'm listening," I assured him, thinking that could be the motto of his young life.

WHEN I GOT BACK to Southern Pines in the late afternoon, Mrs. Cutler's log cabin looked like a postcard of Dixie splendor set back in its towering grove of spreading hardwoods.

I opened a cold beer and turned on the TV and discovered nothing had worked out the way anyone expected at the U.S. Open. That was the joy of the game of golf, a perfect four-letter metaphor for life.

Goosen and Gore had both free-fallen from the lead and were just finishing up their business at the seventy-second hole as I joined the telecast. "If you'd said these two between them would be twenty-four over par," I heard commentator Johnny Miller say, "people would have thought you were out of your cotton-picking mind."

South African Goosen tapped in for an untidy eighty-one, a score I would be ecstatic to claim on No. 2 but hardly a decent day's showing for a two-time Open champion with alleged ice water in his veins. Young Gore, meanwhile, bless his big teddy-bear heart, hobbled off the final green marking fourteen over par on his card, smiling bravely, fighting tears, accepting hugs.

"Good on you, mate," I said, quoting my philosophical golf

and drinking pal, Tom Stewart, lifting a sweating bottle of Sam Adams in silent tribute to Gore's noble efforts on behalf of full-figured guys everywhere. The Little Pro had been right about Gore. He was a kid worth keeping an eye on, exactly what the Tour needed in order to generate new fans.

The cabin phone rang. It was Wendy.

"Is this great or what?" she declared excitedly. "Are you watching the Open?"

"I am," I confirmed. "But I have no idea who won." I explained that I'd taken a lazy Sunday afternoon drive through the country.

"Everything okay?" She sounded a little alarmed.

"Fine. Just needed to clear my head a bit. Tell you about it when I'm home tomorrow. No big deal. So what's happened?"

"I feel *so* sorry for Jason Gore," Wendy said. "He's such a cute guy and everyone seemed to want him to win. But you have to feel good for Michael Campbell, too. I guess he almost won the British Open years ago and then nearly gave up on the game. You should have seen it when he tapped in his last putt. He looked around in utter shock and then he cried."

"The Open reduces grown men to tears," I said. "I'm assuming this means Campbell won the Open?" In a month of summer Sundays, I'd never have picked Michael Campbell to win the U.S. Open. Evidently nobody else had either.

"Yep. He was so great. He was talking about his ancestors being out there with him today. He said winning today was like being reborn."

"That seems to be a prevailing theme around here," I remarked, suddenly thinking of Hogan and Harvie, watching the screen where big Jason Gore was presently being interviewed by

Jimmy Roberts. Once again, the Pinehurst cure had salvaged a career.

"I don't want to see this happen to anyone," a visibly drained and emotional Gore was telling Roberts, squinting into the setting sun. "But that's golf. I've had an incredible week. Seeing my wife and kid coming up the eighteenth put it all in perspective. It's just a game of golf. That's all it is."

The big fellow had taken the words right out of my mouth.

I PUT IN A LOAD of dirty laundry and, despite a distant rumble of thunder, went out for an evening walk around the neighborhood, turning north toward the Weymouth Estate and the Weymouth Center for the Arts and Humanities.

Weymouth was formerly the home of novelist James Boyd, a member of the famed Algonquin Round Table and friendly contemporary of Thomas Wolfe and Scott Fitzgerald, both of whom came to stay at the house during troubled intervals of their careers. I wanted to see the Boyd estate's restored gardens, plus I had recently become interested in the original owners, Jim and Katharine Lamont Boyd, who were, at least indirectly, responsible for my being there in the first place. Not long before his sudden death in 1944, Jim Boyd had purchased the area's leading newspaper and served as both publisher and editor until he died, at which point his widow, Katharine, assumed a similar role at *The Pilot*.

I'd been reading up on the Boyds during dinner breaks in Open week. The civic-minded Boyds—wealthy Pennsylvania horse people who underwrote the construction of roads, organized banks, and introduced water and electrical lines to bustling little Southern Pines, which was founded after the Civil

War by an enterprising Carolinian who realized a fortune could be made peddling house lots on played-out timber land to wealthy Yankees with winter complaints—became the center of Sandhills community life. One of the ailing Northerners who hopped off the train about 1890 to check out reports in Boston newspapers of miraculous Sandhills "cures" was James Walker Tufts, a wealthy Boston soda-fountain magnate and social do-gooder who eventually bought up thousands of acres of useless sandy land and attempted to create a workers' health resort in the desolate longleaf pines, but wound up creating something else entirely—America's first golf resort.

As life in the once forbiddingly remote region slowly evolved, though they existed only a few miles apart, the differences between the quaint Town of Southern Pines and the even quainter Village of Pinehurst, which James Tufts eventually created in his own Brahmin Yankee image, were far deeper than they initially appeared—a social and cultural divergence Jim Boyd himself got to the comic heart of when he fired off a famous letter of "protest" to the editor of the Raleigh *News and Observer* in 1927, vigorously complaining that the newspaper had maligned his reputation by describing him as a "resident of Pinehurst." That editor, coincidentally, was none other than David Woronoff's famous grandfather, Josephus Daniels.

Dear Sir,

   At a single stroke your powerful newspaper has destroyed my happiness and ruined my reputation. Although for nearly thirty years I have been a citizen of Southern Pines, you describe me as coming from Pinehurst. The difference is immense.

Pinehurst is a resort visited by golfers. Southern Pines is a town inhabited by foxhunters. In the summer, Pinehurst ceases to exist. It is merely an empty village haunted by the ghosts of departed golfers. But all year round, Southern Pines may be seen vigorously flourishing, its noble civic life distinguished by sectarian disputes, town dogs, corner loafers, Kiwanians, caucuses, literary gents, beauty shops and all other attributes of organized metropolitan society.

You can, therefore, conceive my grief at your misapprehension. Especially when I tell you I am a foxhunter, and that all foxhunters are ex-officio Nature's noblemen whose luster no amount of lying, liquor and vaingloriousness can dim. If it could, that luster would have been dimmed long ago.

Golf, on the other hand, is merely the most expensive and depressing form of pedestrianism. It renders its victims on the one hand gloomy and self-pitying, and, on the other, tediously and interminably loquacious. I know of no other practice, except the purchase and consumption of bad liquor, wherein good money can be spent for so pitiable a result.

From all this, you can see the wrong you have done me, and when I add that I never visit Raleigh without making your office into my social club where I try and persuade your City Editor, your Special Writers, your Staff Correspondents and reporters, and the sons of your distinguished owner to desert their labors of getting out the paper and listen to my tales of foxhunting, you will feel, as I do, that you have made me a mighty sorry return.

I am, Yours Truly,

James Boyd

As I FINISHED my walking tour of the grounds, a cleaning crew was tidying up the terrace of the Boyd mansion from a final U.S. Open party. Hearing another rumble of thunder, I hurried up a set of stone steps from the lower perennial garden and ran smack into an old friend.

Cadaverously thin and smoking a cigarette, Brent Hackney was sitting cross-legged at an ornate wrought-iron table, having drinks with a well-dressed middle-aged couple.

The last time I'd seen Brent in person was the night Richard Nixon resigned from the presidency. I was the wire boy in the newsroom of the *Greensboro Daily News,* my dad's and Dirty Derr's old paper. In the mid-1970s, Brent was the Raleigh capital bureau chief for the *Daily News,* a star figure in the state's newspaper cosmos. I recalled his kindness to me, a wide-eyed newspaper apprentice, a generosity I'd never forgotten. Years later, it didn't surprise me to learn he was serving as press secretary to Jim Hunt, the state's popular four-term governor.

When Hackney saw me coming up the steps, he smiled. "Well look who just came out of the woods," he remarked dryly. He stood and extended a hand, offering me a seat. "I heard from David Woronoff that you were coming to work at the paper," he said. "Welcome back to North Carolina."

Brent introduced me to the couple. They ran a nearby art gallery during the winter and were preparing to mount an exhibition in the fall featuring the works of several local artists. The woman handed me a terrific print of a group of the famed Moore County hounds—the riding group founded by James Boyd—sitting in profile.

"We're talking about a possible cover story for this," Brent said, handing me an attractive monthly arts magazine called

PineStraw. "We just got started up, but I think it might have a decent future," he said.

"So you're the editor?"

He nodded. "A group of us locally got it started. It's kind of fun."

I congratulated him on the new publication and suggested we get together for a beer and catch up sometime soon, momentarily forgetting that I might not be sticking around for more than a brief vacation with my family.

The couple turned out to be from Massachusetts and knew my landlady, Lloyd Cutler. They divided their time between Connecticut Avenue and Nantucket Island.

Brent, taking a long drag, drawled: "Bouser says you're here for a year as the paper's writer-in-residence. That's pretty swell."

Steve Bouser was the paper's somewhat impassive editor. It was my impression that Bouser, a veteran newsman with an impressive vita of his own, had decided that young David Woronoff had lost his mind hiring a writer-in-residence for a community newspaper, even one with the literary antecedents of *The Pilot.*

"They just don't know what else to call me," I explained, and left it at that.

"How long will you stay?" Brent wondered.

"Not sure yet."

"Well, you know what they say around here, don't you?" injected the woman pleasantly. "If you get the sand in your shoes, you'll never leave."

I smiled at her, remembering Harvie Ward had said exactly the same thing during one of our pleasant Pine Crest breakfast chats.

"So you think it's true?" I asked her.

"Absolutely" Brent said. He gave me a tired smile. "Stick around and you may find out for yourself."

I RETURNED TO THE CABIN to find an angel standing in the twilight. She was a pretty, older woman dressed entirely in white—white jogging suit, white sneakers, a cowl of thick graying hair. She even had a little white dog. For a crazy moment, in the fading half-light I really did think she might be an angel walking her dog.

"Hello," I said, a bit startled to find this apparition hovering in my driveway, with a storm flickering overhead and threatening to break loose any minute.

"Well, *hi* there," she said with a soft, fluting drawl, smiling at me. "You're the new writer in town, aren't you? I'm your neighbor Myrtis Morrison. And this is Rex. We're from down the block on Pine Grove. The brown wooden house with all the landscaping."

"The yard with the fantastic camellia bushes?" I asked.

"That's right. Camellias are my husband Max's truest love in life. I'm, well, second at best." She gave a cute, husky laugh. "That's where he is right now, as a matter of fact, out in the garden. Weather and darkness rarely stop Max."

We shook hands. I reached down to pet her dog, a Jack Russell. He growled at me.

"Now, Rex, *behave*. I don't want to have to take you home for being rude. This is our new neighbor, Mr. Dodson."

"Jim," I said cordially. "No problem. We have a golden retriever version of him. His real name is Riley but we call him Bummy because he acts like one most of the time."

"Is your family here with you?"

"No, ma'am. I'm going up to Maine and fetch them this week."

She nodded and said, "I was out walking Rex and saw your light on and thought I'd stop in and officially welcome you to the neighborhood. You must be relieved to have all the Open craziness done with."

"Yes, ma'am. I was out for a walk myself to get better acquainted with the neighborhood. It reminds me a lot of the one where I grew up in Greensboro, except that everyone around here seems to have a dog."

Myrtis smiled. "Max says there are more dogs than people in this neighborhood—and half of them more intelligent than their owners."

I took an instant liking to Myrtis Morrison. She possessed the gestures and mannerisms common to a certain generation of Southern women, one that included my mother. I placed Myrtis to be about sixty-five or seventy, fifteen years my mom's junior. Remembering my manners, I asked if she cared to come inside for a glass of wine.

"Another time would be lovely," she said. "I just thought I would come say hello and let you know that this town will become a ghost town for the next five or six weeks. It used to be worse, of course, come summer—Pinehurst shut down completely. Now everybody heads for either the mountains or the beach to cool off."

"I've heard that. Do you and Max stick around?"

She gave her sweet husky laugh. "My daughter Jean and I go off to the beach every now and then, mostly to shop. But Max and Rex won't budge. I don't like to leave Max for long. He lives out in his garden most of the year. We have a pool. Before I forget, that's *really* what I wanted to come and tell you. You should feel free to jump in anytime you'd like to cool off. Only I and our grandchildren ever use it, and they aren't coming until late July this year."

I thanked her for the kind offer and said I might take her up on it, especially when my wife Wendy and our four kids arrived on the scene in a few days. I explained that we were a second marriage and that her boys, Connor and Liam, spent their winters with their dad in Syracuse and their summers and holidays with us. Meanwhile, my two teenagers were back at their mom's house in Maine, plotting their latest intrigues. We were, I joked, one big overextended family.

"These modern marriages," Myrtis said. "I don't see how you all manage to keep everything straight—like who goes where. I see you've been up to Weymouth . . ."

She was looking at the materials I'd brought back from Jim Boyd's upper terrace. I'd returned with a dramatic print of the hunting dogs and Brent Hackney's current issue of *PineStraw.*

"Yes, ma'am. I bumped into a guy I knew thirty-five years ago when I was the wire boy at the newspaper in Greensboro. Talk about a small world. He's the editor of the local arts monthly now."

"It is a small world," she agreed. "What do you think of that particular piece of art?" She indicated the print I'd taken a fancy to half an hour ago.

"Very nice. I think it might be by N. C. Wyeth. I'm sure you know he was a pal of Boyd's and an occasional visitor to Weymouth."

Myrtis Morrison smiled. "That's true. But, actually, my

daughter Elizabeth painted that picture. It was the nicest thing she ever did. People said it was her best. She finished it just before she died."

She provided this information so gently and matter-of-factly, I wasn't certain I'd heard her correctly. Then I saw the water welling up in her large soulful eyes.

"I'm so sorry," I said, taking her arm. "When did that happen?"

"A year ago."

We stood in the deepening dusk without speaking for a moment as she gathered herself, and I tried to imagine her suffering. The thought of losing one of my children before their time—or mine—remained by far my most potent fear.

"You know . . ." Myrtis cleared her throat. "I believe the cancer actually enhanced Elizabeth's artistic talents. Her paintings became more beautiful, almost luminous near the end. Her most productive time as an artist were the two years she was dying from cancer." She gave me a brave smile. "It was almost like we were all being compensated for having to lose her."

A LITTLE WHILE LATER I walked Myrtis Morrison home. She took my arm, moving with a slowness I simply didn't have the courage to inquire about. By then I'd learned that Max Morrison was a retired eye surgeon—the town's longtime eye doc—who was even more of a gardening golf nut than yours truly.

"You'll have to pardon my slowness," she suddenly remarked as if reading my mind. "But after the long ordeal with Elizabeth, I was diagnosed with polymyalgia rheumatica. Prolonged stress can sometimes trigger it. It's an autoimmune disorder that causes severe inflammation of the joints. Some people can barely walk with it. I'm lucky. I've started on medication and have only had to give up tennis. I swim in the evenings. That helps."

"*You* sound like a doctor," I remarked, as we slowly proceeded down the block.

"As a matter of fact, my father was the town doctor over at Red Springs. I guess I'll always be a doctor's daughter."

Before I could comment, Myrtis Morrison squeezed my arm and said almost playfully, "I think that was a sign."

"What's that?" I asked.

"Your showing up with Elizabeth's painting. I believe in signs like that. I think we were meant to meet."

"I do too," I agreed. The older I got, the more I did seem to detect prevailing patterns and signs in the seen and unseen movements of life.

"Listen, if you don't have plans for tomorrow night, come to supper."

"That's very kind, but I wouldn't want to impose on you." I didn't tell her I planned to shove off for home in a matter of hours. Something about her reminded me of my late mom.

"Don't be ridiculous. Max already has some early tomatoes and fresh corn and I'm thinking of doing a flank steak on the grill. Nothing fancy. It'll be nice to cook for someone besides Max." With this she let out a sweet, endearing laugh.

Max was in the garden behind their magnificently landscaped house, an older gent in shapeless pants and brightly banded straw hat. As we approached, Dr. Morrison glanced up, scowling, and Myrtis squeezed my arm warningly and whispered, "Don't let Max's grumpiness throw you. He hasn't smiled since Elizabeth was diagnosed. Under that gruff exterior he's really a dear fellow. She was a wild thing but had her father wrapped around her finger."

As she said this I thought of my own wild thing of a daughter, Maggie, who had her father wrapped around her finger, too. One summer that now seemed only a few moments ago, Maggie and I and our old dog Amos had spent several weeks camping and fly-fishing our way across America. Basically most anything that could go wrong did go wrong. We lost the dog for a while in Yellowstone Park, caught very few trout, and blew up our aging truck in Oklahoma. In short, we had the time of our lives. That was a decade ago, and my seven-year-old traveling companion was now busy looking at potential colleges. I harbored a secret hope that a school in North Carolina might catch her fancy.

"Max, I want you to meet Jim," Myrtis Morrison said. "He's our new neighbor. Lloyd's tenant in the cabin."

"Our new neighborhood *word*smith, huh?" Dr. Morrison pronounced *wordsmith* like it might be something one should scrape from the sole of one's boot before entering the house.

"Nice to meet you, sir." We shook hands. He had the grip of a golfing gardener or maybe it was the other way around. I figured him to be an extremely fit seventy-five, give or take a few years for natural contrariness.

"You from North Carolina?" Doc Morrison demanded, eyeing me as if I might be yet another rich carpetbagger come to the Pines just to ride ponies or chase a golf ball. I could tell from his slow and easy accent that he hailed from somewhere west of Mayberry and east of Mount Pilot.

"Yes sir, I am. Many generations in fact."

"Well," Doc Morrison said, "you never know where folks come from *these* days. Everyone moves around so doggone

much. Lot of 'em round here still come from the North, you
know. Yankees trying to escape the cold. Can't say I blame 'em.
Southern Pines was started by Yankees. Bet you didn't know
that, did you? Almost nobody's actually from *here* anymore." He
snapped his pruning shears to emphasize the point.

"They have that same problem in Maine," I agreed.

"I thought you said you were from North Carolina?" He
sounded suspicious *and* grumpy. I was really warming up to
this guy, even if he still wasn't sure about me.

"I am. I've just lived in Maine the past twenty-five years. But
I'll never be considered a Mainer." I told him a joke about being a perpetual flatlander from "away" in the land of lobsters,
and how my Maine-born children would never be considered
native. "Just 'cause your cat has kittens in the oven," goes the
punchline, "don't make 'em biscuits."

Max gave a faint smile. "That's kind of *cute*. So what are you
doing back here?"

"Jim's writing a Sunday column for *The Pilot* for the year,
Max," Myrtis provided brightly. "He's planning to stay the
whole year if he doesn't miss his wife and children too much.
They're still up in Maine."

Max grunted. "Hope you know your grammar. Most media
people these days seem downright illiterate."

"I'll do my best, sir."

I complimented him on his garden, waving my hand over
his impressive domain. Even in the thundery dark I could make
out camellia bushes stretching far into the forest. "How many
camellia bushes do you have out here?"

"Have no idea," Max grunted. "Over a hundred different varieties, though. You a gardener?"

"I am."

"Jim is writing a book about gardening," Myrtis provided as cheerfully as a press agent.

"That so?" Max glared at me as if he couldn't believe what an unfortunate state the honorable pastime of gardening had sunk to.

"Yes, sir. My ancestors from Carrboro were all crazy gardeners."

"Jim's coming to dinner tomorrow night, Max," Myrtis persisted sweetly, "before he drives home to Maine on Tuesday to get his children and bring them back for a visit."

"You're *driving?*"

"Yes sir." I pointed out it was only fifteen hours from one door to the other, assuming you don't stop for more than flushing a toilet and gassing up in New Jersey. Long-distance driving, I added, provided me with excellent time to think and make notes for writing projects.

"Good heavens. You *write* as you drive?" He looked horrified at the menace I posed to the traveling public.

Then he surprised me with a sudden wintery smile, as he stooped to pick up weeds and cuttings. "That reminds me of a bumper sticker I saw on the way home from the golf course yesterday. It said, 'Sometimes I wake up Grumpy. Sometimes I let her sleep.'"

"That's a good one," I agreed, smiling, pleased to hear he was a golfer after all. But Myrtis looked at me and rolled her eyes.

"If you like that, one day I'll tell you my talking dog story. It's quite humorous." Doc Morrison continued picking up clippings.

Myrtis's eyes widened in mock horror, and, as her husband's

attention went elsewhere, she silently mouthed, "Oh, no! Anything but the talking dog story!"

Then she informed her husband, "Guess what Jim found over at Weymouth, Max? Someone gave him a copy of Elizabeth's painting of the Moore County hounds."

"It's really wonderful," I said. "At first I thought it was N. C. Wyeth."

Holding an armful of brush, Dr. Morrison straightened up and nodded faintly, his smile gone.

"Glad you like it," he said, turning back to his garden. Over his shoulder he added distantly, "I suppose we'll see you tomorrow night then."

CHAPTER FOUR

Idle Knights Adventure
and Philosophy Club

B Y THE TIME my neighbor's rooster let loose, I was already at my desk, using my extra day in the Sandhills to finish up some promised work. When an unexpected loud rap sounded at the kitchen door, I opened it to discover Tom Stewart, dressed in a faded Michigan sweatshirt and grinning like an Irish wood sprite with a dirty secret.

"The dawn breaks, O, Idle Knight! The reservoir awaits! Grab your shoes and let's go! Not a minute to waste if we're going to honor our sacred vows to the ladies."

"What vows are you talking about?" I asked, making him come inside.

Tom bounded into my kitchen. "Say, this is one great place. Wendy's going to love it. Who knew *you* had such good taste!"

I loved Tom Stewart. We met one afternoon during the 1999 U.S. Open when I came to his shop to sign copies of *Final Rounds,* and the friendship had deepened with every encounter.

The Old Sport and Gallery, off the village square in Pine-hurst, was perhaps the most eclectic and fascinating golf shop in the world, filled with fine sporting art, rare prints, strange col-lectibles, exquisite first-edition sports books, and Russian folk art that Tom's beautiful wife, Ilana, a longtime senior flight at-tendant for Delta Airlines, brought back from her regular trips home to Russia. Before coming to Pinehurst, Tom had served as head professional at two of the country's most distinguished private golf clubs and traveled the world on the Australian and South American professional golf tours. He'd also run ten mara-thons on three continents, read more books on philosophy and politics than anyone I knew, and taught former Soviet Premier Mikhail Gorbachev to play golf. He'd been a childhood golf chum of Tom Watson in rural Michigan and was buddies with Tour star Bernhard Langer. He basically seemed to know every person in the golf world by first name. He also kept an inex-haustible supply of Irish jokes—although he'd shamelessly ap-propriated some of mine and called them his own.

A friend who can make you laugh, as the Koran points out, is a gift from God—and Tom was perhaps the only guy I knew who'd read the Koran. Among the lesser known facts in the Stewart vita, he had come close to taking vows as a Jesuit priest and still carried himself off annually for a spiritual re-treat to the same Kentucky monastery where his hero, Thomas Merton, had lived and worked.

Sri Tommy, as I'd taken to fondly calling him, helped himself to the last of my morning coffee. I asked what *vows* to our wives he was talking about.

"The first night you arrived? We told Wendy we'd agreed to inspire each other to exercise, to shape up our bodies and our minds! A successful life is about wise revision! We agreed to start at dawn the morning after the U.S. Open. That would be today, mate."

"I guess I forgot." I told him how he would have found a dark cabin if it hadn't been for my neighbor Myrtis Morrison's dinner invitation. By now I'd have been somewhere around the Delaware Bridge.

"So, you see," he piped up. "It's a sign. The invisible shaping hand of Providence! We're Idle Knights meant to inspire each other to heights of service and thinner selves." He picked up a blueberry muffin and began to nibble on it. "So what are you writing about?"

I explained that I was finishing up a piece on Jack Nicklaus's farewell to St. Andrews, having announced that he would be playing in his final British Open this summer, further evidence that the end of an era was upon us.

"Who are you doing it for?" Tom asked.

"An editor friend at the *London Times.*"

"Well, London can wait. There's no time to waste, young Kajeido wanderer! Golf, like life, is subject to change without notice. Grab your sneakers and let's get to the reservoir before the dog-walking crowd gets there. I want to show you something that will blow your mind, and tell you about my new ten-year plan."

"Ten-year plan?" Realizing there was little point in resisting, I went to find my sneakers. "And what exactly is a Kajeido wanderer?"

"Colman McCarthy started calling me that back when I was running for Congress in Michigan. I don't know where he came up with it, but its supposed to be a spiritual seeker, a warrior in training, a guy in search of greater meaning in life, ready to be of service to all. McCarthy called me that after I came back from Findhorn in Scotland. I had a full beard in those days. So I guess I looked like a wanderer."

"You were at Findhorn?"

I knew a little about Findhorn, a New Age community not far from Donald Ross's hometown at Dornoch. It was where spiritual pilgrims grew otherworldly vegetables and believed angels whispered to plants. During my year of living horticulturally, I'd been half tempted to go there to see what all the fuss was about. But getting so close to Ross's birthplace would have sorely tempted me to abandon my time in the wilderness in favor of playing golf, so I never reached Findhorn. I should have guessed Tom Stewart had.

"Studied Chinese philosophy and calligraphy there." He gave me a sly wink. "Actually, I was mostly there for the hippie girls. But don't tell Ilana."

I located my sneakers exactly where I'd placed them, one under the bed, the other by the front door. Living like a bachelor again had both pleasures and drawbacks.

"Did I hear you say you ran for Congress?"

"I did. Had to shave my beard off, though. Almost won, too—a progressive Democrat in a district full of conservative Republicans. It was the golfers who nearly sent me to Washington."

Tom followed me to the kitchen, bouncing on his heels like an aging prizefighter chomping to get in the ring.

"Is there anything you haven't done?" I asked, remembering maybe the most surprising thing in Tom's past—during his Tour days when he went to see Mother Teresa in the slums of

Calcutta and wound up working several months for the future saint.

"I could give you a short list. Stop global warming. End this absurd war in Iraq. Persuade you to speak at the Sandhills Men's Breakfast Fellowship next Tuesday morning at eight."

Tom also directed the monthly breakfast program at the Pinehurst Resort and arranged an impressive roster of speakers. The event had featured retired five-star generals and Nobel Prize winners, some of whom were passing through the area, others who called the Sandhills home. I was flattered that he wanted me to speak. I just wasn't sure which category I fit into.

In truth, if Harvie Ward first placed the idea of returning to my boyhood haunts in my head, Tom Stewart was probably the reason I actually did it.

The morning after I said goodbye to Harvie, Tom picked me up in the dawn darkness at the Pine Crest Inn and drove us through the ancient Uwharrie hills west of town to meet golf entrepreneur Bill Perry and his son, Taylor, at the Old North State Club in Asheboro for a round of golf I'd decided would be my last until I returned from my golf sabbatical.

The remote Uwharrie hills were regarded as the sacred navel of the earth by the Native American peoples who originally inhabited the rugged hills that begin west of Pinehurst. Marking the boundary where the upland Piedmont commences and a prehistoric ocean ends, the sparsely populated Uwharries were best known by me as the place my father used to bring my brother and me to hunt for arrowheads and other traces of a lost race around Town Creek Indian Mound.

As I explained to Tom that day during the hour's drive

through the darkened hills, my father's grandmother was a full-blooded Cherokee whom everyone around Dodson's Crossroads near Chapel Hill knew simply as Aunt Emma, a gifted healer whose farm on Buckhorn Road had been my father's favorite spot as a boy. He was proud of his Indian blood and shared her view that nature was sacred, a holy place meant to be honored and cared for by the generations.

It was on the way home after one of our arrowhead-hunting expeditions to these very same Uwharries that my father brought my brother and me over to nearby Pinehurst to have a look at what he affectionately called "another kind of birthplace." I was eleven or twelve when I first laid eyes on the gorgeous, whimsically meandering avenues and grand old houses of James Walker Tufts's idealized Yankee village in the longleaf pines.

"He took us to look at No. 2 and then to the Carolina Hotel for dinner, telling us about the greats of the game who'd come here to play—Jones, Hagen, Sarazen, Snead, Hogan, even my hero at that time, Arnold Palmer," I explained.

Tom grinned. "So, technically speaking, you could call yourself a *native* son of the game."

"Now that you mention it," I agreed, "I suppose I could. I certainly will now."

"Did you get to play No. 2?"

"Oh, no. That didn't happen for many years. But I took up playing golf seriously after that and eventually got decent enough to be invited to play with my dad and his buddies at his club in Greensboro. You may recall my embarrassing beginning."

Tom smiled, remembering the story I'd mentioned in *Final Rounds*. "That's right. You missed a putt and slammed your putter into the green and your dad made you fix the damage and go apologize to the head pro. You never got to complete your first round of golf on a regulation course . . . He threw you off or something like that."

"That's right. But that's not the proverbial rest of the story."

"What's the rest?"

The very next Sunday after church, I explained, I was still moping around, feeling sorry for myself when my dad calmly instructed me to fetch my clubs and put them in the car. Without saying where we were headed, we drove out of Greensboro toward some unknown destination.

"Ostensibly we were taking fruit baskets to a couple of maiden aunts who lived together in a log house near Hillsborough. But after that we headed south through the countryside, talking about everything except golf. Suddenly we rolled into Pinehurst. It was exactly the way I remembered it from that first visit, so beautiful and serene, a postcard golf paradise."

Tom shook his head. "Please don't tell me the first golf course you ever played was Pinehurst No. 2."

"Nope. That didn't happen until I was fourteen, a year or so later. He did, however, drive me to Mid Pines Golf Club a few miles further down Midland Road. We parked the car and walked inside the pro shop, and there stood none other than Julius Boros, the U.S. Open champ, chatting with his brother Ernie, the head professional there. I was speechless. But my dad knew Ernie Boros, and he, in turn, introduced me to Julius Boros, who kindly took a Mid Pines visor, autographed the brim, and gave it to me. He asked me if I enjoyed playing golf. I told him that I did. 'In that case you should take care of the game,' he said to me, 'so others can enjoy it, too.' I assured him I would do that from now on."

"Wow," Tom said admiringly. "Do you think your dad set the whole thing up?"

"I never thought to ask him. He might have. After that, he and I walked outside to the terrace and watched a group of guys play the eighteenth hole. He casually said to me something like, 'Beautiful, isn't it? You know, Bo, this can all be yours if you figure out how to calm down and behave properly on the golf course.' I vowed on the spot I would never throw a golf club or beat up a green as long as I lived. 'Good enough. In that case,' he told me, 'let's get our clubs and play.' So we did. Mid Pines became the place I played my first full eighteen holes of golf." I thought for a moment and added, "It's still probably my favorite golf course. I can't wait to take Jack there."

Tom smiled again. "That'll be like passing the torch. What a great story. Did you ever throw a golf club again?"

"Not when my dad was anywhere in sight."

With that, Tom began telling me about his own golf beginnings in Northern Michigan, a boyhood idyll that sounded straight out of Hemingway's Nick Adams stories. The son of a nurse and a rural mail carrier from tiny Petoskey, Tom still carried the hickory-shafted mashie niblick his father used to win the Michigan state high school golfing championship in 1931. Tom grew up playing golf in the summer with Tom Watson and his older brother, Ridge, at the Walloon Lake Country Club, where he also worked as the waterman.

"Before that, though, my first job was caddying at the Petoskey-Bayview Country Club," he remembered. " I followed my older brother Bob there. I was barely tall enough to carry a bag. My dad was a working man who basically quit playing golf after high school. One of the happiest moments of my life came when Bob and I put our caddie money together and paid Pop's green fee at a municipal golf course. He hadn't touched those old hickory clubs of his in over twenty-five years. He went out that day, though, and shot seventy-four. Bob and I both cried."

By the time we reached the parking lot of the Old North State, the two of us had revealed many details of our lives, including my unexpected need to get away from the game for a time in hope of finding some useful perspective. I told him about my plan to take a year's sabbatical and gave him an abbreviated summary of the sequence of unsettling events beginning with my mom's death and ending with the loss of the Last Amateur that made this escape necessary.

"It's kind of nice to be able to speak to another guy about stuff like this," I confessed to Tom.

"I agree," he said. "A good golf buddy is nature's compensation for being unable to pick your relatives. Golf is hard but life is harder. Welcome to middle age, mate, the loneliest time of the modern American male's life." He gently punched my arm. "Fortunately, I have just the remedy for what's ailing you . . ." He sounded like he'd been speaking to Harvie Ward—which, as I later learned, he had.

"What's that?"

"*Me.* You go off to Africa and do what you have to do with plant hunters —think of it as your biblical sojourn in the wilderness—then come back to Pinehurst, and we'll set off together to rediscover our inner golf lads. Mother Teresa used to say you have to save yourself before you can save the world."

"You're probably right," I agreed. We were sitting in the

empty parking lot of the Old North State Club, an hour or so before the course opened for play. I felt better just airing my problems to a kindred spirit like Tom.

"Of *course* I'm right! Come here and we'll help each other find our games again. Mother Teresa once said to me that the greatest measure of your life's success is what you leave behind. I know two great things we can leave behind."

"What's that?" I asked.

Tom smiled, for once not fooling around. "Jack and Bryan. If you come here, we can help them become true sons of the game the way we did. Can you think of anything better to pass along to them than the simple joy of playing golf with a buddy?"

I nodded. The older I got, the more I decided that was all golf was really about. "I think that's why Harvie gave me the putter for Jack," I said.

"That *exactly* why he gave you that putter for Jack!"

And with that, he told me a dirty Irish joke I'd recently told him.

"So TELL ME ABOUT your big ten-year plan," I asked Sri Tommy now as we hiked vigorously along a narrow sandy path above the glittering Southern Pines reservoir, a spectacular spot with tall longleaf pines swaying in a mild morning breeze.

"Pretty simple," Tom said between ragged breaths. "I'm fifty-nine years old. In a year I'll be sixty, and Ilana and I will have been in Pinehurst for exactly ten years. Bryan will soon be heading out the door to college. It'll be time to make a new life plan. Every ten years or so, see, I reinvent myself."

I asked if this talk on "reinvention" had anything to do with his brother's recent unexpected death.

"Bob's death reminded me how precious little time we have to make a contribution to this world. Mother Teresa taught me this. I was one of her biggest miracles, after all."

"How's that?" I asked as we huffed and puffed along the narrow trail.

"As you know, I was playing the Asian Tour, and I went to play in the Calcutta Open one day in 1979. What you don't know, though, is that I was a cocky, self-centered young dude who had no clue why he was really on this planet other than to make birdies, see the world, and meet pretty girls. But I'd just finished reading Malcolm Muggeridge's *Something Beautiful for God* and knew that Mother Teresa was operating a home for the dying in Calcutta. On a lark, inspired by that, I thought it might be interesting to hang around and see if I could somehow be useful to her for a couple days. So I went to morning mass and walked up and brazenly introduced myself to her. What a *tiny* woman she was, with a face like a wise old root vegetable! I told her what I wanted to do and she just . . . *smiled*. 'Can you drive a car?' she asked me. 'Yes, ma'am,' I replied. 'Good,' she said and made me follow her. Turned out, the pope had sent her a brand-new ambulance. She handed me the keys, and I began that same day picking up dying people from the streets of Calcutta and bringing them back to the home—shaving and bathing them, changing their soiled bedclothes, performing jobs I could never have imagined I'd be doing. It was disturbing and yet moving and oddly . . . liberating. Mother Teresa had a favorite saying—'Your results are unimportant. Your effort is all that matters.'

"She wasn't like the press made her out to be—an icon or a saint. She used to say saints were just dead people who got things done. She was one tough little lady, very much alive, extremely human. I saw her get angry and shout at people and weep over the world's injustices. But she was passionate and unbending about what she did, plunging ahead on faith and hard work, running two hundred houses for the poor far more efficiently than any CEO in America."

Tom smiled, shaking his head, sweat dripping off the end of his pug nose. "Let me tell you, if the chairman of General Motors had spent a few days with Mother Teresa, that company wouldn't be in the mess it's in. The experience fundamentally changed me. I planned to stay two weeks. I stayed two months and came home a very different guy."

I asked for more details.

"I went back to my club pro job in Michigan but also became an activist for the poor. I still loved golf—like you, that was in my blood since I was a kid—but I decided to run for Congress on a platform promoting fiscal conservatism and social justice. I was the only golf pro in America running for Congress that year. Thanks to golfers, I nearly upset a six-term conservative Republican who outspent me fifty to one."

Tom suddenly veered left onto a rutted path that wound up a sandy ravine recently washed out by heavy rains. I dutifully followed. He seemed to know exactly where he was headed.

"So how'd you end up in Pinehurst?" I suddenly realized that I didn't know this part of the Stewart saga. His life sounded like a golf version of *Pilgrim's Progress*.

"Another little miracle," he said with an impish grin. "Or maybe I should say a wild leap of faith."

He fell silent. We pushed hard up the hill, wordlessly sucking in the cool morning air. We eventually paused to catch our breath at the top of the hill, from where we could see several handsome brick buildings in the middle distance. It looked like some kind of school.

Tom placed his hands on his hips, breathing hard.

"This getting back into shape can be dangerous for your health," I said, also gulping air.

He grinned as if in pain. "Nine years ago, I had a job most guys would die for. I was head professional for one of the top private clubs in America, had a young son and a fabulous wife, all the money I needed, lots of influential friends — everything our society values and claims will bring you happiness. On paper, it was the perfect deal, except for one thing. You can probably guess what it was."

"You wanted a crazy sheep dog."

He laughed. Tom's dog, Scotty, was perhaps the craziest sheep dog on the planet.

"You're right, I did. But Scotty came later. No, it was simpler than that. As the Buddhists say, my joy bell was broken. One day I woke up and knew something vital was missing."

What he told me next, in the privacy of this glorious pine forest, was both surprising and oddly comforting to hear.

"I was fifty years old and suddenly realized I was sick and tired of the golf world — maybe even fed up with playing the game, as unthinkable as that might sound." He glanced at me thoughtfully and added, "Sound like anybody you know? See, you thought you were such an original head case — the only guy to hit the midlife wall."

I nodded, eager to hear more. Tom appeared to be one of

the happiest and best-adjusted guys I knew. Over a beer at Dugan's Pub he once told me, "There are no bad days. Only poor attention."

"So what did you do?"

"Jumped on a plane to North Carolina. During college I spent a great year in Chapel Hill and always intended to go back there and have a second look. I thought perhaps I'd open a bookstore specializing in philosophy and classic sports books, something like that, though nothing was very clear in that department. But something told me I needed to come here, so I did—leaving it pretty much in God's hands. Poor Ilana thought I was having a mental breakdown. This was just after we'd gotten her parents settled here from Russia. The timing couldn't have been worse, in many respects."

After a few days of snooping around Chapel Hill, however, he realized that wasn't where he needed to be.

"Some old friends from my first pro job in Michigan had retired to Pinehurst. I phoned them up, and they invited me to come down for a visit. Naturally I knew all about Pinehurst and Southern Pines—what golfer doesn't?—but strangely enough I'd never been there. So I decided to go see my friends and have a look at No. 2 to see if it was a good as everybody said. Frankly, I was unprepared for what I found."

He went for an afternoon stroll through the village, charmed by its timeless avenues and cottages, and passed a beautiful brick building with a for-rent sign in the window. Within an hour, he'd tracked down the realtor and placed a rental deposit on the Harvard Building.

"That's a leap of faith," I agreed.

The Old Sport smiled. "I didn't even know *why* I'd rented the building. I just knew we were *supposed* to be in Pinehurst. I telephoned Ilana and asked her to fly up and give me her opinion on something important, though I didn't dare tell her what I'd done. Fortunately, as soon as she saw Pinehurst and the building, she felt exactly the way I did. Our future was *here.*"

Now the Stewarts owned the cute little Harvard Building, and the Old Sport and Gallery was known far and wide across the world of golf.

I had a sudden worrying thought—his *new* ten-year plan might involve giving up Old Sport and making a new leap of faith to someplace else—maybe off to Findhorn to grow mystical rutabegas.

Sri smiled, shaking his head. He had obviously already given this topic considerable thought.

"Are you *kidding*? Coming here was a new beginning for us, a genuine rebirth of the spirit. We couldn't leave the Sandhills. I've been a lot of places on this planet, but I've never seen a place that has such healing energy. I don't mean to go metaphysical on you, pal, but when you stop to think about it, there is absolutely nothing in the Sandhills that should physically appeal to people.

"Think about it. We're three hours from the mountains and three hours from the ocean, dead center of nowhere, with no big cities or recreational lakes nearby, and nothing but these scruffy old sandy hills with soil of little agricultural value and a million acres of lonely pine trees in all directions. Yet people have flocked here and found their true selves. This place is heaven in a wasteland."

Sri Tommy poked me on the shoulder like he was choosing up sides for a game of tag. "That's the mystery *you're* here to figure out. What is it about these old Sandhills that gets so deep into people's hearts and minds? Harvie and I used to talk about this. We decided a seasoned golf writer or an investigative reporter was needed to finally solve the mystery. That's where you come in, Ace. You've been both."

I smiled. "Sounds good. But I have a confession to make. I played hooky yesterday from the Open—couldn't bear to watch another day of golf. I'm not sure whether I've lost interest in playing golf or it's lost interest in me. Either way, it seems like a chore now. Never dreamed I'd say that."

Tom didn't seem fazed by this news. "When I arrived here, I didn't care if I ever played golf again. It's true. I was that burned out. In time, however, I realized it wasn't this four-hundred-year-old game that was the problem, it was the golf business and all the stuff around the game. What the PGA Tour has become is an excellent example of the problem. To the Tour and its players, this is no longer a game. It's an industry, a bottom-line corporation, a commodity. The money's too large, the passion too small. Those guys look like they're having root canals out there. You know who else felt this way when he came here—at the same age as we did, by the way?"

"I can't imagine."

"Harvie Ward. He told me he had to fall back in love with the simply joy of playing golf and finding his missing inner golf child. Teaching young people to play the game brought that back to him. This place is really about the amateur, not the professional. Richard Tufts, after all, wrote the Amateur Creed."

He was right, of course. The grandson of the founder was so dedicated to the proposition that golf should be played for the joy of competing against a friend or simply Old Man Par, he eventually stopped the professional segment of the famed North and South Open, which had saved Ben Hogan's skin in 1940, fearing what the growing influence of playing for money and corporate sponsorship could do to the game.

"So how about you?" I asked Tom pointedly.

"I think I just needed to shake things up a bit, maybe strike off in some once and future directions. The old Mother Teresa activist in me, I guess, is eager to get to work. Issues of poverty and justice are calling me again."

"Maybe you should toss your golf cap into the ring and make another run for Congress. There's so many golfers around here, you're bound to win."

"Maybe I will after Bryan finishes high school. Meanwhile, I'm delighted to know you're going to be here for the year. We can continue to shoot the breeze and bat these ideas around on a regular morning walk around the water. One of my favorite poets said sometimes the answer is simply a good walk around the lake — or in our case, the golf course."

"Sounds good," I said, recognizing a line from Wallace Stevens, trying to remember if the poet played golf, too.

WE WALKED AROUND a building and came to the entrance of a gorgeous garden.

"Voilà," Sri said, waving an arm. "Here's what I wanted to show you."

"What *is* this place?"

"Sandhills Community College. This is the school's botanic garden. There's a new Japanese garden just ahead. I wanted to be the first to show it to you."

An hour later, we arrived back at Tom's van, exhausted but

happy. I thanked Tom for prying me loose from Jack Nicklaus and work—and, for that matter, luring me back to the Sandhills, however long I wound up staying. His speech about how the pro game had changed but Pinehurst essentially hadn't, and how we had an opportunity to pass along the real point of a four-hundred-year-old game to our sons the way our dads had faithfully passed it to us, was now giving me serious second thoughts about my previous second thoughts about staying.

"We ought to do this at least twice a week—when we're not playing golf," Tom proposed, mopping his brow with an old golf towel from the back of his car. "A long hike and good talk are beneficial in more ways than one."

"We could start a club," I joked, "for Idle Knights and armchair philosophers like us. A walking, talking, golfing club."

"The Idle Knights Adventure and Philosophy Club," Tom said out loud. "It has a nice ring. Everyone else in Pinehurst belongs to a club or society of some kind, so why not us? I can think of half a dozen excellent candidates. Dirty Derr, Corso, and Dempsey to begin with, maybe even David Woronoff if he's old enough to drive or shave yet. Kelly Miller and Doc Morris would be naturals. We'll be the new Tin Whistles."

The Tin Whistles, a famous club within a club at the Pinehurst Country Club, began as a drinking association and turned into a legendary golf association with members across the map.

As for Idle Knight prospects, I knew John Derr and Pat Corso. Derr and I were old friends from the Hogan trail, and Corso was the dynamic executive who'd been at the helm when the Pinehurst Resort mounted its first U.S. Open in 1999. Kelly Miller was the delightful chap who ran my favorite golf resort just down the road, Mid Pines and its sister, Pine Needles, soon to host its third U.S. Women's Open. All three were good fellows and philosophical types. Walt Morris was Harvie's physician, about the same age as David Woronoff. Walt and I had tried to get together for a round of golf for years but had never managed to. He had a great sense of humor and a load of Harvie stories to tell.

"Remind me," I said, "have I met brother Dempsey? What are his qualifications for Idle status?"

"Dempsey is the president of this college. Heck of a storyteller, completely mad for golf. He turned this place into a dynamo. Great short game."

"He's in," I said, warming to the proposition. "Maybe Dempsey can be official keeper of the Sacred Sand Wedge."

"Good choice," Tom agreed. "Do we *have* a Sacred Sand Wedge?"

"Memo to self: Buy Sacred Sand Wedge," I said.

"I'll get to work on the official Idle Knights blazer patch. Maybe traditionally crossed golf clubs, an open book, a burning candle symbolizing wisdom, and a pair of feet propped up comfortably at the end of the day."

We solemnly shook hands to officially establish our new club or secret society—whatever it was going to be. Or maybe not so solemnly. That seemed to be the point.

"Say, what's our club motto?" I wondered. Organizational details were already piling up in my head.

"How about . . . To walk the walk *and* talk the talk. To elevate man's higher nature and serve his lower needs. To play golf, buy the beer, and argue civilly at all times."

"Excellent," I responded. "Maybe we could also work in something about women and inappropriate male humor."

"Absolutely." With this he told me a joke about three nervous Pakistanis attempting to pass a quiz about the meaning of Easter, administered by the Reverend Jerry Falwell, and sneak into Christian heaven.

"Should this be a secret golf society?" I wondered after I quit laughing.

"Not unless somebody tells our wives."

AT DUSK, WITH A bottle of Greg Norman cabernet in hand, I walked down the street to the Morrison house and rang their doorbell, reliving an unexpectedly fine day in my head and feeling more relaxed and happy than anytime since I had arrived in the Sandhills.

Whatever else was true, the impromptu hike around the reservoir with Tom had done my uncertain mind a world of good—and perhaps helped revise my plans once again.

Inspired by our Idle Knights silliness, with a summer afternoon to fill up before my appointed dinner engagement at the Morrison home, I'd finished my essay for the *Times* and sent it on its merry way through the Internet, then shouldered my Hogan clubs and set off with an Idle sense of curiosity to check out the venerable Elks Club golf course five blocks from the cabin.

I'd never laid eyes on the place but knew it by reputation. Originally it had been the Southern Pines Country Club, a former private club now owned by the Benevolent and Protective Order of the Elks. I'd long heard what a "gem in the rough" the old Elks course was, supposedly an original Ross layout that hadn't been altered much.

I found the Elks Club swimming pool chock full of kids and moms, and the adjacent golf course sitting under a dome of intense afternoon heat, devoid of human activity. The friendly head professional drowsing inside the air-conditioned shop collected twenty-two dollars from me and waved me on to the first tee.

In light of my morning conversation with Tom, another real question was whether I had a game even worth rehabilitating—not to mention the motivation to do so. Perhaps the steep falloff I'd experienced in both desire and skill simply indicated I was growing older and finding wider interests. Golf had always been close to the center of my being, but lately it didn't seem nearly as important as it used to—or, more accurately, actually seemed irrelevant in a world that appeared to be coming apart at the seams.

I walked to the first tee and pegged a new Titleist Pro V1. The first fairway, an elk's eyelash over 350 yards long, swept downhill to a tiered green, moderately bunkered left and right, a relatively easy but classic Ross opener.

It was a lovely hole, and I wished Jack had been playing it with me. On impulse, before I hit my drive, I took out my cell phone and dialed his number. The phone rang twice and his voice came on. "Hey, it's Jack. Leave a message, and I'll call you back." *Beep.*

"Hey, Ace," I said cheerfully. "It's your old dad. I'm standing at the first tee of a golf course I'd love to play with you sometime, a hidden Donald Ross gem. Maybe we'll play it when you get down here. Hope you're having a nice afternoon. I'll call you later."

I struck a fine opening drive, splitting the fairway into neat halves.

As I set off, I found myself remembering the delightful

father-son trip to Scotland that Jack and I hosted for PerryGolf a few years back. Jack, ten at the time, wasn't old enough to play at most of the famous linkslands we visited, a roster that included the Old Course at St. Andrews, Carnoustie, Nairn, and Royal Dornoch. But he caddied uncomplainingly and seemed to have a fine time getting to know the other fathers and their adult sons. At Nairn we teamed up to beat another father-son duo, and down the stretch at Dornoch, in a seesaw match with scratch golf paper and his son-in-law, Jack's eagle eye found my hooked second shot on the difficult par-four sixteenth hole lying half buried in the sand just inside the tide line out on the shingled beach, leaving me a blind shot to a small green in the dunes.

Jack scaled a dune to serve as a human aiming post and yelled out his calculation of the distance to the hole—175 yards—through hands cupped against the brisk sea wind. A moment later, I struck a five-iron flush and watched it soar straight over my son's head. As the ball passed overhead, he pirouetted and thrust both his arms into the air—a human exclamation point of joy. The ball had finished three inches from the cup, and we made a birdie to take a lead we never relinquished. It was the best shot I'd ever made.

The evening after the group supper, Jack and I went out to the "wee" course at Dornoch and played until dark, finishing most of the holes. "Dad," he said to me as we were walking back to our hotel through the streets of the village where Donald Ross grew up and fell in love with the game, "I can't wait to play a real golf course with you." I assured him I felt exactly the same way.

Two days later, that chance came at the newly opened Kingsbarns Golf Links near St. Andrews. On a cool windy morning, Jack and I went out with a man named Scott Whittaker and his grown son, Nathan, and played a full eighteen holes on a championship course that would soon host the vaunted Dunhill Cup. Jack shot a very respectable 120, with no mulligans. That evening, after an emotional goodbye supper during which the other fathers and sons presented him a silver plaque recognizing his contributions to the pilgrimage, Jack and I walked around the Old Grey Toon, checking out Old Tom Morris's grave in the ruins of the cathedral, and looking at the infamous road hole bunker on the Old Course, where I'd recently spread some of my father's ashes. We crossed the Swilcan Burn and finished our day drinking grape sodas and sitting on the steps of the magisterial Royal and Ancient clubhouse, enjoying the sunset over the West Sands of St. Andrews, the birthplace of the game.

"Dad," he said to me, "would you ever want to be in the Royal and Ancient Golf Club?"

I admitted that I would. The R and A, after all, was the governing body of golf throughout the world outside the United States, and besides, I was already a member of the USGA. Also, something about the way the game was respected and played in Scotland greatly appealed to me. "Over here," I explained to my son, "it's really about the game and who you play with; it's the pleasure of the match. I like that. I once played the Old Course with a town butcher and a fellow who owned a castle."

"I think you should join the Royal and Ancient," Jack decided.

"Well," I allowed with a smile, "if they invited me, I probably wouldn't say no. They have to invite you in, though."

"They probably will," he assured me, drinking his grape soda.

"You think so?"

"Oh yeah. Then we can come back and play the Old Course, too."

"It's a date," I promised. "Even if they don't invite me to join."

THE BERMUDA FAIRWAYS of the Elk's Club course were choked with dandelions and chickweed and actually bare to the sand in many spots. But they marched smartly up and down a tidy set of pine-forested hills in a charming demonstration that the famous author of Pinehurst No. 2 and Mid Pines—or perhaps it was some Ross wannabe (a local historian contended that Ross may not have been the designer of the Southern Pines Club, whose records were lost in a fire)— certainly knew what he was doing in terms of routing a golf course naturally over the existing terrain.

The trademarks of Donald Ross were evident to me—small, open-fronted greens, slightly crowned putting surfaces, unforgivingly sloped in places, fairways that were kind to the rank beginner but cinched like a prairie schoolmarm's corset in the spots where the better golfer would choose to fire his tee shot.

The course powerfully recalled Mid Pines and even Augusta National in spots, and I wondered what its state of neglect meant. Rumors around town hold that several groups were attempting to gain control of the layout and restore it, but the Elks stubbornly refused to relinquish it. In any case, I was fairly sure my wife, a relatively new golfer, was going to like the place. Hopefully Jack would, too.

I played at a brisk but pleasant clip all the way to the final hole, finishing in just over two hours, enveloped in a kind of sweet summer reverie that reminded me of being fifteen again, alone on the course save for a few circling hawks and darting cardinals and the occasional lizard, dropping extra balls and swatting them for the sheer pleasure of doing so, marveling at the cleverness of the course's simple design.

At the seventeenth green, I played up onto a couple older guys in a cart. After I putted out and walked to the eighteenth tee, they invited me to play up the hill with them to the home green. Their names were Hank and Lester. We shook hands.

"We're a couple old retired farts," Hank explained with a languid smile. "I'll bet you're working on a good number," he added. "I watched you play seventeen."

"I don't know. I'm not keeping a scorecard. That's the quickest way to ruin a nice afternoon."

They laughed. In fact, even though I'd been playing a lot of second and third balls for fun, on my first ball I was close to level par—proving that maybe I shouldn't quite abandon hope that I still had a respectable game in me.

"My wife and I are enjoying your column in *The Pilot*," Lester said as we started up the fairway, he and Hank riding while I trod beside them, the low sun hot on my neck. "Bet your old man would be mighty pleased you've come back here."

I looked at him, surprised. "You knew my dad?"

"I sure did. He ran the Sunday-morning men's class at First Lutheran Church that I attended for fifteen years. We had some wonderful Sunday-morning debates. I miss those—and him."

Les was a retired professor of business ethics from the University of North Carolina at Greensboro. "I took this crazy game up a year before I retired. I would have loved to play with your dad. I know he had a regular Saturday-morning group. He used to tell me the golf course was the best place in the world to figure things out—and not just your golf game. I loved that book you wrote about him. Bet you miss Opti the Mystic."

"I do. That's one reason I came back to work here, I think. Being here connects me with him again. Everything seems remarkably unchanged."

"Do you have a son?"

"Yes, sir. His name is Jack."

"For Mr. Nicklaus, I'll bet."

"No, sir. His Scottish great-grandfather who once won his club championship in Glasgow. Jack's middle name is Braxton— for Opti the Mystic."

"Well how about *that*," said Les, sounding genuinely pleased. "That kid's got a legacy to live up to. How old is Jack?"

"Almost fifteen. He certainly has golf in his blood line."

"Has he beaten you yet?"

"Not yet. But I look forward to the day." I explained that my son was coming to the Sandhills in a week or so to play golf and swim before he went off to church camp in Maine.

"You'll have to come and play with us sometime"—Hank joined the conversation from behind the cart's steering wheel— "assuming you don't mind old fart golf."

"That would be fun," I said, a little dazed by the heat and

the climb up the hill and how unexpectedly revealing my un-planned day in the Sandhills had turned out to be.

"I love old fart golf. I plan to play it myself any moment now."

"LET ME GET THIS STRAIGHT. You're planning to *drive* from here to Maine every few weeks, then turn around and come back here?" Doc Morrison handed me a large tum-bler full of crushed ice and bourbon and frowned, taking a seat across from me at the large round wooden table in the cheerful Morrison kitchen. He had come inside a moment before from picking the last of his French endive before the heat wilted it.

"Yes sir," I said, explaining about my teenagers still being in high school up north, but eager to come visit whenever their schedules permitted. I reminded him that Southern Pines and Pinehurst had been founded by Yankees who divided time be-tween here and their homes in the north.

"That's true. But most sane people do it every season, the way Lloyd Cutler does. Not every *month*. Why on earth wouldn't you fly?"

I replied that I had been flying somewhere on the map for my job for over thirty years. It was time to be grounded.

"Besides, I love to drive. Driving long distances is therapy for me. The phone can't ring unless I want it to. I can stop and see friends along the way. I can even write down ideas for my Sunday column as I go. It's only for a year. I can do anything for a year."

I sipped my iced bourbon, hoping I sounded convincing.

Part of making this unconventional career arrangement work was convincing myself I could actually pull it off. My second thoughts had brought me back to thinking I'd stay at least until the end of summer and see how things panned out, play it one day at a time.

Grumpy Morrison sipped his scotch and shook his head as if this was the dumbest arrangement he'd ever heard. He also gently nudged a bowl of microwave popcorn in my direction.

"Quit interrogating Jim," Myrtis insisted. "I'm sure he's got it worked out, Max. Life sorts itself out. Not everybody gets up and goes to the garden or bird hunting according to their wristwatch, you know."

"Actually," I admitted, "up until a few hours ago I was having some strong doubts about sticking around. I'd pretty much made up my mind to thank David Woronoff for the two-week writing vacation and get along home to my own neglected garden in Maine."

Myrtis smiled sympathetically. "You are probably homesick for your wife and children."

"Yes, ma'am." She was an intuitive lady. "And my dogs and garden."

Max grunted as if I'd merely confirmed his worst suspicions. "So what happened to change your mind?"

I sipped my bourbon. The iced liquor tasted wonderful on such a hot night, and I found sitting at the Morrison's large table with its delightfully cluttered lazy Susan oddly relaxing. Dinner was simmering in covered pots on the stove, and the smells were enticing. Myrtis had said she had new butter beans, braised cabbage, and a roasted pork loin, with homemade peach cobbler for dessert.

"I was walking home from the golf course when it suddenly hit me what an absolutely fantastic day it had been."

I recounted my refreshing hike around the reservoir with Tom Stewart and the discovery of the Sandhills Horticultural Gardens and how happy I felt after rapping out my essay for the *London Times* and then shouldering my golf bag and setting off like a kid again though the neighborhood and discovering a great little golf course right around the corner. On the eighteenth hole, I added, I even met a chap who had been in my father's Sunday-school class. What a small world this was, after all.

"This may sound crazy. For the first time since I arrived here two weeks ago, it felt like I wasn't just visiting friends or passing through town. I almost felt like I actually *live* here."

"I don't think that's crazy at all," Myrtis declared. "Living somewhere happens in ordinary things, not in special events like some big golf tournament. You'll feel better when your wife and children get here and you can settle into things." She sipped her red wine and smiled at me.

She glanced at her husband and remarked, "Many of the camellias in the horticultural garden were donated to the college by Max. He'll have to give you a tour."

"I'd like that," I said.

"Do you bird hunt?" Max asked with a grunt, sounding as if he hoped I didn't.

"Grew up bird hunting," I confirmed. "Haven't done it in thirty years, though."

Max shook his head as if he wasn't the least bit surprised by this fact.

"There you go interrogating Jim again, Max," Myrtis said. "Cut it out."

"At least you play golf, I gather." He ignored his wife's gentle protests. "So what did you shoot today? Any good?"

I said it was a fluke, probably because I was so relaxed and playing with no expectations, thinking mostly about a golf trip my son and I once took together to Scotland and hoping we might take again soon.

"Well what *was* your score?" He seemed a trifle annoyed by my stalling.

"One or two over. But I didn't write it down."

Max shook his gray head. "You're too good to play with my bunch. I *was* going to invite you to play with me in the Dornocher this fall. Forget it."

"What's the Dornocher?"

Frowning, he explained it was a one-day member-guest event that happened in early November over at the Country Club of North Carolina, so named for some original members who fancied playing golf in Donald Ross's birthplace. "But you probably won't still be around here then," he added.

I smiled at him, pleased to learn he meant *that* Dornoch.

"I'd love to play with you. Hope you've got good strong shoulders, though. Carrying me won't be easy."

For an instant, I saw the faintest flicker of a smile. But it disappeared as quickly as it came.

We sat talking for another half hour, waiting for their youngest daughter, Jean, to arrive home from her physical therapy job in Hamlet. During that time I learned that Myrtis had been the first girl from tiny Red Springs to attend Duke University, and that she once served as an L&M cigarette girl, making appearances with TV actor James Arness of *Gunsmoke* fame.

She showed me a photograph of herself standing with Arness and three other L&M hostesses. The actor's arms were spread around the three dewy young coeds.

"Look how long his arms are," Max grumbled. "Like an ape."

"What a dish you were," I said to Myrtis, wondering if I should have said "are." She was still a regal beauty.

Just then Rex began barking excitedly and a pretty dark-haired woman wearing a white lab coat breezed in, flush from the heat but smiling. The resemblance to her mother was striking.

"Hi, I'm Jean," she said, coming straight over and offering me a friendly hand. Rex growled and snapped at the air east of my left knee, a warning shot fired over the bow to stay clear of his womenfolk.

"Oh, Rex, knock it off," Jean said, and scooped him up in her arms. He attempted to lick her face.

"What kind of doctor were you?" I casually asked Max, forgetting that Myrtis had already told me and feeling the soothing effects of the bourbon. Good thing I had only two hundred yards to negotiate on foot to my angel-watched cabin.

"A really grumpy retired one," answered his wife, laughing unselfconsciously.

"I was the eye doctor here for almost fifty years. Gave up my practice a few years back. Now I just play golf and fiddle in the garden."

"Two of my favorite things," I confirmed.

"Daddy's got a new friend," Jean said to her mother in a girlish singsong, smiling first at me and then her father.

Myrtis laughed. "You two may be made for each other."

Jean grinned. "A regular Grumpy Junior."

OVER THE MOST sensational home-cooked, Southern-style dinner I'd had in a long time, we talked well into the evening. I gave them the bare bones of how and why I'd come there, speaking of Harvie Ward, Tom Stewart, and David Woronoff, emphasizing my work with *The Pilot* and skipping the bits about my pending midlife crisis.

"So what sorts of things are you planning to write about in the Sunday paper besides golf?" Max Morrison asked.

I was eating the delicious peach cobbler. "I don't know. Whatever catches my attention. My dad used to say it's the business of a columnist to write about whatever is none of his business."

"Careful you don't stir up the fundamentalist Baptists," Max warned. "They seem to be on the warpath over *The Pilot* these days. Stick to golf and horses. That calms people down around these parts. Religion gets 'em lathered up."

"You know why, don't you?" I asked seriously. Grumpy gave me a blank stare.

"It's because the Jews refuse to recognize Jesus as the Messiah, while the Catholics refuse to recognize the Jews as the Chosen Race. The Muslims, meanwhile, refuse to recognize Catholicism as the one true faith. And the Southern Baptists refuse to recognize each other in Hooters."

Grumpy Morrison snorted, while Jean burst out laughing.

"It's a joke, Daddy."

"I got *that* much," Grumpy snapped and offered something dangerously close to a real smile.

"So how is Lloyd Cutler's cabin working out?" Myrtis asked, changing the flow of table talk. "Seems like half the people in town have lived there at one time or another."

"A woman at church told me the same thing. She also said

there is a resident ghost, but I have yet to meet up with it. It's a great little place. I've slept like a baby there."

"Maybe the spirit is glad you're there," Myrtis calmly observed. She was silent for a moment, then added in a reflective tone, "I never put much stock in spirits until one day not long after Elizabeth died. She appeared to me early one morning after I'd just awakened. I wasn't the least bit afraid. I saw this light, and suddenly there she was standing in front of me. I wanted to wake Max, but I couldn't take my eyes off her. She looked so beautiful, young, and very much at peace. She was wearing a white dress — which, if you knew Elizabeth, wasn't her style at all."

I glanced at Max. He was looking at this peach cobbler, silently spooning it into his mouth. Jean was gazing at her mother affectionately, and I saw moisture gathering in her eyes as she listened.

Myrtis continued in a steady voice. "Elizabeth, you see, was as wild and free-spirited as some of the horses she was able to calm at the stable where she worked for many years. But there she stood, looking so happy and dressed all in white. She said to me, 'Hi, Mother. I came to tell you I am fine and very happy here. Don't worry. I'm here with my friend whose name is also Elizabeth,' and she indicated someone else standing off in the light. I couldn't see who it was, but I got the feeling she was with a new friend, someone else who perhaps also just died."

I glanced at Max again. He was listening intently, now watching his wife, jaw set but his expression one of pained tenderness. Max saw me looking at him and sighed, shaking his head a little. "I didn't see this. But she obviously did. She woke me and told me about it."

"At first I wasn't sure if it was a dream or a visitation," Myrtis continued, her large brown eyes suddenly reddening with emotion. Her voice softened and cracked. "But whatever it was, it really *was* Elizabeth speaking to me and it made me feel . . . *okay*. I was so grateful afterwards. It was the first peace I'd had in such a long time."

"Tell Jim about the hawk," Jean prompted. She seemed on the verge of tears, too. She blinked at me and smiled.

Six hundred friends and neighbors turned out for Elizabeth Morrison's funeral, Myrtis explained, filling Brownson Memorial Presbyterian Church. Near the end of her struggle with ovarian cancer, Elizabeth had told her parents about repeatedly seeing the same hawk circle the trees around the cottage she and her husband, Chuck, were remodeling. "As everyone was filing out of the service, someone pointed to the steeple of the church and there was the hawk. Chuck recognized it."

"We all saw it," Jean said. "In Native American culture, I guess, hawks are sacred creatures. They are messengers or guardians or something. A few weeks later, Chuck and a group of her friends put on a fund-raiser for an art scholarship in Elizabeth's name at Sandhills Community College. In the middle of it, the same hawk reappeared. People were astonished."

"Tell him the other part of the story," Max suddenly insisted, now staring with gently haunted eyes at his wife.

Myrtis glanced at me and I thought again what a beautiful college girl she must have been. Still was.

"A little while after this happened, Max learned that the daughter of his first cousin had been killed in a plane crash in the Blue Ridge Mountains. Her name was Elizabeth. I'm

convinced she was Elizabeth's new friend and that they both
are at peace . . . somewhere." She fell silent and looked out the
sliding glass door at a birdfeeder where a pair of cardinals were
dining late.

"It was like being visited by a pair of angels," she said, her
voice cracking.

After supper Jean walked me home to the cabin. I thanked
her for allowing me to come to dinner and apologized if anything I'd said had upset her parents. What they'd been through
was a family's worst nightmare. I couldn't get the returning
hawk out of my head.

"Are you *kidding*," Jean said with surprising vigor, taking my
arm. "You have *no* idea what happened tonight because of you.
You'll have to come back when my sister Marianne comes up. I
know she'd love to meet you, too."

We were standing at the end of my driveway. I asked her what
had happened. Perhaps I'd missed something.

"That's the first time I've seen Daddy relax and *smile* since
Elizabeth got sick four years ago. He likes you, I can tell. And it
was so helpful for Mother to be able to talk openly about what
happened. She's kept it all inside."

Jean smiled at me. "I believe Mother actually saw Elizabeth,
and I think you may have been sent to help us end the grieving
and get back to normal life. You *have* to come back and bring
your family with you."

I didn't know what to say to this. Before I could reply, however, Jean gave me a warm good-night hug.

"And, by the way," she added, turning to go back down the
street, "don't feel obliged to play golf with *Grumpy* Morrison

and his buddies. They're a bunch of old coots who like to get together and complain about politics and their wives."

"It so happens that I'm an old coot in training." I said I would soon bring my family to meet hers, and they would confirm this.

"I can't wait. Have a safe trip home, Grumpy Junior," she declared with a musical laugh, waving good-night.

CHAPTER FIVE

An Ideal Sport

For our fifth wedding anniversary I took Wendy to the Pine Crest Inn for dinner. After just one week in the Sandhills she was glowing with relaxation. The day after she arrived she had a comprehensive tune-up lesson at the beautiful Pine Needles Lodge and Golf Club with Bonnie McGowan, daughter of LPGA hall of famer Peggy Bell, one of the game's most accomplished teachers. After that she went out and shot two of the best rounds of her life at the Elks Club, scoring in the low nineties. Suffice it to say, she'd fallen hard for the easy elegance of Pine Needles and the faded charms of the Elks Club.

By all indications, our kids were having a swell time, too. Wendy's younger son, Liam, a nine-year-old dude in love with college basketball and the NBA, had wandered down to the town courts in the heart of Southern Pines and somehow insinuated himself into the regular evening pickup games with kids twice his size and mostly black. They affectionately dubbed him Little Man, and he quickly established himself as a long-range three-point bomber. Meanwhile, his brother, Connor, twelve, a budding cross-country runner, was in heaven because he could take our two lazy golden retrievers on leisurely evening runs through beautiful Weymouth Heights and the Boyd estate. Maggie and her best chum, Liz, had been in town only nine days but found themselves being wooed every evening by a trio of high school Lotharios, taken out for movies and ice cream, while Jack and Bryan Stewart had picked right up where they'd left off on the links, playing one local course or another almost every morning and spending the balance of their afternoons cooling off in the swimming pool at National Golf Club.

As for me, I had no complaints whatsoever.

The speed at which I'd slipped back into the rhythm of a small Southern town was a little surprising and entirely welcome, given my decades of unpredictable schedules that always seemed to have me getting on a plane to some distant destination or coming home wearily from a distant interview. Though I knew it had grown considerably since my days pedaling a borrowed bike around town, Southern Pines felt eerily familiar — like the neighboring village and town in Maine, Topsham and Brunswick, had felt when my first wife and I moved to the midcoast in 1985 — a blend of newcomers and friendly natives, home to retirees and big-city refugees who preferred small-town American life. In recent years, however, nearby Portland had experienced explosive growth. A new bypass, carved through the heart of our formerly sleepy New England village, had brought a wealth of change, including a two-fold increase in the population along with major development issues that had never been part of our contented life there.

In any case, early every morning after Idle Knight Tom Stewart and I hiked the Southern Pines reservoir, swapping jokes and arguing politics, we grabbed coffee at Java Bean or the Short Stop, and I put in my two or three hours of writing on the Seminole history project or read over the first proofs of my book on the gardening world, then set off on foot for the office of *The Pilot* five blocks away, eager to get better acquainted with my colleagues, pleased to discover that the little newspaper was more of a splendid refuge for burnouts like myself than I'd first realized.

For instance, Steve Bouser, the paper's seemingly austere editor, and sunny Tom Bryant, the chatty advertising director, were respected veterans of the major daily newspaper racket who'd seen the light and returned to a more civilized pace of life. With his cheerful office off the lobby of *The Pilot,* David Woronoff greeted people who came through the door as if they were family, not just customers or readers.

And so, following my successful fortnight in the old stomping ground, and feeling like a relieved tour guide, I'd brought Wendy to the Pine Crest to celebrate our fifth wedding anniversary, introduce her to the owners and the dining room's famous pork chop dinner, and have her meet my old friend Marmalade the cat. Perhaps subconsciously, I'd finally committed to making the shift to Sandhills living, at least part-time, and was anxious to get Wendy's reaction to the place. She'd grown to love small-town Maine, after all, for the same reasons Pinehurst and Southern Pines appealed to me. But she'd had only passing exposure to Southern life until now. Thus her reaction, when it came, was a relief.

"I can see why your mom and dad loved coming here," Wendy exhaled as we sat with glasses of wine in the big white rockers on the porch before going in for dinner, watching a thundery summer evening expire over the village square. "I can just picture your mom here." She smiled at me, offering her glass for a toast. We touched rims. "Here's to them *and* us. I could get used to this, too.

"My only complaint," she added, "is that you've kept this place all to yourself. You took me everywhere else in the golf world but here. Why is that?"

I thought about it. She was right. During my decade as golf correspondent for a large travel magazine, which more or less coincided with the years we'd been together, I'd introduced a nongolfing Wendy to the game by inviting her on many of my research trips to leading spots of the game. After only rudimentary lessons, for example, I'd tossed her shamelessly to the wolves at Pebble Beach and she'd handled herself superbly. She'd eventually accompanied me on several trips to Britain, and together we'd golfed our way across France and Hawaii. During the first night we stayed at the spectacular Lodge at Sea Island, Georgia, just two days after the magnificent new hotel opened its doors to the public, I proposed to her on a balcony overlooking the handsomely refurbished Plantation Course, presenting her a diamond ring my mom had worn for almost sixty years. This was a few months after my mother passed away. We'd decided to get married in our backyard in Maine on my parents' fifty-sixth wedding anniversary.

"I don't know," I admitted, "maybe I wanted to save the best for last—like marrying you."

"That's so sweet," she said. "But I think it's because you feel more comfortable here than anywhere else. It's home to you. You don't share home with just anyone."

"You're not just anyone."

"I know. That's why you're now sharing it with me."

"Is that why you tossed me my car keys and pushed me out the door to go see Harvie?"

"Somebody had to. I knew you wanted to come here. You get visibly happier just talking about this place. I'm learning why." She smiled. "What was it Harvie called it?"

"The Pinehurst cure." I took a swallow of my wine. "You've been here two weeks. What do you think that means?"

"Maybe he meant all the great golf," Wendy replied. "That would be a good place to start. This is, after all, the home of golf."

"Actually, they like to say the 'Home of American Golf.' But golf wasn't here when Pinehurst got started. Golf was an accident in the Sandhills—one of those things that found its way here and took root like kudzu."

"You're *joking*."

"Whatever makes people feel the way you're feeling, give or take a glass of chardonnay, was present here long before golf arrived. Pinehurst became the home of American golf by accident."

My wife sipped her wine and shook her auburn hair. "We still have a whole half hour before dinner, and you haven't given me my anniversary gift yet." She poked me playfully. "Tell me how golf came to Pinehurst, and maybe I'll give you your gift later. I promise you'll like it. It has nothing to do with golf."

I reached down to scratch the top of Marmalade's head and said to her, "Close your ears, old girl. This is no conversation for an impressionable hotel cat."

For her part, Wendy had no idea that my anniversary gift

to her was a pair of white rockers like the ones we were sitting in. David Woronoff and I had bought them that morning at a presale of U.S. Open outdoor furniture, beautiful handmade rockers broken in by the backsides of highly knowledgeable U.S. Open patrons.

"Well *I'm* all ears," said my rapidly improving golf wife. "And I'm still waiting."

So I sipped my wine and told her about the accident.

PINEHURST, I EXPLAINED, BEGAN as a noble social experiment that wound up becoming something much different than its founder intended.

Seeking relief from the winter congestion of the crowded industrial Northeast and hoping it was true what he'd read in the Boston papers about a place in the desolate Sandhills of central North Carolina that could ease his aching sinuses and fragile lungs, Boston soda-fountain magnate and aspiring civic do-gooder James Walker Tufts, who was sixty at the time, disembarked from the Seaboard Air Line Railroad at the rustic resort town of Southern Pines one evening in the early spring of 1895, checked into a hotel, and took himself the next morning on an extended nature walk to the west.

No records indicate what captured Tufts's fancy in the grim, stump-covered, sandy terrain five miles northwest of Southern Pines. But in June of that year, he put down a deposit on a parcel of land, and by year's end had shelled out a total of $7,400 to purchase nearly six thousand acres of land. Locals who heard of this startling transaction shook their heads in wonder and amusement, sensing another rich Yankee who'd been artfully separated from his money.

As residents in the sparsely populated region knew, the land Tufts paid more than a dollar an acre for was useless, a moonscape of sand and piney stumps, the result of a once-thriving longleaf forest that had been savagely clear-cut for its timber and high pitch content and the remaining stubble left to rot under an even more savage sun. The prevailing view, as more than one periodical from the time makes clear, was that James Walker Tufts was a friendly madman who would soon go broke. Initially at least, Tufts's family back in Boston reached this same unhappy conclusion.

But one man's madness is another man's epiphany, and Tufts had an almost evangelistic vision of what he planned to create: a Southern utopia built in the timeless style of a quaint New England settlement, a healthful retreat in the pines for every class of weary traveler.

In short, James Tufts's motives were pure. And his timing couldn't have been better.

The impulse to do something significant for America's exploding poor and working classes was a growing movement across post–Civil War New England, thirty years after the end of the nation's greatest nightmare. As major cities of the Northeast grappled to accommodate waves of immigrant workers and the skies clouded with the discharges of a booming industrial economy, nostalgia for the idealized New England village with its pristine white houses, friendly village common, civil meetinghouses, and tranquil church steeples proved irresistible for many who feared that an entire world and way of life were being sacrificed. Others, meanwhile, dreamed of simply making better lives for themselves.

Influential writers like Harriet Beecher Stowe, for example, yearned in print for "our New England villages in the days when people were of our own blood and race, and the pauper population of Europe had not landed upon our shores."

Yet as distinguished Colby College Professor Richard Moss points out in *Eden in the Pines,* his short but indispensable history of the Village of Pinehurst, the patriarchal thinking of James Tufts was probably given shape by the evangelistic musings of a cheerful Dorchester reverend named Benjamin Goodridge, who, upon hearing tales of the amazing curative powers of the desolate Sandhills, packed his seriously ill wife off to Southern Pines in 1885 and soon witnessed a miraculous recovery.

"Goodridge's first and largely negative impressions gave way to the magic of the place," Moss recounts. "His decision to stay, he admitted, was 'not the result of any profound reasoning.' Simply, the weather got him. Two days of 'delicious spring weather' nearly unhinged him and he 'knew that [he] had reached the land where there is real spring, not that pious fraud of the almanac, which is our portion in New England.'"

As Professor Moss further stresses, at first glance the ground that became Pinehurst hardly suggested the presence of a new Eden. Though ground water was clear and abundant, and the air was sweetened by surrounding longleaf forests, the sand was ten feet deep in places—remnants of an ancient seabed that once covered the central region of the Old North State—and suitable for growing little more than wild peach trees and rabbit tobacco. Photographs of Tufts's early village starkly attest that the landscape was home to few trees taller than a man and was covered in places by useless native vegetation called wire grass.

Even so, Tufts pressed ahead with his town-building scheme. He first considered naming the place Pinealia, or even Sunalia, but soon adopted the German Pinehurst, which first appeared in correspondence mailed in November 1895 to various physicians in Boston announcing his plan to create a "town . . . eminently adapted to benefit invalids." He took the name, some believe, from a predominantly German working-class community near his home in suburban Boston, by some accounts advanced by the Reverend Goodridge himself.

However it happened, Tufts aimed his business enterprise at helping "decent people of modest means recover their health," generally from the early stages of tubercular infection, or as it was then commonly called, consumption. With Yankee thrift and entrepreneurial acumen, Tufts dedicated himself to creating a self-contained and fully functional community that was "semi-philanthropic in character" and would "attract only a refined and intelligent class of people."

To help support this new Eden, noting that Sandhills peaches went for as much as four dollars per crate in the bustling marketplaces of Boston and New York City, the ambitious founder set out to promote agriculture in general and a budding local peach industry in particular, hoping to make his new Pinehurst a major producer of the cultivated fruit.

Tufts wasted no time creating his working town. Weeks after purchasing the land, he signed up the design firm headed by renowned landscape architect Frederick Law Olmsted to create a working blueprint for the new Village of Pinehurst. The creator of New York's Central Park had recently completed Biltmore House in Asheville but was in rapidly declining health, believed to be suffering from the early stages of dementia. Contrary to some published accounts of Pinehurst's early days, Olmsted never laid eyes on the village his firm was hired to design.

As a popular story goes, Tufts ordered a railroad spike to be driven into the ground (adjacent to the site of Given Memorial Library today) so Olmsted's designers could create a blueprint of curving lanes that radiated out a thousand yards in all directions from the village center, with streets intersecting at odd angles, producing housing lots of irregular dimension, a brilliant deviation from the prevailing grid system of the turn-of-the-century American town.

The whimsical lanes and narrow byways were romantically named for Southern flowering trees and shrubs, most of which — like the citizens who would reside there — had to be imported from someplace else, and an ambitious nursery and landscape scheme were created to beautify the new village. A trolley line was also laid along the remains of the old Yadkin Road that bisected North Carolina from east to west, with a spur running from the Seaboard railroad depot in bustling Southern Pines directly to Tufts's new village.

By Christmas 1896, a crew of 170 laborers, a majority of them African-Americans directly descended from freed slaves, completed the Holly Inn, a general office building (also called "the casino"), a handsome village hall, and several smaller commercial buildings, plus a row of appealing cottages.

Within the first decade of Pinehurst's life, more than a quarter of a million seedlings were planted through the village proper, transforming what had previously been a desolate wilderness into a blooming garden of flowering dogwoods and crepe myrtles, azaleas, magnolias, camellias, loblolly and longleaf pines. At the center of this botanical paradise, Tufts installed a classic New England village green (where the trolley would deposit and pick up guests) and made plans for a settlement of "shanties" west of the village, plus a "workers' district" designed to put roofs over the heads of his ever-expanding army of seasonal employees.

To facilitate the flow of northern guests to his resort, Tufts worked out favorable steamship rates to bring them from Boston, New York, Philadelphia, Baltimore, and Washington to the docks in Portsmouth, Virginia, where train service linked them to Southern Pines. The trip from New York to Southern Pines on the Seaboard Air Line took sixteen hours and cost about twelve dollars.

A room at the Holly Inn lavishly equipped with costly electric lights and in-house telegraph ran about five dollars per night, roughly half what a comparably equipped hostelry in a major city would cost. A cottage in the village proper rented for about $120 "for the season," which ran from November to May—widely deemed to be, as one upper-crust Philadelphian described it in her newspaper, "the only civilized weather down in that wild and forgotten place."

Though such tariffs sound remarkably modest by today's standards, in the late nineteenth century the average middle-class American made about four hundred dollars a year. Thus as Brad Klein, Donald Ross's biographer, notes, "For all the claims about drawing a middle-class population, Pinehurst was always a decidedly upscale undertaking."

JAMES WALKER TUFTS would die six years after his first resort guests arrived, but he lived long enough to see his splendid utopian experiment radically transformed by several unforeseen developments.

The first was the stark realization that tuberculosis was in fact deadly contagious in *all* its stages—not simply the latter ones, as commonly believed by medical authorities of the day. This discovery prompted Tufts to reverse course and to alter Pinehurst's image as a place that welcomed victims of the nation's most feared contagion.

Newspaper and magazine advertisements previously extolling the healthful effect of Sandhills "ozone" on ailing consumptive lungs suddenly appeared with a consumer warning label, unambiguously advising those contemplating a sojourn to sunny Pinehurst that "no consumptives will be accepted."

"Tufts," writes Moss, "made sure that anything written about the village contained this message." Given the choice between abandoning a few of his cherished social principals or seeing his dream go bust, Tufts chose to exclude the very souls he'd once hoped to help.

Then, in 1897, probably borne by a flying insect invading from the swamps of eastern Georgia, a blight called San Jose scale attacked and decimated all the peach orchards in the area — scuttling Tufts's ambitious scheme to create a self-supporting peach industry that would provide fresh fruit and a steady revenue stream.

Ironically, at this low and precarious moment, another kind of bug invaded the meticulously landscaped lanes of Pinehurst, one that would prove the place's salvation. This friendly contagion was quietly brought by the hotel guests themselves.

In the early days of the resort, winter guests played badminton or took themselves on picnics and nature walks through the surrounding pine forests. They played tennis on specially made clay courts, and roque, a form of croquet favored by the founder himself. In the evening, they played billiards, attended high-minded lectures on social issues of the day in the village

hall, and watched homegrown entertainment, including a popular "baby show" in which local African-American mothers presented their newborns and competed for cash prizes awarded by
judges chosen from the all-white audience.

The year after the Holly Inn opened for business, however, during the winter of 1897, workers reported to the boss
that guests on their own had appropriated one of the resort's
dairy meadows and were playing a "peculiar" game involving
rudimentary clubs and some kind of ball. Golf had been on
American shores only about a decade but was rapidly gaining
popularity in the suburbanized North where affluent businessmen were forming clubs and taking up the imported Scottish
game at a feverish pace. Once Tufts heard what his guests were
up to in his dairy meadow, he ordered a nine-hole golf course to
be laid out so that it would be waiting for his guests upon their
return for the winter season in 1898. The resort's original nine,
featuring rough ryegrass fairways that quickly expired with the
arrival of intense summer heat, and packed clay putting surfaces
covered by sand, measured 2,291 yards with a standard "bogey"
score of thirty-five. Tufts thus provided guests with a timely new
outdoor activity, and not a moment too soon, they gave him a
social amenity he could aggressively promote.

"Everybody can play it," the founder proclaimed in the resort's early promotional materials, "some excellently, others indifferently. It keeps the player out in the open air; it keeps him
moving over wide spaces; it exercises all his muscles and all his
wits. It is an IDEAL sport for the maintenance of bodily and
mental health."

Within a year, responding to rapidly accelerating fascination with the "ideal sport," the resort hired its first professional

teachers, rounded up local men and a small army of boys to serve as bag carriers or "caddies," and erected a handsome new clubhouse with separate men's and women's changing rooms and a four-sided veranda for viewing the action on what many enthusiasts had taken to calling "the links." Technically speaking, a linksland golf course is a seaside layout, though Pinehurst claimed, not without justification, that the sandy terrain and wire-grass vegetation recalled elements of a classic Scottish linksland.

In March of 1900, the newly expanded eighteen-hole Pinehurst Resort course hosted a four-day exhibition featuring British golfing legend Harry Vardon, already a three-time British Open champion and golf's first supreme stylist, touring the former colonies en route to adding a U.S. Open title to his vita at the Chicago Golf Club. Vardon's ball-striking was so elegant and pure, it was said, he rarely took a divot. His unusual overlapping grip (which he actually copied from an obscure club pro in Britain) came to be called the "Vardon grip" and, some argue, revolutionized the game.

More important, in a country where only a hundred or so golf courses existed, but the concept of elite private "country clubs" had become a distinguishing feature of Gilded Age wealth, Vardon's effect on the large crowds that flocked to see him at Pinehurst was nothing short of electrifying. The resulting publicity that poured out of the Sandhills onto the sports pages of the nation's newspapers helped establish Pinehurst as a vanguard of the game, a paradise where the auld Scottish game was taking new root and flourishing.

That same summer, James Tufts began scouting around for someone to direct his emerging golf program and heard about an agreeable young professional who had distinguished himself with the membership at the Oakley Country Club in Watertown, Massachusetts, by rebuilding their course and teaching the members how to play it. Though he'd been in America scarcely a year, Donald Ross was ambitious, with exactly the kind of broad experience Tufts desperately needed. A true son of the game from Dornoch, Scotland, Ross had apprenticed under Old Tom Morris at St. Andrews and honed his craft as a clubmaker, teacher, and greenskeeper at two of Scotland's most hallowed linkslands before he set off in 1899, with just thirteen dollars in his pocket to find his fortune in America.

Ross's fortuitous encounter with James Tufts — who knew little about golf but possessed a canny eye for a man's work ethic and character — resulted in his being offered the position as Pinehurst's new head professional, caddie master, and clubmaker. The duties Ross accepted included running the newly formed Pinehurst Country Club, supervising the growing ranks of caddies, giving lessons to resort guests, and overseeing the maintenance of the golf course. "Thus," as Richard Moss puts it, "Donald Ross joined the staff at Pinehurst and like so many on that staff, he became a migrant of sorts, coming South for the season in late autumn and returning to the North in the spring . . . an essential element in the growth of Pinehurst."

What quickly became apparent to both Tufts and Ross was that the existing eighteen-hole course was insufficient to accommodate growing customer demand for play, so Tufts asked his Scottish polymath to design and supervise the construction of an additional nine holes north and east of the existing clubhouse. "This short layout," Klein notes, "all of 1,275 yards in length, occupied the area presently taken up by the 1st, 17th and 18th

holes of what would soon become the famed No. 2 course." By
the time the expanded course officially debuted to the world five
years later, Pinehurst was a name synonymous with the game of
golf in America, and Ross was a designer whose services were
in demand.

When the resort opened to business at the start of the winter
season in January 1901, Tufts's crowning touch, the Carolina
Hotel, with 250 luxurious rooms beneath a vast central pavil-
ion and ballroom capped by a spectacular copper cupola, was
heralded by the Northern press as one of the finest hotels in
America—"the Queen of the South," as one New York paper
labeled it—signaling the birth of modern Pinehurst and a bold
change in the direction of the resort. The goal of luring the
middle class was a thing of the past. Unlike the adjacent incorporated town of Southern Pines, with its growing commercial
interests, diverse economy, and mix of upper-crust and working-
class neighborhoods, the pristine Village of Pinehurst, owned
and controlled by one aging and avuncular patriarch, became a
living symbol of the newly emerging American leisure class.

As the *Pinehurst Outlook* unabashedly conceded, the lavish
Carolina Hotel was built "to minister to the wants of a class that
is each year becoming more numerous," made up of "wealthy
and fastidious people" whose demands were "more luxurious
and exacting" with each winter season.

Just over a year after his glamorous hotel opened to breath-
less reviews, attracting the cream of Eastern society and wooing
such international celebrities as Annie Oakley and John Philip
Sousa, the Yankee visionary who'd set out to create an American
utopia in the southern pines where all classes of people could retreat to heal whatever ailed them, passed away in his sleep. The

elder Tufts left no record of his thoughts on Pinehurst's ironic social and economic evolution. Pragmatic Yankee businessman to the end, however, he left his son Leonard a rapidly expanding community that had become, in relatively short order, the preferred winter colony of America's sporting elites.

He also left Leonard a hundred thousand dollars in cash to promote what he once hailed as the "ideal sport," a game that had unexpectedly cured his own financial troubles and given birth to America's first comprehensive golf resort, securing a future for Pinehurst that appeared thoroughly promising.

MY IMPROMPTU DISCOURSE on the history of Sandhills golf, and of Pinehurst in particular, had taken Wendy and me from drinks on the porch all the way through the dessert course in a cozy corner of the dining room. Afterward, as a nightcap to a fine evening, I proposed that we take a crack at the Pine Crest's infamous Chipping Board.

Not surprisingly for a Friday night, the Pine Crest was buzzing with a happy clientele, and we had to wait our turn to play the popular game in the main lobby of the hotel.

The Chipping Board, which in my partisan opinion perfectly summarizes the easy grace and timeless charm of Pinehurst at its best, came about in the early 1960s when a man named Lionel Callaway (no relation to Ely of golf equipment fame) created the original game, which consisted of a large piece of plywood with a couple of foam frames set strategically against the parlor fireplace.

Its devious ingenuity lay in irresistible simplicity. A hole eight inches in diameter provided the target of Callaway's novel creation, intended to simulate the challenge of pitching a golf ball

from a tight lie into a hole. The game's yeoman appeal established a nightly competition among locals and regular patrons
that has crossed the decades and bewitched golfers of every
skill level. The object is to see how many balls one can chip
from a distance of ten feet, through the opening and into the
fireplace—a feat, according to Pine Crest lore, that golf great
Ben Crenshaw accomplished ten times out of ten, ranking right
up there with winning the Masters when he was in his midforties. Among the Chipping Board's many devotees, which in-
clude movie stars and Tour players, Pine Crest regular Payne
Stewart supposedly matched Crenshaw's record a few nights
before he won the 1999 U.S. Open at Pinehurst. To celebrate his
accomplishment, the story goes, Stewart signed his name on the
wall over the door in the downstairs men's room, a bit of graffiti
now preserved beneath Plexiglas.

Our shot at the board came after a mixed foursome of
drunken couples finished their failed efforts to chip a single
ball through the magical hole and disgustedly handed over the
shooting irons to Wendy and me.

"You go first," Wendy said, eyes brightening from the challenge. "I need to see how it's done."

I chipped ten balls with a nine-iron, and managed to slip
four of them into the fireplace. Every time a ball missed the
target or found it, a cluster of anesthetized folks watching the
action from the wings either groaned or made noises like it was
the last stroke of a major championship. Pine Crest lore is also
full of colorful tales of wagers that grew higher proportionate
to the consumption of alcohol. With all due respect to Donald
Ross and James Tufts, both dedicated teetotalers, the Chipping
Board was the *ideal* game for golfing drunks.

Wendy tried her hand, choosing a seven-iron, thumping her first shot off the board.

"Durn," she sniffed, wrinkling her nose.

Then she shifted her grip and popped her next chip cleanly through the hole, prompting a cheer from the attending gallery. Groans and cheers accompanied her attempts. As her last ball leapt through the opening, the tidy throng applauded and whistled, and she blushed, handing over her seven-iron to the next player in line.

"So how did I do?" she asked as I handed her a brandy nightcap and we headed back for the quiet of the front porch.

"Six out of ten," I said. "Bonnie McGowan would be proud of you. You'll soon have your autograph under Plexiglas in the ladies' room."

"What's your best?"

"Six out of ten," I repeated, pointing out that my dad had once gotten nine—but then, he'd learned his chipping game in England during the war and was one of the best chippers I'd ever seen. Luckily, I added, Jack seemed to have an instinct for his grandfather's short game.

"You really miss your dad, don't you?" Wendy said after we'd settled back in the white rockers.

It was now softly raining, and Dogwood Road wore a sheen that reflected the hotel's lights through the dripping boxwood hedge. Marmalade the cat was in her bed at the porch's end, curled up and bedded for the night. I yawned, realizing it was at least an hour past my bedtime. But I hadn't felt this contented in a long time.

"Yes, I do," I admitted, remembering what I'd said to Lester that afternoon at the Elks club. "The older I get, the more I wish

I had him around to play golf and talk about things with. I do miss those talks we used to have. Being back here helps bring him back."

"That's why you have Jack." She was gently rocking, her eyes shut, holding her scarcely touched brandy, breathing in the night. Whenever I got flustered or was stressed out from too much work and not enough play, Wendy had a habit of taking my arm and saying, "Just breathe, babe."

"I hope you're right. He used to be so passionate about golf. But these days I can't tell what's up with him. He's impossible for me to read."

She smiled, rocking back and forth. "He's a teenager. You're not supposed to know what he's thinking. You were one once, too."

As I sat considering that, a familiar face came out the hotel's front door. I was pleased to see Andi Hofmann, Bobby Barrett's wife. Bobby and his younger brother, Peter, owned the Pine Crest. They had inherited it from their father, Bob Barrett. Andi and I were old friends. Her son, Patrick, was Jack's age and a rising sophomore at Pinecrest High, as well as a rising golf star on his high school team. Year in and out, to nobody's surprise, Pinecrest was the perennial golf champion of North Carolina. We'd discussed getting the boys together for a round of golf when Jack came to visit.

"What are you doing here on a Friday night?" I asked Andi, who along with desk clerk Linda Tufts pretty much ran the Pine Crest from dawn to dusk on weekdays.

"Oh," she replied breezily, "some friends came to stay the weekend and I popped in to say hello. Someone inside told me you and Wendy were out here. I wanted to come meet the woman you've kept secret from us all these years."

"My best kept secret," I said, introducing my wife to my favorite innkeeper. Within minutes they were chatting away like sorority sisters.

"By the way," Andi broke off at one point after I'd wandered down the porch to give Marmalade a good-night scratch, "Peter was planning to call you. He hoped maybe you and Jack would enjoy playing with him and Patrick on Sunday morning."

I smiled and nodded. As a rule, I never play golf on Sunday mornings. Also, at the suggestion of Grumpy Morrison, with whom we'd dined already twice that week, Wendy and I planned to check out Brownson Memorial Presbyterian Church. Grumpy assured us the minister knew how to give a "pretty decent sermon." Grumpy also sang in the choir, and he cracked a wintry smile when I asked if he was naturally a soprano or an alto. But golf with Patrick and Peter seemed like an opportunity not to be missed. The only way a young player improves, as any good player will tell you, is to play with better players.

"May I check with Jack and give you a call tomorrow? I know he'd love to meet Patrick."

Andi asked how we'd enjoyed our dinner. The Pine Crest possessed one of the premier dining rooms in the Sandhills.

"It was lovely," Wendy replied. "I can see why Jim feels like this place is his home away from home."

"Room 322 is his anytime he wants it."

As we walked across the darkened parking lot, holding hands, Wendy asked what I meant when I called Tom Stewart the "model Idle Knight."

"Everybody in this town belongs to some kind of club or organization," I explained. "John Derr is a Tin Whistle. That old group dates back to the early days of the Pinehurst Golf Club. Tom and I are organizing a band of aging philosopher-golfers who are starting out on the back nine of life."

"Sounds like just what you need—new playmates." She gave me a pert kiss. "Let's go home and I'll give you your anniversary present, Mr. Knight. I think you'll like it. And that's no idle boast."

I kissed her back, and she asked, "So what *is* this mysterious anniversary gift you're giving me?"

"There's two of them." I hoped Jack had remembered to put the rockers out on the terrace of the cabin before he and Bryan Stewart went off to the movies. I wanted Wendy to see them sitting there in the moonlight as we drove up. "One for you. One for me."

"Sounds intriguing. Think I'll like them?"

"Hope so. If you don't, you're off your rocker."

CHAPTER SIX

Sons of the Game

As I watched Jack warm up on the practice range at the Country Club of North Carolina, a line from an old Anglican hymn jumped into my head: "The Father speaks from Heaven's height / This is my son, my well beloved son / In whom I take delight."

"Hey, Ace, slow down. Might try loosening that grip a little, too."

Jack gave me a tense sideways glance. He teed up another ball, placed his club behind it, and made a powerful cut, sending a soaring shot deep to the far left portion of the practice range. He thumped his driver against the sandy turf, sending up a whorl of dust.

I thought I knew what was bothering him: the prospect of playing against Peter and Patrick Barrett. Patrick was one of the most promising young players in the state, a friendly and polite son of Pinehurst who was already climbing in the national schoolboy rankings and being courted by the UNC–Chapel

Hill golf coach. Jack was clearly nervous, pressing to recover a game that had been on ice for ten months. During the first few days he'd been back in the Sandhills, he and I had played several rounds with Bryan Stewart, and his game had shown rapid improvement.

But this was a match against highly competitive players neither of us knew anything about, on a golf course we were both unfamiliar with. Jack teed up another ball and sent it soaring in a long hook. He shook his head in disgust. I stepped closer.

"Jack, you can't fix everything in a day or two. I learned that the hard way up at Pine Valley a few weeks back."

He teed up another ball, looking miserable, and I suddenly regretted saying yes to Peter's invitation to play a round with Patrick, who at that moment was tuning up for the Donald Ross Junior Championship at the Pinehurst Resort. What initially seemed like a nice way to jump back into the heat of competition now appeared to be a formula for a long and distressing afternoon.

It was easy to forget Jack was only a year older than I'd been when I played my first full eighteen holes of golf at the Mid Pines Golf Club in 1967, perhaps because he was miles ahead of where I was at his age in terms of exposure to the world and the quality of his swing.

The major hurdle faced by any parent who hopes a son or daughter might take a shine to life's most socially engaging game is to strike a balance between promoting the virtues of golf in a consistent and healthy manner while not shoving it down their throats with evangelistic zeal. With my own children, perhaps because they had been exposed to the golf world from an early age, I'd always been on guard against overselling the game—hoping, I suppose, they would someday choose to take up golf and would naturally come to appreciate its assorted charms the way I had. Judging by the reactions of Maggie and Jack, this strategy thus far was only mildly successful.

For instance, Maggie, who in high school was cocaptain of her varsity field hockey team, is naturally athletic and had developed a promising golf swing with relative ease. She could have been something to write home about with the application of elbow grease. But alas, she appeared to have less interest in playing her old man's game than in, say, nude bungee jumping.

Her brother, on the other hand, had expressed genuine interest in the game from an early age, and his simple, beautifully groomed golf swing only needed regular usage and a few tweaks before it began producing fine results. I wasn't alone in this assessment. Beginning with Hank Haney and ending with my Idle Knight pal Tom Stewart, almost anyone who had occasion to watch Jack swing a club commented upon the grace and rhythm he displayed. In my view, time and experience were the only missing components. As I had admitted to Hank Haney on that first practice day of the Open, however, for all his time around the game and his obvious natural abilities, I wasn't convinced the golf bug had actually bitten Jack. Or, for that matter, that it ever would.

I saw benefits of Jack's developing a life with golf near the recreational center of it, especially as the years progressed. Golf provides a chance to spend four or five hours in the intimate company of another soul, briefly removed from the demands and cares of life's daily grind. Several of my more enduring friendships had sprung directly from relationships born on the links. Like my dad, I saw golf as a splendid way of staying connected to my son through the ups and downs of life. If ever a pastime encouraged participants to stay rooted in the now and enjoy the journey in another's company, that game was golf.

On a more personal level, Jack was decidedly reserved in expressing his golf passion, a young man who observed everything but often kept his feelings close to the vest. He reminded me of myself at his age—quiet, maybe a little too much inside his own head. In time, however, playing golf with my dad and eventually a larger group of buddies helped draw me outside my anxious teenage head. It taught me to respect traditions, to honor the rules of fair play, and most of all to have a hell of a good time using little more than a pitching wedge and my imagination to solve problems and overcome obstacles—serving, at the end of the day, as a reminder that everything is a game if you choose to make it so.

That's what I thought—and hoped—golf could do for Jack. Silly dad.

We rode silently in a cart from the CCNC practice range over to the putting green near the first tee where Patrick and Peter were waiting for us.

I made the introductions, and we shook hands.

Jack went off to a corner of the green and dropped a handful of balls, rapping putts in quick succession, taking little time to think about what he was doing. I was pleased to note, however, that he was using the old White Hot putter Harvie Ward had sent home to Maine. I walked over and patted my partner on the shoulder, hoping to lighten his mood. In retrospect I should have skipped the Gipper moment and simply passed on to him the latest inappropriate joke Tom Stewart had told me.

"Hey, buddy," I said, "we're just here to have some fun and

see the golf course. Don't try to compete with Patrick. He plays golf almost every day of his life. You haven't played since, what, before Halloween? So let's relax and play for fun and have some laughs. Sound good?"

Jack nodded dimly. He was like a field biologist studying a specimen under the microscope, thoroughly processing everything before coming out with his true feelings on any given topic.

"Dad," he said quietly, "I need to tell you something."

I dropped a ball and casually rapped it toward the same cup, using a technique John Derr told me Hogan showed him one evening before the British Open at Carnoustie, placing the head of your putter half an inch away from the ball at address, which promotes a low forward stroke and therefore desirable overspin. It seemed to work. My ball went into the cup like it had eyes.

"Sure, boss. What's up?" Prefaced by this qualifier, and factoring in his mood, I didn't like the sound of whatever was coming next but resolved to keep the atmosphere light and breezy, no matter what. Jack stalled for a moment, examining the dimples on his Titleist.

"I like golf. I really do. I just don't, like, *love* golf the way you do. Golf isn't that important to me. I play because my friends play."

I nodded, startled. The day was already beastly hot, predicted to reach one hundred degrees that afternoon. My shirt was sweated through, but I felt a cold place the size of a grapefruit begin to open in my gut.

"That's okay," I managed to say, forcing a smile and glancing across the green to where Peter and Patrick were putting and chatting pleasantly. I wondered what I could say in response to this confession. I would be lying if I didn't admit feeling envious of the Barretts and suddenly worried about us.

In truth, I'd long suspected — or feared — that Jack's interest in the game was exaggerated or perhaps manufactured out of deference to his old man. That he registered only the faintest blip of disappointment over missing a chance to be a standard-bearer at the Open, for instance, struck me as revealing. The competition for those jobs had been fierce, and most kids who professed to love the game would have jumped at the chance to walk along inside the ropes with a Tiger Woods or Phil Mickelson, or even a jolly Jason Gore.

And yet, as I struggled to remind myself, this was a minor disappointment when compared to the pride and admiration I felt for my son — the thoughtful kid he'd been and the accomplished man he was becoming. In truth, the world around us hadn't changed one iota, so what the hell was I *really* expecting from him? Jack was still the same great kid he'd always been, and the dreamy summer clouds were floating overhead this peaceful summer morning. The air was sweet with the bosky scent of longleaf pine and a heady gardenia bloom nearby. Ahead of us, a group of geezers was teeing up on the first hole of the Dogwood Course, swapping barbs. Across the practice green, Patrick Barrett said something that made his Uncle Peter laugh heartily. On our side of the green, meanwhile, my heart sank like a chip shot in a pond. Just then CCNC's delightful head pro, Jeff Dotson, passed and waved from a cart, and I smiled and waved back, suddenly feeling lonely and foolish.

I took a deep breath and tried not to show my surprise and disappointment at Jack's revelation, though it must have been obvious to anyone paying even the slightest attention to the conversation via our body language that I was reeling inside.

"I see. Well, gee, Jack, in that case why don't we skip this match and go get some lunch. I'm sure the Barretts will understand. They're focused on getting Patrick ready for the Donald Ross, anyway."

I dropped another ball onto the green and gave it a ludicrously firm rap across the undulating putting surface toward a plastic flag sixty feet away and watched without enthusiasm as it curled around the gentle contour and fell into the cup.

"Nice *putt*," Jack said with a grin. "Were you trying to do that?"

"Absolutely," I lied. "I'm a putting fool." Or maybe just a father fool, I thought. Jury's still out.

Truthfully, I hadn't even seen the cup. Maybe that was because my eyes were stinging at this point. Though it sounds melodramatic to say, I imagined that, there in the rising heat of a perfect Sandhills summer day, my hedge against growing old was vanishing like a mirage before my eyes.

Did I really care if Jack's lovely golf swing carried his game to a level of excellence on par with Patrick Barrett's or other top amateur players? Not really—or, to be more precise, I cared only if *he* did. In point of fact, given my acute disapproval of the direction professional golf had gone in the past decade or so (and even the way many high-level amateurs approached the game these days), I had no hopes or expectations of Jack's becoming a young champion.

Despite his frequent proclamation that he would someday win the Maine state high school golf title and thereby possibly earn a scholarship to college, I viewed the game simply as a way to escape the pressures of life and have a little fun and possibly make the best friends a fellow can make on the journey through his days. That had been my good fortune in golf, almost since that transformative summer afternoon with my dad at Mid Pines Golf Club. At a minimum, that summarized my best hopes for my son.

I took another breath. "Is there anything else you need to tell me?"

Jack nodded. "I don't know—yeah, maybe. I don't know if I want to, like, go to Sea Island or play with Uncle Pat tomorrow." He seemed embarrassed. "I was also thinking how I might like to go home early and hang with Drew and Andy before I go to summer camp. I mean, if that's okay . . ."

I nodded hollowly, gutted, hearing the words but trying not to let them batter my heart any more than they already had. Peter and Patrick had become invisible on their side of the green. Despite my emotional dizziness a relevant question did somehow surface.

"Gosh. Wow. I see," I fumbled. "I guess this means you might not even try out for the golf team this year—"

"Actually, I don't know. Maybe not. I can't stand Smokey. None of us can."

Smokey was Jack's JV coach. Smokey was course superintendent at the municipal golf course where the JV team played in Brunswick. Smokey wasn't a bad guy, more of a babysitter than a golf coach, an unshaven lug with duct tape on the toe of his work boot who rarely had much to say to his JV charges. When Jack heard that his school's varsity team might move to a nine-hole course I'd helped design in our village across the river, he'd made a point of announcing that he was going to make the varsity in his sophomore year. Golf is an autumn sport in northern New England. The tryouts were in four weeks — two of which Jack planned to spend at church camp, his final summer at good old Camp Bishopswood, in Camden. Hiking, canoeing, and swimming would be his daily pursuits for the fortnight. So essentially he had merely two weeks of golf in the Sandhills and a week or so at home before his golf team tryouts.

I straightened up and looked Jack in the eye. I suddenly realized he was almost as tall as his old man, lean and broad-shouldered and blue-eyed, not to mention better looking than I'd been at his age. Less than a month earlier he'd asked if I thought he might be good enough by his senior year to earn a golf scholarship to a decent college. I'd replied that with his golf swing anything was possible — though he would have to play a lot and improve before college recruiters would give him as much as a glance. Far from discouraging him, this reply seemed to fire him up. Today, however, that conversation might only have taken place in my imagination.

"Fair enough. I'll fly you home tomorrow if that's what you want."

"Sorry, Dad . . ."

He gave me another embarrassed smile. The Barretts were waving us to the first tee of Dogwood, swinging their drivers, raring to go. I suddenly wished I was floating in the Elks Club pool, chilling out on this wiltingly hot day, surreptitiously admiring the pretty middle-aged pool moms. I wished I were anywhere but here.

Jack looked relieved and reached to pat me on the shoulder as if nothing had happened. "Okay, Dad. Thanks. But we can play today. It's *really* okay. I mean, are you mad at me?"

"No, Jack. I'm not mad. Let's just go do this." I went to collect my ball and whatever remained of my scattered wits.

"Are you . . . *sure*?" His hand stayed on my sweaty back as we walked to the tee.

"Really. I promise. Let's play," I replied without looking at him.

We all shook hands, flipped a golf tee, and the Barretts won.

Patrick teed up, went through a fine preshot routine, then drilled a gorgeous three-hundred-yard drive to the right center of the short opening hole. Peter swatted a nice drive that wound up just shy of his nephew's. He had what I call an "old pro" swing that could direct the ball to almost any spot with minimal effort. I wondered if Buck Adams, CCNC's late beloved head pro and a longtime pal of Harvie Ward's, had perhaps given it to him, then recalled that Peter's dad, Bob Barrett, had been on a first-name basis with every great golfer who had come through the Sandhills since the days of Ben Hogan.

As we watched Patrick and Peter tee off, my son leaned over, touched my bare arm, and whispered, "Dad, I'm sorry if I hurt your feelings . . ."

I patted him on the shoulder and summoned up the cheeriest smile I was capable of under the circumstances. "I'm fine, Jack. *Really*. Why don't you hit first, buddy. Everything will be fine."

WHAT HAPPENED NEXT proves that golfers—or maybe just teenage boys and their overanxious fathers—really are a mystery, perhaps most of all to themselves.

Patrick Barrett played as expected, which is to say splendidly, pounding his tee shots over most of the doglegs and hazards on the handsome Ellis Maples course, while his Uncle Peter skillfully maneuvered his way using his old pro swing that identified him as a true child of the sixties. Both were at or near par by the turn.

I, who had recently brought the venerable Elks course to its knees, played laughably bad golf, reminiscent of the crimes I perpetrated at Pine Valley, foozling along with bogeys and doubles, trying to find my focus and force a game that couldn't be coaxed out of hiding, while feigning a bonhomie that had vanished like summer dew back on the putting green.

At least the kid was going out with style, I decided. I had to give him that. Jack launched several booming drives that matched or even outdistanced Patrick's, chipped and putted like his late Carolina grandfather, and reached the halfway hut with a respectable forty-one, only four behind Patrick, his lowest nine-hole score ever on a championship-caliber golf course. More important to me, I was pleased to see him laughing and chatting with Patrick, at ease and apparently having fun as they strode briskly along the fairway.

Peter and I hung back, talking about various people and things. Hoping to divert my mind from the shock of the practice range and the corresponding awfulness of my game, I summoned enough geniality to ask Peter if the rumor was true that during Open week the Pine Crest had done a million dollars in bar business. Twice during that crazy week I'd attempted to duck my head into my favorite inn to offer a quick hello to Patrick's mom or Linda Tufts, but both times got turned away by the volume of thirsty patrons standing ten deep at the tented bar erected in the adjacent parking lot.

Peter gave a thin smile. "Two might be closer to the truth."

Worrying him, Peter related with creased brow, were more recent rumors circulating through the village that the newly installed Pinehurst Village Council was working on a comprehensive plan for dramatically expanding and altering the footprint of the existing village—which some locals affectionately called Old Towne—and possibly taking part of the Pine Crest property with it. One of Peter's favorite expressions, which I'd used in a recent travel piece on the place for a national magazine, was that the beloved, anachronistic Pine Crest, with its old-fashioned bedrooms and cozy chenille bedspreads, its gently bossy waitresses and unmatched air of Southern hospitality, was "a second rate-inn for first-rate people," an artful self-assessment that came close to explaining why its thousands of devoted patrons, myself included, would go to the barricades if anyone attempted to fool with this Pinehurst institution.

A perfect example of the passion the Pine Crest evoked in kindred golf-loving souls was handsomely expressed at a dinner I'd recently attended at the Pine Crest, hosted by President John Dempsey of Sandhills Community College, who turned out to be as golf-crazed and friendly as Tom Stewart had said he was. Every year since the late 1960s, Dempsey had hosted a group of his colleagues who had all been young professors together at the College of Charleston but who eventually had scattered to the winds. Since then they always faithfully returned to the Sandhills for their annual early May golf rendezvous, coinciding with the end of the college term.

"When we started this thing there were only two constants— Pinehurst and the Pine Crest," President Dempsey informed me one afternoon over a bourbon at the Pine Crest bar, where generations of golf scribes have gathered to lick their wounds and swap stories. He related how, after serving as president of two distinguished small colleges, he was on the fast track to presidential jobs at several major universities when he happened to be invited by a golf pal from Pinehurst to come interview for the head job at tiny Sandhills Community College. Dempsey was in his midforties at the time, in the prime of his administrative career. "As I admitted to the board when I came for the interview, the only reason I did so was because I love golf and I love Pinehurst, more or less in that order. In my wildest dreams I couldn't have imagined *downsizing* to a community college.

"But the spirit and attitude of the people I discovered here struck me as rare, even extraordinary. By the time I left, I was in love with Sandhills Community College. And so, entering the back nine of life, instead of going to the major leagues of higher education, to use a baseball metaphor, I realized I needed to go back to the minor leagues. I decided this was where I could make a greater contribution and have an impact. Some of my colleagues were astonished. But in retrospect, it was the smartest career decision I ever made."

Whatever measure one chose to apply, Dempsey's impact had been impressive. During his sixteen years at the helm, Sandhills had grown from a sleepy technical school to a sprawling community college with an ever-expanding curriculum and a top national ranking, creating, among other things, a horticulture program and culinary school that were the envy of the major institutions in the state. His annual fund-raising golf tournament for the school attracted support from across the region and had raised millions of dollars that would be used to improve the educational outlooks for thousands of young people and older folks returning to school.

"Through all of the changes in my life and of Sandhills," he said by way of conclusion, "the one thing that hasn't changed, I'm happy to say, is the Pine Crest Inn. In a world where nothing stays the same, the Pine Crest stays serenely and gloriously *unchanged*."

I lifted my bourbon in salute to his dedication and golf-fueled vision, pleased to meet someone else who'd left the major leagues for a smaller place on the road. "For this reason," I chose that moment to inform him, "you have been chosen to be the bearer of the Sacred Sand Wedge for the Idle Knights Adventure and Philosophy Club."

"Great," Dempsey said enthusiastically, "but what the blazes is the Sacred Sand Wedge, and what the hell is the Idle Knights Adventure and Philosophy Club?"

"Your new secret golf society. Forget the Tin Whistles, forget the Royal and Ancient. You're an Idle Knight now. But please keep this under your golf cap for the time being—at least until Tom Stewart can get a blazer patch designed and produced."

"Wonderful," Dempsey declared. "Can I at least tell Evelyn?"

"Who is Evelyn?"

"My wife. I'm very attached to her."

"If you must. She'll probably hear it from our wives anyway."

Not surprisingly, endless delightful stories like Dempsey's wove through the lore of the Pine Crest, tales of annual family reunions that had gone on since the days of Donald Ross, accounts of anniversaries and other life events that could occur at no other place than the porch and public rooms of the funky, beloved hotel. I had more than a few of my own.

"Everything in Pinehurst and to some extent the Sandhills at large is connected by three main things," Peter said, expanding on Dempsey's theme as we followed the boys along the back nine of the Dogwood Course. "One is golf, the other is family relations, the third is Pinehurst politics. Whatever the resort wants, it gets, for the most part."

In many minds, including my own, the family-owned Pine Crest was more an enduring symbol of Pinehurst's timeless charms than either the stately Carolina Hotel or the lovely Holly Inn next door, both owned since around 1980 by massive ClubCorp of Dallas. So, like a canary in a coal mine, whatever happened to the Pine Crest was bound to affect life in the self-described home of American golf.

This was no rap against the Carolina or the Holly Inn. World-class hostelries, logically evolved from the remnants of James Tufts's original utopian scheme, these first-rate resort hotels aggressively catered to large and sophisticated travel segments, including a major portion of the state's corporate convention trade.

But the Pine Crest was something else entirely, folksy and soulfully threadbare in the same welcoming way as certain older golf clubs in Britain, conveying a patina of grace and conviviality that many golf travelers find irresistible. Once, while playing golf with former Pinehurst Resort General Manager Pat Corso, a delightful Dempsey golf crony and potential Idle Knight in his own right, I casually wondered why the resort had never made a play to acquire the Pine Crest. After all, they owned the

Holly Inn on one side of the Pine Crest and the Manor Inn on the other.

"Oh, believe me, that possibility has been discussed by management since the days of Leonard Tufts," Pat responded without hesitation. "Fortunately we've always had the wisdom to realize the only thing we would do if we were ever lucky enough to acquire the inn would be to thoroughly screw it up. Why ruin a perfect anachronism like the Pine Crest? Folks would hate us."

IN MAY OF 1920, James Walker Tufts's son, Leonard, filed the first certificates that legally incorporated Pinehurst, an entity owned by himself and a handful of minority stockholders of the newly created Pinehurst Corporation, among them Donald Ross. By then Ross had created the championship course at No. 2 and three more golf courses that he would tweak until his death in 1948, giving Pinehurst an unprecedented seventy-two holes of championship caliber golf, making it the undisputed golf Mecca of America—arguably the first village ever expanded by, and expressly dedicated to, the game of golf. Scotland's St. Andrews, it's worth remembering, was a thriving seaport market town and home to a distinguished college and cathedral long before golf became its principal source of fame and revenue.

In order to promote this pioneering concept of "the golfing lifestyle," as one prominent periodical of the day labeled it, to a nation of newly prosperous sportsmen, an adman named Frank Presby dreamed up a clever corporate signature for the thriving resort, an engaging mascot called the Golf Lad, a whip of a boy turned out in baggy blue pants and a floppy straw hat, a folksy "native son" of Pinehurst toting a golf bag or a single club, often depicted in evocative newspaper ads boarding a train in some chilly northern city for the sunny climes of central North Carolina.

Presby is also credited with inventing the concept of the corporate "golf outing," a winter event that came directly out of his League of Advertising Interests, an organization he formed in order to generate positive feedback among groups of visiting businessmen and travel writers, luring them to the Sandhills for fraternal competitions that typically concluded with formal award banquets and gifts. As the *Outlook* summed up these golf-themed social fetes: "All business talk is taboo in Pinehurst . . . and the man who is found soliciting business from his partners or his opponents on the links soon finds that his presence is no longer desired."

And yet, as the new American leisure class emerged, Presby confided to Leonard Tufts that no place was "better suited for the generation of excellent ideas and agreeable flow of commerce" than a golf course in the Carolina Sandhills. Simple discretion in mingling one's business objectives and sporting passions seemed to be the accepted rule. Thus the American corporate outing was born.

Buoyed by the brisk sale of property and construction of cottages in the village proper, Leonard Tufts expanded his vision into adjacent Knollwood, which lay along the trolley tracks linking Pinehurst to Southern Pines, envisioning a posh new club, smaller hotel, and quiet residential community that catered to an even more discriminating crowd.

"For some, the Carolina . . . and the village had become *too lively*—if you can believe that," writes Lee Pace in *Sandhills*

Classics, his delightful account of the creation of Mid Pines and the Pine Needles resorts and the eventual arrival of the Bell family, the other great family that helped transform this once-bleak pine barrens into a Mecca of golf.

The new club, built for about half a million dollars by investors that included Thomas Wilson, the founder of Wilson Sporting Goods Company, Frank duPont of the Delaware duPonts, James Barber of the Barber Steamship Lines, and New York publisher George Dunlap, originally called for thirty-six holes of championship golf to be constructed by Donald Ross. Renowned society architect Aymar Embury II, who had designed the home of the Boyds in Southern Pines and many of the finer homes of Weymouth Heights, created a distinctive three-story hotel and clubhouse in Georgian style that made the newly named Mid Pines Inn, when it opened for business in November 1921, the preferred getaway of the golfing elite.

The success of Mid Pines spawned a second project across Midland Road, the even more ambitious Pine Needles Lodge and Golf Club. "This enterprise, like Mid Pines," relates Pinehurst historian Richard Moss, "was clearly driven by a desire to promote the real estate between Pinehurst and Southern Pines." The original Pine Needles Lodge, imagined on a grand scale of luxury, included a Tudor-style brick building, outfitted with the latest luxury conveniences, set atop a piney bluff that commanded a sweeping view of the surrounding countryside, which included a golf course designed by Donald Ross. With its lavish public appointments and luxurious fireproof suites, the second hotel opened in the winter of 1928, celebrated by an impromptu women's golf exhibition in which outstanding amateur Virginia Van Wie beat Glenna Collett on the fourth extra hole. Collett, who resided at Pine Needles and sold real estate there whenever she wasn't practicing on the golf course, later became the most celebrated women's champion of the 1920s and '30s, collecting six U.S. Women's Amateur titles and the nickname "the female Bobby Jones."

As the Roaring Twenties ended, Leonard Tufts's aggressive expansion into real estate and various other schemes (including breeding new varieties of cattle) set the tone for explosive growth — and near financial ruin, once the merry ride on Wall Street came to an abrupt halt on Black Tuesday 1929.

Before this unforeseen development, however, catching the investment fever of the day, Ross himself ventured into the game by purchasing and restyling the cozy Pine Crest Inn on Dogwood Road with a golf partner named James McNabb. The inn was next door to his employer's own Holly Inn — thus making the son of Dornoch a direct competitor of the very resort upon which he'd fashioned his national reputation as a golf course designer.

The Pine Crest had been built by a woman aptly named Emma Bliss, who arrived in the village from Rhode Island, sometime in 1903, and first managed a boardinghouse before raising the Pine Crest in 1913. Emma Bliss was an able housekeeper and a devoted golfer — said to have been the only person in Pinehurst history to win two separate golf tournaments, playing one left-handed and the other right-handed. "A delightful little hotel created for and by golfers," as one national travel magazine of the day described Emma Bliss's decidedly modest Pine Crest Inn, establishing its reputation as the preferred stopping place for a less fussy breed of golf traveler.

During the twenty-seven years he owned the Pine Crest,

Ross, a teetotaler who appreciated the importance of having the friendliest bar in town (even during the darkest days of Prohibition you could always get a drink at the Pine Crest), took pleasure in sitting on the wide and welcoming porch to welcome arrivals to his hotel.

In the early 1960s, Bob Barrett, a newspaperman from Erie, Pennsylvania, brought his wife, Betty, for a vacation to Pinehurst and fell in love with the unpretentious Pine Crest and, upon their fourth visit, used his wife's family inheritance to make an offer on the premises. For $125,000 the Barretts, who had of course stayed in hotels but had no experience operating one, found themselves owning a beloved but down-at-the-heels institution that had kept the same staff for nearly fifty years.

"People always wonder how we manage to keep the Pine Crest the way it is. The truth is, after Mr. Ross left the scene in 1948, not much was done to keep up the place—that was the secret to our success," the elder Bob Barrett told me with a wry chuckle one afternoon when I visited with him shortly before his death. "We had moments when we weren't certain we hadn't made the biggest mistake of our lives. So many improvements had to be made, and we were such complete novices. In the end, we did what we thought would make *us* happy if we were still paying customers at the Pine Crest Inn. That became our guiding principal. The improvements came later."

AS WE FOLLOWED the older Barrett grandson and my son around the Dogwood Course at CCNC, I asked Peter what kind of improvements he and his brother had eventually made to the inn. Half the charm of the Pine Crest, as Dempsey was quick to remind, was the impression that no major changes had taken place since the days of Ross.

"The rooms were tiny and only a few had bathrooms," Peter explained. "The first order was to tear out walls, add plumbing, and make most rooms larger. As for the staff, we inherited a staff that had been there a very long time and was set in its ways, including the chef, Carl Jackson, who wound up working there more than half a century, and popular housekeepers like Tiz Russell and Peanut Swinnie treated guests like they were family—including making sure they ate breakfast before going out in the morning. Dad decided you shouldn't fool with tradition—something money can't buy—so he left things alone and concentrated on quietly upgrading the rooms, making changes appear less sudden."

As he related this, I thought about my first visit to the Pine Crest as an "adult" the year I graduated from college. Hoping to impress a new girlfriend, I drove her to Pinehurst for dinner at the Pine Crest. At one point, I ordered a Schlitz beer and attempted to further impress her by chipping six of ten golf balls through the hole in the Chipping Board.

"Some college tournament was in town," I explained to Peter as we trod the final holes of CCNC. "The place was packed with college guys. While I was attempting to impress her with my golf prowess, my date began chatting with a couple of fraternity boys. Not long after that she was dating one of them. I lost the girl but found the Pine Crest."

"We're glad you did," Peter said with a laugh, then asked if I had given more thought to purchasing a cottage in the village. Andi Hofmann had once phoned me in Maine to let me know a widow's tiny cottage, diagonally across the street from the Pine Crest, had come up for sale.

Before I could act on her tip, though, the cottage was snatched up by an executive from the Golf Channel who engaged an army of workers to strip, gut, completely refurbish, paint, and lavishly landscape the classic Pinehurst bungalow just in time to rent it out for a small fortune to corporate patrons of the National Open. Most of the time the place sat empty, which was true of many of the classic cottages of Olde Towne Pinehurst: wealthy absentee owners occupied them only a few weeks each year during the winter season. For this reason alone, Pinehurst had always struck me as something more akin to a shrine to the game than a living and breathing place, à la Southern Pines. As much as I loved going there, I'd long ago realized that residing in Pinehurst would be a little like living on the grounds of Augusta National—a beautiful, *too* perfect, outdoor museum.

"No," I admitted to Peter as we approached the final green of Dogwood, "I'm afraid room 322 at the Pine Crest will be the only thing I can afford to call home in the home of golf." And, in fact, within days, not willing to risk the consequences of breaking with my own modest literary tradition, I planned to check into the Pine Crest for an overnight read of the galley proofs of my book about the horticulture world.

"Well," Peter came back warmly, "your bedroom will always be waiting at the Pine Crest. Dad would want it that way."

"Thanks, Peter," I said, pointing ahead to Patrick and Jack. "Looks like our Pinehurst golf lads are finishing up in style."

The boys were striding onto the final green to mark their approach shots, which lay within feet of the flag. Our balls lay well outside theirs. Whatever had been bugging Jack prior to the match was nowhere in evidence now.

I heard him laugh at something Patrick said, and he seemed happy and engaged. Moments later, both boys rolled home birdie putts. Peter and I made our pars. The Barretts beat us handily, four-and-three, but thanks to Jack's good play it was no worse—and bloody well could have been, given my laughable effort.

We shook hands, said thanks, and loaded up our clubs. Jack had finished with eighty-two, his best eighteen-hole score ever.

"Dad," my son said pleasantly as we drove out of the lushly groomed front gates of the Country Club of North Carolina, "do you think we could stop somewhere and pick up some new Titleist Pro V1s?"

I replied that I supposed we could, but wondered why. After all, Wendy, whom I had phoned at the turn, was probably at that moment trying to book him onto a Monday-morning flight home to Maine.

Jack looked at me, flushed from the heat, loose and relaxed, visibly happy, and smiling.

"I'll need them for playing with Uncle Pat tomorrow and Sea Island next week."

I nodded. For the second time that day, I was shocked—though in this case pleasantly so. Life and golf, as Tom Stewart was fond of saying, were both subject to change without prior notice.

"So, I guess this means you plan to keep playing golf for a while . . ."

"Yes, sir." He glanced out the window at a passing golf course—a fairway designed by my friend Rees Jones, Pinehurst No. 7. Jack never said "sir" up north; he sometimes said it down south.

"I've got only three or for weeks before the team tryouts. I *will* make the varsity this year."

"Good for you," I said, thinking how I couldn't wait to ruminate upon this breathtaking reversal with my fellow Idle Knight.

He casually added, "One more thing."

"What's that?" I felt myself bracing for whatever might be coming next.

"You know what I said this morning about not loving golf the way you do?"

"I do," I said, watching the road but feeling him stare at me.

"I didn't really mean *exactly* what I said. I don't know why I said it. I love golf, Dad. Not as much as you do, maybe. But I *do* love it."

"I'm really glad to know that, Jack."

I risked a small, grateful smile—thinking perhaps I should leave things at that and say no more. As Tom Stewart might have said, my joy bell was beginning to ring again. I almost had tears in my eyes for the second time that day.

"I'm looking forward to tomorrow and going to Sea Island with you," I pushed my luck by adding. "That's where Wendy and I got engaged, you know."

"Cool," he said, and slapped my knee. "I didn't know that. I can't wait to play it with you."

I picked up my phone, hoping Wendy hadn't paid money yet to buy a plane ticket we didn't need.

CHAPTER SEVEN

Where the Heart Wants to Be

The day after Jack's stunning change of heart at CCNC, we drove a winding back road to Greensboro to meet Pat McDaid for a round at his club north of town. Pat and I had been best friends since junior high school and had played golf together off and on over the years since.

On the way there, I thought Jack might enjoy seeing his great-grandfather's homeplace near Chapel Hill, the family horse farm where my dad spent many of his happiest summers growing up. This was our family's sacred ground. In one form or another, Dodsons had been on this land back to the late 1700s. Jack knew a great deal about his mom's Scottish forebears but little about my redneck Southern roots. It seemed like a good moment to connect him to his past.

As we drove along the rural road with the windows cranked down and a CD of Jack's favorite band, Guster, playing, he asked what I liked about *The Pilot,* and I told him it was the people who worked there and their passion for what they were doing, explaining how the paper had doubled in size during the decade David Woronoff and his partners had owned it.

"David reminds me of your grandfather in a lot of ways," I said. "He says the only thing he ever wanted to do in life was own a small-town newspaper. My dad had that same dream and managed to do it very successfully for a time. Their personalities are almost identical—same can-do optimism and collegial love of what he does."

"Granddaddy owned a newspaper?" Jack appeared surprised to hear this. I thought I'd told him this story, though perhaps I hadn't.

I explained how I was born while my father was working for the *Washington Post,* selling advertising and writing an aviation column. A short time later, he took a job as assistant publisher of the *Dallas Morning News.* A few years after that, he and my mom sank their life savings into starting a weekly newspaper in Gulfport, Mississippi. The paper was coincidentally called the Gulfport *Breeze and Pilot.*

"I see. Like the Southern Pines *Pilot.*"

"Exactly. We lived on the beach by the Gulf of Mexico." My first memories centered around that little newspaper and the people who worked for my dad. "I even remember my dad's business partner, a state senator who planned to run for gover-nor someday. He turned out to be the problem, though."

"Why? What'd he do?"

I explained that one autumn day in 1959, my dad returned from Memphis, where he had purchased a new offset press for the newspaper—they'd been so successful they were preparing to publish three days a week—only to discover that his partner had cleaned out the newspaper's bank accounts and vanished.

"Where'd he go?"

"Cuba. According to my dad, he took his golf bag, his girlfriend, and the newspaper's operating funds with him. I guess he didn't want to be governor after all. His timing couldn't have been worse, though. Fidel Castro came to power in a coup on New Year's Day." Here I paused and smiled, remembering the funny way my dad described life's comeuppance. "My dad always said he pictured the guy attempting to dog-paddle back to the U.S. towing a golf bag full of cash."

"What happened to his newspaper?"

"He had to close it. Then he had to find a new job in a hurry. He took what was left of his personal savings and gave his twelve employees a final paycheck, locked up the place, and phoned a friend at the *Washington Post*. He had a job offer in about two hours. That's what brought us back to the Carolinas. But that wasn't the worst thing."

Jack, solemn and fascinated, was staring at me. "What was that?"

"Days later, just before we headed for his new job in Florence, South Carolina, my dad's only sister, my Aunt Irene, got killed in a car wreck outside Washington. He worshipped her. The next day, my mom suffered a miscarriage. So my dad lost his job, his newspaper dream, his only sister, and his third child all in the same week. The baby was a boy. I'd have had a little brother. Anytime I have a bad week—sometimes even a bad golf round—I remind myself what an unbelievably hard week my dad once had, and how he managed to come through that tough time all right, maybe even better than before. He liked to say that if you choose to seek joy instead of sorrow, the heart will lead you where you're meant to go. The heart, he said, always knows where it wants to be."

"Do you think that's true?"

I nodded. "Corny but true. During our golf trip to England, for example, he told me that he assumed he might never come back to North Carolina. But when everything he'd achieved crumbled to dust, he decided the only logical thing was to return to where he came from and begin again. He chose to think of it as a new opportunity, almost an awakening." As I said this, I thought of the midlife awakenings of Harvie Ward and Tom Stewart and realized my own life crisis wasn't a whole lot different than my dad's had been at a younger age, only considerably milder. Perhaps I was simply awakening to a fuller life, too.

"The theme of returning to where the heart wants to be is as old as Homer's *Odyssey*," I said, putting it into a literary context because Jack had recently also expressed interest about how one became a writer.

"What did he do back here?" Jack wanted to know.

"After a year or two in the newspaper business, he went to work for the largest advertising agency in the state. That's when we moved back to Greensboro. I was starting the second grade. Among other things, he revived the state's big tourism campaign, 'Variety Vacationland,' from the 1930s and 1940s, and gave it widespread new life, and he helped promote the state symphony's performances in the local schools. He's probably the reason I love classical music so much — and to some extent why you do, as well. Everything gets passed along. You can still find the Variety Vacationland slogan in magazines and on restaurant place mats around the state. That was your granddaddy's touch, good old Opti the Mystic."

A SHORT WHILE LATER, we were sitting at Dodson's Crossroads, a rural country junction a dozen or so miles northwest of Chapel Hill.

"This is it," I said.

"What is?" Jack asked.

"Where we come from. Ground zero for pink-eyed, lint-eared Dodsons. Including you and me, Junior," I drawled like a *Hee-Haw* hillbilly. I pointed to a leaning road sign that had our name painted on it.

Jack looked over. "Oh, wow . . . Cool." *Cool* was his highest accolade.

My grandfather's homeplace sat a few miles away on Buckhorn Road, on the way to Hillsborough. His father—the original Jimmy Dodson, whom the locals had called Uncle Jimmy—was a land-rich, dollar-poor horse trader, fiddle player, and genial country gent who, during the Yankee occupation in the Civil War, was reputed to have sold the bluecoats horses by day and stolen them back by night.

Soon we were cruising along Buckhorn Road itself, and I was searching for a pair of distinctive century-old red oak trees and a wooden gate that indicated the entrance to my grandfather's homeplace. I hadn't seen it in more than a quarter of a century but told Jack how my father used to bring my brother and me there during the holidays to shoot mistletoe out of the tops of the oaks with our shotguns.

Even then, standing at least half a mile off the main road, the family homestead was long abandoned, its windows broken out, its porches sagging, saplings growing through the buckled floorboards. But the farm was sacred ground to my dad and therefore to us. He'd spent his summers there learning about the life of fields and woods from his grandmother, whom everyone affectionately called Aunt Emma. Her father, George Washington Tate, was a rural polymath who forged the bell in the Hillsborough courthouse and founded several Methodist churches on a rough line from Haw River to Seagrove. Tate also served as one of the state's leading boundary surveyors following the Civil War. A prominent street in Greensboro was named for this man.

"Did you ever meet Aunt Emma?"

"Oh, no. She was long gone before I came along. But my father assured us that she found her way into our bloodstreams—the deep love of the natural world, her friendliness with everyone she met. Aunt Emma knew no strangers. My dad was the same way. You seem to have that gene, too. Geneticists say the short-game gene, however, skips a generation—so that accounts for your chipping skills, Ace."

We failed to find the entrance road into Uncle Jimmy Dodson's old homeplace. Large new constructions and farms and swank housing developments were scattered along Buckhorn Road, which had been widened. The distinctive twin oaks and the gate were long gone—as were, it likely followed, any remains of the family home or any trace of the family that once owned it.

So we drove on slowly toward the interstate that would lead us to Greensboro. Jack wondered if any more Dodsons were living along Buckhorn Road. I told him I didn't think so. Time had swept them away, leaving only a family name attached to a lonesome crossroads.

"You mean there aren't any more Dodsons here at *all*?"

"Unless I'm mistaken, Old Champ, it's just us." I realized I'd added one of Harvie Ward's favorite nicknames to my list: *Old Champ.* "I suppose you could say we're the end of the line save for your Uncle Dick and your cousins."

"Maybe that's really why you wanted to come back here," Jack proposed. "Like you said—where the heart wants to be."

"You might be right," I agreed, impressed by his grasp of complicated family issues. "Your granddaddy wanted to buy his grandfather's homeplace—tried in vain, in fact, for more than two decades to do it. But it slipped through his fingers. That was maybe his only lasting regret in life."

"He didn't regret losing his newspaper?"

"Oh sure. Who wouldn't, especially under those circumstances. But he also believed—as a lot of people who live close to the earth do—that life has a way of working out on its own, a natural rhythm you have to get in touch with and accept."

After a moment of silence, I admitted, "That may explain why I always felt more comfortable out in the sticks than in Greensboro, where I essentially grew up."

Jack's brow wrinkled. "Are you kidding?" he asked.

I shrugged. "I call Greensboro my hometown, but it's not. It's where I grew up from the second grade on, but it never really felt like where I belonged. They say the first five or six years of life are critical. During my first six years, we lived in small towns across the South. Those places, I think, shaped who I am today—a small-town guy at heart. That's why I fell in love with Southern Pines, at about your age. That's also why I fell for Brunswick and Topsham. Brunswick felt like a New England version of the southern towns I'd always fancied. Southern Pines was founded by New Englanders. It's really a Yankee village in the heart of the Old South. Greensboro is a big city now, but Southern Pines hasn't changed much. You get the best of both worlds."

I looked at my son. "Does any of this make sense? Probably not."

He nodded. "No, it does." He was still looking around, soaking up the countryside. He added, "I like Southern Pines and Pinehurst, too."

"I'm glad to hear that," I said. I asked how he would feel if I did choose to stay on to work for *The Pilot* over the coming year.

"Fine with me," he said as if he couldn't see any problem with the idea.

"You might want to think about that. It would mean I'd be able to get home to Maine maybe only two weeks each month. Sometimes less, once I begin teaching in Virginia."

"But you would come back . . ."

"Of course. Maine's my home. This is a temporary gig, a chance for me to live out a boyhood fantasy."

"Could I come down sometimes?"

"I'd count on that, Nibsy."

We drove on toward the interstate. Our tee time with Pat McDaid was less than an hour away. Jack fell silent, studying the passing woods and fields. Then he spoke up again, obviously processing all this family history and landscape.

"Do you think we could someday try to find Uncle Jimmy's place again?"

The road had widened even more, and newly constructed

houses began to appear on both sides, giant boxy affairs that had postage-stamp lots and no discernible architectural motif.

"Maybe," I said. "Would you like to?"

"Yes, sir."

"Tell you what, you come down here for Thanksgiving, and I'll borrow a couple shotguns from Grumpy Morrison, and we'll go hunt for mistletoe."

"That would be great." Jack sounded genuinely pleased at this prospect. I chose not to tell him I had doubts if any trace of our homeplace existed outside my foggy memory banks.

We came to the entrance of a new development. A stone gate that look like it belonged at a theme park had been erected, along with a large, ornately lettered sign announcing that Hunters Ridge was offering "Luxury Homes from the High 300s."

"Guess we'd better get back here soon," I said. "Before the mistletoe is all gone."

A LOVELY AFTERNOON of golf followed.

My old friend Pat led us to his club north of town, an Ellis Maples layout that was as beautiful as it was unpretentious, and our forty-year golf rivalry picked right up where we left it last, complete with body-specific barbs and idle boasts that made Pat an obvious candidate for Idle Knight status.

One of the advantages of being back in the Old North State, it dawned on me, would be the chance to play golf with Pat on a regular basis. Our pointed remarks, general threats, and genial bullshitting clearly amused Jack. As was customary in our long-standing blood-feud matches, I gave Pat two strokes per side and beat him by a whisker, though it took shooting seventy-seven to do it, and I had to endure the usual litany of complaints about how I'd probably been playing every afternoon in Pinehurst and working on my game for weeks while he'd been earning a paycheck, blah, blah, blah.

"You and Uncle Pat have so much fun playing each other," Jack remarked afterward as we threaded our way through evening rush-hour traffic in Greensboro, making for a quieter road back to the Sandhills.

"That's what God put golf pals on this earth to do," I explained to him in Tom Stewart's words, "divine compensation for being unable to pick your family members."

"I don't know if Andy's going out for golf this year," Jack admitted. "He's not improving much. Besides, I think he wants to play tennis instead. He likes golf, but he loves tennis. I think he played golf because his dad likes it so much."

I nodded, trying not to read too much into this remark.

Andy Tufts was Jack's best friend, his Pat McDaid. Jack was exceedingly loyal to his group of four buddies back home. When one announced he was going to run cross-country, Jack announced he would run, too. When another said his parents were sending him to a private school in the White Mountains, Jack began talking about going to private school as well. When a third went to India on a youth enrichment program, Jack started talking about making a similar pilgrimage. If Andy Tufts dropped off the golf team to focus on his tennis, it was possible Jack might follow suit. Maybe *he'd* played golf, as I secretly feared, only because his dad loved the game so much.

"Well," I said, "you're at an age where guys begin to discover who they are and yearn to go over the horizon. You don't need your parents hovering over you all the time. That's perfectly natural. You want freedom, and your mom and I have to let you go. In fact, I *want* you to go. If you haven't learned whatever lessons I have to teach you, it's probably too late."

"Did you feel this way at my age?"

I smiled at his question. "Are you *kidding*? At your age I had three crystal-clear pictures of my future life. The first one was of me living somewhere in England, writing a column for the *London Times,* à la Henry Longhurst, and playing golf every weekend. The next fantasy involved Paris, working for the *International Herald Tribune,* living with a dark-eyed French beauty who smoked foul cigarettes and had underarm hair—the result of reading too much Hemingway at an impressionable age. The third vision saw me living in a cozy cottage in New England, cutting my own wood, shoveling snow, writing clever essays like my *other* literary hero, E. B. White."

Jack laughed. "Are you *serious*?"

"You have to have a picture of where you want to go in life— otherwise, as your far-traveling granddad used to say, any old road will get you there."

We happened to be passing the Friendly Center shopping mall on our way to Greensboro's southside, a mere half-dozen blocks from the house where I'd grown up, when I suddenly spotted someone off to the side of the road. I slowed the car to a crawl in the thick traffic.

A lone man was sitting on a park bench under a crab apple tree near the overpass. He was about my age, wearing rough clothes and a long ponytail. He appeared to be leaning over some kind of large book, intently focused on it. A backpack lay at his feet. To the world he would appear to be just another homeless soul. But not to me.

"Let's go say hello," I said, pulling into a parking lot on our right.

"What?" Jack looked baffled.

"See that fellow on the bench over there? That's an old friend of mine. He was part of the Gang of Four."

Once upon a time, Pat McDaid, Eddie Snow, and Frank Heberer had been my best chums. We were inseparable in high school. We planned to stay friends forever, regardless of wherever the world and life took us. Frank and I went off to different colleges. Pat and Eddie went to the same university, however, and roomed together. This was near the end of the Vietnam War. Eddie became a protester and fell in with an antiwar crowd and eventually took an overdose of LSD. He began suffering violent psychotic episodes and got caught stealing typewriters to pay for his drug use. Eventually he was booted from college. Then he found Jesus and tried to go back to school, but left a short time later and lived at home until his mother threw him out.

At least that was the official story I'd gotten from sources in my former hometown. According to both Pat and Frank, Eddie found a home first on the golf course where we'd all grown up playing the game, and later on this park bench near the Friendly Center. His older brother and local church groups had taken care of him ever since, seeing after his few material needs and coaxing him indoors whenever the weather turned bad. The church where Pat taught eighth-grade Sunday school helped look after Eddie, too — though Pat said Eddie sometimes failed to recognize people from his past or simply chose not to acknowledge them, Pat especially.

"That's so sad," Jack said with feeling. "How could that happen?"

"I don't know. He didn't have a father like the rest of us did." We got out and started down a sidewalk to the park where Eddie was sitting. "Or, more precisely, he had a father who left his family when Eddie was small. His mom worked hard but didn't have a clue how to raise a son. We were the closest thing Eddie had to a family — the place, I suppose, his heart wanted to be. With us, he once told me, he felt safe — safe and happy."

As we approached, the man glanced up.

There were deep lines etched around his eyes, and his cheeks were ruddy from his long outdoor life. But the eyes were clear and startlingly blue, and I knew this man was Eddie Snow. Besides, Pat had kept me up to date on Eddie for years. I knew this bench was his home now, and that he rarely ventured far from it.

"Hey," I said casually. "I'm looking for an old friend of mine named Eddie Snow. I'm told he's often around here. Have you seen him?"

The man calmly stared at me, betraying no trace of recognition — no anger or surprise, either, and no joy that an old friend had just appeared from the ether. For his part, Jack obviously wondered why I was asking Eddie Snow if he'd seen Eddie Snow. But this was Eddie who wasn't Eddie, as I'd heard Frank Heberer say.

After a moment, the fellow gently shook his head. He glanced at my son, his gaze lingering, then looked down at his big book again. I was fascinated to realize what he was studying so intently: a road atlas. Eddie was studying Pennsylvania.

"You see," I said, "I'm an old friend of Eddie's, here for the afternoon with my son. I was hoping to see him and say hello. This is my son, Jack."

Eddie who wasn't Eddie looked up at me again, his placid gaze holding directly on mine. Then his blue eyes shifted a second time to Jack, who smiled and made a nervous gesture with his hand.

"Hey," he mumbled.

"I'll tell him if I see him," the man said evenly, regarding me briefly again. His voice was barely above a whisper, but it held the faintest note of challenge—as if he wanted us to go and leave him alone.

"That would be great," I said. "Thanks. Can I do anything for you?"

"No." He was already looking at Pennsylvania again.

HALFWAY HOME TO THE Sandhills, Jack fell asleep with his head against the passenger window.

It had been a long but satisfying day exploring our family roots and playing golf with my oldest golf buddy. Jack had surprised and impressed Uncle Pat with the quality of his evolving game. He'd shot a respectable eighty-three at Deep Spring Golf Club, and blushed and grinned when Pat told him he expected soon to hear that Jack had won the Maine high school championship—or at least "kicked your old man's ass, the way I've been doing for decades."

The car window was slightly open, the warm night rushing past. I'd switched off Jack's music and tuned up a classical station out of Wake Forest. The summer night was full of stars, made pale by a bright full moon, which reminded me of a typical winter night on our hill in Maine. For an instant, I felt like a sojourner between two worlds, or homes, wondering where my heart really wished to be.

A husky voice in the darkness beside me asked, "Do you think he ever regrets how things turned out?"

Surprised to find my companion awake, I wasn't certain whom he meant. Did he mean my father and the losses that brought him back to a rediscovered fuller life in North Carolina? Or maybe fatherless Eddie Snow who dreamed of going far but wound up on a park bench a few blocks from the golf course we all once called home? For that matter, might he also have been talking about my older brother, Dick, who phoned as we came off the golf course with Uncle Pat to say he couldn't get back to Greensboro from a shag dance festival at Myrtle Beach to meet us, as planned, for supper. Jack knew most of the details about the rift in our relationship. He also knew how eager I was to repair that rift and start anew. I decided he meant my brother.

"Well, between you and me, Junior, one reason I'm glad to have this year down here is so he and I can get back on track. Your Uncle Dick and I used to be extremely close. I'd like that to be the case again."

"*No,* I mean your friend Eddie," Jack said. "It was almost like, I don't know, he didn't even *know* who you were, Dad. Are you sure it was him? Could he have forgotten you?"

"It's possible. We came up on him unexpectedly. Eddie and I haven't seen each other since 1979. Uncle Pat says his awareness of people comes and goes, due to his illness. Eddie has become acutely schizophrenic."

"It's really sad," Jack said, stifling a yawn. "I mean, how could he end up there?"

This was the second time he'd asked this question. I said I wasn't certain. But every life has a purpose; it just might take years and a great deal of heartache and searching to figure out what that higher purpose was. Having said this, I was fairly certain my old friend Eddie would never venture far from his bench. As Pat liked to say, that bench was his home, the place he felt most comfortable and secure, the place where his heart wanted to be.

"Why didn't any bad stuff happen to you?"

I smiled, thinking of my father and this beguiling question. Some *bad stuff* had happened to me, of course, depending on what one chose to classify as "bad." It happens in every life — nobody gets out alive, as my dad once quipped to a depressed Scottish barman on our final golf trip to Scotland.

And yet, with the notable exception of loving a girl who was shot and killed during a botched robbery of a country club where she was working during my senior year in college, and the repercussions of a divorce I never saw coming at age forty-three, few really bad things had happened to me. It was possible to say that I'd weathered the ordinary ups and downs of life with a certain grace and good humor, all of which I could directly attribute to my father's example and influence. It wasn't just a deep love of the game he'd passed on to me through all those years on the golf course — but a means of looking at broader life, as well.

Boys dream their fathers' dreams, Carl Jung said. No doubt Eddie's problem, apparently one of many we weren't equipped to notice or understand at the time, was that he hadn't had a father of any kind. It may have been a simplistic explanation, but Eddie was left to make his own way in the world without a dad to guide and encourage him through the inevitable good times and bad.

But that failed to address Jack's haunting question: Why hadn't more of the bad stuff happened to me? The easy answer was that every life is as different, as individual, as a thumbprint. A golf swing.

"I don't know," I said to Jack, after filling him in on how my own Gang of Four had turned out, "maybe I just got lucky." The older I got, the more I'd realized how fortunate I was to have a father and mother who were smart enough to teach me to follow my heart and to do whatever I did with passion and honor. That simple formula encouraged me to go over the horizon in search of my own life. This was, of course, precisely what I was aiming to do with Jack.

Jack was silent for a while as we motored along through the summer moonlight, still leaning against the car door, possibly imagining what might lie ahead for him and his gang of four.

A road sign revealed that we were passing Level Cross, a junction town south of Greensboro where I did my first big newspaper interview, with Richard Petty, the King of NASCAR, after joining my father's old newspaper in 1976. During that interview, which helped me snag a bigger job in Atlanta, I asked Petty what the most important thing was that he'd learned from his success on the track. "Never forget your raisins," he answered without a moment's hesitation.

"I'm sorry," I said, thrown off by his strong Southern accent, "never forget *what*?"

Petty looked at me and smiled almost tenderly. "Never forget where you *come* from, son — the important values and people who raised you up. Those are your *raisins*."

Jack and I were approaching the Sandhills, and the end of our first golf road trip ever — or maybe just the beginning. The good news was, there would be another one starting on the morrow, a two-day jaunt down to Sea Island, so I could chat with Jack Lumpkin and his son about a book project they hoped to write together. The elder Lumpkin had become Davis Love's mentor following his father's untimely death in a plane crash. With only a couple weeks left before Jack went home to Maine for church camp and then golf tryouts, I wanted him to see the Lodge at Sea Island and perhaps meet Davis if he was there, and, of course, play the famed Retreat Course where I'd first played with my dad when I was about his age.

After considerable silence, I assumed Jack was asleep, but he again surprised me by asking, "Hey, Dad. Can I ask you something? Tell me honestly."

"I'll do my best," I said.

"Do you think I could be as good a golfer as Patrick Barrett before the end of golf this year?"

The answer was an unqualified no, but I took a few seconds to consider his question anyway. Given how little he practiced and played, it was either a testament to Jack's unusual natural abilities or to Hank Haney's superb teaching skills that he could play as well as he did—sometimes frighteningly well, an indication that not even he had a clue how good he might become. For her part, Jack's mom had a theory that his passion was genuine, but that he was simply the most disorganized young dude on the planet. There was validity to this point of view. My mom had said essentially the same thing about me when I was Jack's age.

"Probably not," I answered. "You have to remember that Patrick Barrett has been playing golf the way you've been ice skating since an early age. He lives and breathes the game, attends a high school that is famous for producing great student golfers, and plans to try for a golf scholarship to college. His parents, I know for a fact, spend a fortune taking him around to national tournaments where college scouts are watching. A small industry has grown up around this sort of thing."

Jack was silent again. I could almost hear the gears grinding in his head. I hoped I hadn't done more damage than good by being so straightforward.

"But I do think," I added in the next breath, "that you could, with patience and hard work—assuming it's really what you want to do—be one of the best golfers in Maine and maybe New England at large."

"I think I could, too," he agreed with a determined voice.

"No question about it," I said, reaching over and patting his knee, realizing my heart was exactly where it wished to be at that moment. Days like this one, I decided, were a splendid cure for anything that ailed me, my own Pinehurst cure. With all due respect to Carl Jung, I truly didn't want Jack to dream his father's dreams. I wanted him to find his own dreams and go make them happen.

"But it *would* take hard work. You have to realize that, Jack. It's a nice ambition. But you haven't played a lot of golf compared to Patrick, or even half the kids you'll be competing with up in Maine. Until you got down here two weeks ago, I'll bet you hadn't played a full eighteen holes of golf this year. And summer's already half over."

There was a long silence in the car. "Yeah," he admitted. "I know. But Bryan and I have played almost every day since, and I know I can get a scholarship if I work at it."

He shifted in his seat, getting more comfortable. I saw him tilt his head against the window and close his eyes.

"I think you could do anything you make up your mind to

do, son." I thought for a moment and added, in my best *Hee Haw* voice, "And that's the gospel truth, Junior."

"Thanks, Pappy," he said back to me, though a bit distantly, in an exaggerated hillbilly voice of his own. "I'm really glad you came down to Pinehurst."

I smiled into the darkness ahead. The radio was playing Brahms. My dad loved Brahms. The older I got, the more I did, too.

"I am, too, Old Champ," I said, sounding like Harvie Ward and hoping that wherever he was, the Last Amateur was taking in this unexpected and exceptional conversation.

CHAPTER EIGHT

Go Do Good

Late on a spectacular October afternoon, just back from Maine, while on my way to Dugan's Pub to meet my brother for a beer, I ducked my head into the Old Sport to check on the progress of our blazer patch and to give Tom Stewart an update on the end of Jack's sophomore golf season. I'd arrived at the cabin the previous evening and found myself surprisingly happy to be back in the Sandhills.

After tuning up his game at Pinehurst and Sea Island, Jack had gone home brimming with enthusiasm and had missed making the varsity team by only a single stroke.

Despite this disappointment—not to mention his dislike of the JV coach and the fact that his best friend actually did quit the team—I was proud of my son for sticking with it and finishing his JV season with a nearly perfect 6-1 record, his only loss coming during a match in which he was leading three-up but was forced to forfeit after growing faint from hunger. That was vintage Jack. He'd been so excited to play that he'd skipped lunch. As he walked off the course, his coach chewed him out pretty good, but Jack, to his credit, remained silent and respectful.

October had come to the Sandhills, and the winter residents were beginning to trickle back, opening up cottages in Pinehurst and filling the shops of Southern Pines. I was eager to check in with my fellow Idle Knight and catch up on the gossip and scandals that had unfolded in my two-week absence. A small town newshound never rests.

In the Old Sport, I waited while Tom showed several well-dressed gents a spectacular original landscape of St. Andrews by Richard Chorley, an English golf-course artist he'd recently introduced to American audiences.

I picked up a copy of Sandy Herd's rare 1923 classic *My Golfing Life* and continued reading where I'd left off. Herd, a lovable son of the Old Grey Toon, found his game at about age fifteen and came out of thin air in 1902 to snatch the Claret Jug from two-thirds of the Great Triumvirate (Harry Vardon and James Braid), using a newfangled, rubber-cored ball that sent the faithful gutta-percha ball rolling into the dustbin of golf history. It was a watershed moment for golf. No "guttie" ever won a major championship again. Neither did sweet Sandy Herd, alas, but Herd nevertheless became one of the early inspirations of the game, best known for his friendship and generosity in the pub. "The only thing sweeter than Sandy's swing, such a thing of natural beauty," wrote Bernard Darwin, "was his perfect disposition and hospitality. There was never a man met who wasn't Sandy's friend."

As I read about him, I was struck by the similarities to my own Jack, whose great-grandfather John Sinclair had been a golf-club champion in Netherlee, Scotland. Herd's memoir was priced at three hundred dollars and thus out of the range of my book budget, but owing to the Old Sport's busy trade and the natural garrulousness of its proprietor, I'd nearly finished the book during summer afternoons while waiting for Tom to get free of his customers.

"So how did you fellows play today?" Tom asked the trio of men who'd clearly dropped in straight from the course. "Was it No. 2 you boys played, or No. 8?"

"It was No. 2," one of the three answered with a grimace. "Amazing golf course—everything I ever heard it was and more, I'm afraid. Let me tell you what happened . . ."

Tom slipped me a wry but familiar look. If there truly was such a phenomenon as the Pinehurst cure, which I was beginning to accept, there was conversely something Tom and I both regarded as the Pinehurst curse—whereby your middle-aged male golf pilgrim to the so-called home of American golf becomes a thundering bore, droning on ceaselessly about his life-changing round on one of the area's famous layouts, replaying every shot in laborious detail, blow-by-blow. Many was the time I'd sat contentedly on the porch of the nearby Pine Crest with a libation and my good friend Marmalade the cat for companionship and listened with amusement as some lonely golf knight on a corporate outing recounted his day to a distant, long-suffering spouse. I'd heard women do this, too—though that was distinctly rarer. In any case, Tom instantly recognized the symptoms of the curse and cut the poor fellow off before he'd finished his detailed account of the first hole.

"Excuse me, sir," he said pleasantly, lifting a genial hand, "but if we're going to do the full eighteen, I'll need to go get a riding cart."

The man's companions burst out laughing. The man reddened but then laughed as well.

"You're right," he agreed. "I'll save it for my wife. If she's getting a nice guilt gift for letting me come here, the least she can do is listen to how I played."

After sending the pilgrims on their merry way, each with "guilt gifts" for their wives, Tom strolled over to where I was reading about Sandy Herd in a discreet corner of the shop.

"Are you going to ever buy that book, sir, or just finger it to death?" he gruffly demanded.

"Why pay for it when I can stand here and read it for free? This place is better than a lending library or even a bookseller's kiosk on the streets of Paris." In truth, Tom had tried to give me Sandy Herd's book, but I'd refused to take it. I made a mental note, however, to purchase it someday for Jack, if he ever got close to competing for the Maine schoolboy golf championship.

"How much will you take for the autographed photo of Ma Teresa?" I pointedly asked, motioning to the Calcutta saint on the wall. At least once or twice a year, some callous shopper asked Tom to part with his treasured memento of Mother Teresa, a move that never failed to work up his dander. The photograph, signed to Tom, hung in a spot of honor over his cluttered desk and next to an Augusta flag signed by Jack Nicklaus.

"It's not for sale. Besides, you wouldn't have enough money if I did sell it. You're no Donald Trump, you know."

"Well, you're no Mother Teresa—if you know what I mean."

A gray-haired woman had paused by the door, staring at us quizzically.

"He always does this," Tom explained to her, jabbing a thick index finger at me. "Comes in here and bothers my customers."

"I'm his parole officer," I calmly explained to the woman. "We're hoping he keeps this job for a while, or else he may have to go back to the big house."

She laughed nervously, shook her head, and left with the bell on the door jingling behind her.

Tom, grinning, punched me on the arm. "Welcome back, mate. I missed you. It's lonely walking the reservoir by myself."

"Missed you, too, brother. Just popped in to say hello and see if I could buy you a beer. I'm meeting my *real* brother at Dugan's in ten minutes. Want to come? I'll tell you all about how Jack's golf season ended."

He said he would join us after he closed the shop but demanded to know immediately how Jack had fared, so I told him.

Tom listened to my account, visibly pleased, then conveyed an unexpected bonus.

"Something really nice happened to Bryan after Jack left town. He quit playing video games almost entirely and began going each afternoon to the golf course by himself. When I asked what was up, he told me Jack had said he should knock off the video games and work on his golf. So he's done just that. His game is starting to improve—because of Jack."

"It doesn't hurt having you for his dad," I said, pointing out the obvious. But it was nice to hear, suggesting some part of the message was getting through to Jack, as well.

"I suppose. But it sometimes takes a buddy to drive those lessons home and help you get your game on track."

"I'm living proof of that," I said. "Look how my game has improved thanks to you and Woronoff."

Without question, owing to the golf I'd been playing with Tom at Mid Pines or the Elk Club, and with David Woronoff at CCNC, my game had finally begun to creep out of hibernation. In a recent charity event at National Golf Club to benefit the Moore County schools—what David Woronoff playfully called one of the area's "Majors"—I'd shot even par and come within two inches of scoring my first-ever ace and taking home a Toyota Camry. My matches with David were typically casual affairs in which we simply hit balls and talked shop and rarely wrote down our scores. With Tom, however, I played matches that were increasingly close affairs. I still had yet to beat him, but that day seemed to be edging over closer. In short, these two had put the fun back in the game for me. As a bonus, I'd even played several delightful rounds of golf with Grumpy Morrison and tied for first place in his "Dornocher" best-ball event at CCNC.

"So how's our official blazer patch coming along?" I asked as I slipped Sandy Herd back into the bookcase.

Tom gave me an annoyed look. "I'm working on it," he snapped with mock irritation. "These things can't be rushed. I'm studying classic heraldic designs. Go have a beer with your brother. I'll be there in an hour. And leave some beer for real working men, if you don't mind."

As I sat at Dugan's waiting for my brother to arrive, gazing out at streets beginning to stir with new life, I mentally relived the trip I'd had to Sea Island with Jack, recalling how he'd been one hole away from breaking eighty on the Retreat Course when a huge thunderstorm chased us off.

After supper that night at the Lumpkin house, Jack Lumpkin had given Jack Dodson a few pointers on his swing and had graciously videotaped him in action. The next day, Jack and I went back to Retreat, and he shot eighty. The day he flew home to Maine, we played golf with a close friend named James Maynard at his club in Raleigh, and Jack finally broke eighty for the first time ever, scoring seventy-eight on a demanding Carolina Country Club course where Arnold Palmer once played with his dad, Deacon. It was the perfect ending to his summer Pinehurst sojourn.

At home in Maine, however, his game inexplicably wasn't the same. On the naval base course where Mt. Ararat High School played its junior varsity matches, he could scarcely break forty-five for nine holes. The school golf season was brief, barely six weeks long, and I'd made two sixteen-hour trips home to watch him play. As his scores refused to come down and his frustration mounted, he made a point of asking me not to follow him around the course—merely to wait for him to finish. With reluctance, I honored his request, resisting the urge to sneak out and tag along with the other parents.

The afternoon before I returned to the Sandhills, he'd come off the course from his final match of the year having notched his sixth win of the season, but nonetheless downcast.

"I can't believe it," he'd fumed, tossing his TaylorMades angrily into the back of my car after signing his card, shaking his opponent's hand, and climbing in beside me. The wind had a sharper bite. Come October in Maine, winter closes fast.

"Believe what?" I'd cheerfully inquired.

"How awful I played *again*. Down south I played great on really hard courses —better than anybody on the varsity up here probably would have! But now I can't play worth a *crap* on this crummy course. I can't even break forty-five. It's totally humiliating, Dad."

"Bobby Jones said there are two kinds of golf," I said, easing in a bit of historic perspective. "There's golf and then there's *tournament* golf."

At the risk of deepening his gloom, I pointed out that the pressure of playing in a tournament or high school match made even highly skilled players do peculiar things. It had to do with jangled nerves. Bobby Jones quit competitive golf after capturing his famous Grand Slam, in large part because he was tired of playing in tournaments that made him an emotional wreck. He wanted to rediscover, as middle age settled on him, the pleasure of playing the game "for the fun of it."

Ben Hogan, I reminded my frazzled lad, took more than a decade and failed three times to make it on the PGA Tour before he mastered his nerves and finally learned how to win a tournament. "After he broke through," I said, "there was no stopping him. Hogan's fabled reserve was the mental bulwark he constructed to contain those destructive nerves.

"So how'd you actually do in your match today?" I asked mildly. In truth, I already knew Jack had won his match in a romp; one of the other parents had told me he was three-up standing on the final tee. I just wanted to hear him say it, so he'd perhaps realize what a decent year he'd had after all, given how relatively little formal match experience he had compared to most of the other guys on his team.

Jack sniffed, shaking his head dismissively. "I won. But it was only because the other kid sucked."

I hated that word. Jack knew this and rarely used it. But, of course, it's a young man's obligation to shake up his old man's world.

"Well, that's just great," I said enthusiastically, determined to keep my side of the conversation on the up note. "What's that make your record for the season?" I already knew the answer to this, too, but I wanted to hear him say it out loud. We were behaving like two determined toddlers on a seesaw, forcing each other up and down in the air.

He shrugged indifferently. "I don't know. Five-and-one maybe."

"Actually, someone told me it was six."

"I guess. Big deal. I'm still playing like crap."

"That's fantastic, Jack. I'm proud of you. You'll be ready to go by next season, I'll bet."

He gave a dim nod. "Maybe. But if I don't make varsity," he said in a quiet but emphatic voice, "I won't play golf next year. For one thing, I hate this course."

I sighed and continued steering us along the coast road that led out the south Harpswell Peninsula to where Pat Robinson, just out of the hospital from difficult heart surgery, was recuperating at her daughter Jane's seaside cottage. Earlier that afternoon, I'd driven out to East Watch Cottage and sat with the recovering grandame in the garden, looking across the inlet at Orr's Island, where Harriet Beecher Stowe spent her happiest summers in Maine. For two splendid hours we talked about everything from Pinehurst to poetry. Among other revelations, I learned that Pat and her late husband, Ray, had planned to retire to Southern Pines when Ray left the navy in the late 1960s, but they wound up returning to Maine and buying East Watch Cottage instead.

At her request, I filled Dame Pat in on my summer adventures in North Carolina—how I'd been adopted by Max and Myrtis Morrison and about Jack's rapid improvements on the courses down there. She listened with keen interest, balancing her teacup on her knees, occasionally interrupting like an Oxford don to pose a question. When I mentioned Jack's mystifying struggles with the game at home in Maine, she leaned forward with urgency and said, "You musn't let him lose heart. Golf is the most difficult game on earth to master! I advise you, dear boy, to tell him to go do good and don't look back! That's what seventeenth-century Dutch sailors said to each other, you see, before embarking on perilous voyages. Most applicable in this instance. It'll help him get around the golf course."

I had to smile at her sweet Old World advice. As she walked me slowly to my car, clutching my arm, I asked Dame Pat if she'd returned to the Sandhills since nearly purchasing a cottage there. "No, we never went back. To tell you the truth, part of me always regretted that—which is why I'm so pleased you've rediscovered your game and made new friends there."

She paused and looked me in the eye. I kissed her pale cheek. "I think you belong there the way I belong here." She lightly squeezed my arm. "Ray used to call this cottage 'the laughing place.' I see that laughter in your eyes again."

IN THE AFTERMATH of Jack's disappointing season, which wasn't all that disappointing to his old man, I suggested, "You should start practicing much earlier next year so you're guaranteed to make the varsity."

Jack responded with silence. So I pushed on.

"I've agreed to stay at *The Pilot* until the end of next June.

We could even stick around through the summer, if you like. You could come down and play with Bryan every day until your tryouts. His game is improving thanks to you. Tom wanted me to let you know that."

I conveyed this last bit in my finest hillbilly voice, hoping that might make a dent in his gloom. He gave me a look as if I was simply incapable of understanding the disappointment he felt.

"That's great, Dad. Good for Bryan," he said gloomily.

"Hey," I tried cheerfully, patting his knee, "you won six matches, dude—and only lost one due to hunger pains. That's amazing! A first for Dodsons!"

I told him how I'd attempted to qualify for the Maine Amateur Championship six years in a row and missed by a single stroke five out of six times, which had to be some kind of modern record for screwing up. I typically went around my longtime golf home at Brunswick Golf Club in no worse than seventy-five or seventy-six, yet during Amateur qualifying there, I couldn't break ninety.

"Unfortunately, maybe it's a case of like father, like son. You'll have to break the family curse next year."

"I probably won't even *make* varsity next year," he muttered, looking out the window. "By the way, just so you'll know, I've decided to go out for hockey again."

I nodded. This was a big surprise. Jack hadn't played hockey in over three years, a small eternity for that violent game. His mother wasn't going to be thrilled. Truth told, I wasn't either.

"Okay," I said, remembering what it felt like to be so young and full of disappointed golf dreams, hoping he didn't get his handsome head handed to him by the other kids.

"Hey, bro. Sorry I'm late," a familiar voice said, pulling me back to my barstool in Dugan's Pub.

Dick looked older, thinner, and grayer than the last time we'd met. But he looked good, nonetheless. Seeing him, I realized how much I'd missed him.

"Sorry I missed Jack," he said after he ordered a draft beer and sat down across from me. "How are things going in Maine?"

I filled him in on the drama that had moments ago replayed through my head, telling him about the six wins and one loss and how Jack planned to go out for the hockey team. My brother loved hockey.

"So what's Maggie up to?"

I explained that Jack's big sister was cocaptain of her field-hockey team and on the verge of applying to college. He seemed astonished by this fact and wondered where she was interested in going. I told him the short list of colleges she was investigating but in the next breath admitted I was quietly championing St. Andrews University in Scotland because that would make parents' weekend a lot more interesting. Coincidentally, that very afternoon while motoring through Greensboro on my way back to the Sandhills, the friend who'd proposed me for membership in the Royal and Ancient Golf Club of St. Andrews had phoned to say the wait was over. I would soon be officially notified that I was eligible for membership in the oldest organization in golf. Naturally this news thrilled me. The first thing I thought about was the conversation I'd had years ago at Dornoch with Jack, shortly before I struck the finest shot of my life and won our match—his unwavering youthful belief that someday I'd be invited to join golf's most venerated organization. He seemed to know something then I could only fantasize about at that point.

If I couldn't break this big news to Jack, my brother and Tom Stewart would suffice. Tom had yet to arrive, so I went ahead and told Dick about being invited to join the R&A.

"That's great," he said, sounding pleased for me. "What's it mean, exactly? They give you a break on the greens fees at the Old Course or something? A free golf shirt? Tickets to the British Open?"

"I have no idea," I admitted. "But I think Dad would be pretty happy."

"Yeah. He would."

We drank our beers, and he caught me up on the doings of his family, then finally got around to asking, "So what are you actually *doing* here in Pinehurst?"

"Working," I said, giving him the simplest answer. I took a deep drink of my stout. Guinness, after all, was supposed to be good for you. So was seeing my big brother again.

"On a book or for your magazines?"

I told him I hadn't worked for my magazines in over two years, and that I'd agreed to work for at least a year as the writer-in-residence at *The Pilot* newspaper, describing the unexpected way I'd come back to North Carolina and stayed on to try and locate my inner golf child and possibly inspire Jack to deepen his connection to the game.

Dick nodded. "So are you writing golf or just playing it?"

"Mostly playing it for fun. I'd almost forgotten how much fun golf can be when nothing except bragging rights are on the line."

He nodded again. "So how long will you stay?"

"Hard to say. Probably at least through next summer."

For the next half hour, we had a nice time talking about how our parents had loved coming to Pinehurst and Southern Pines. We reminisced about other old times, too.

"So . . . are you and Wendy okay?"

"Fine," I said. "Never better. Why do you ask?"

"You're here by yourself in Pinehurst. She's still up in Maine."

"True," I said. "But I drive home to Maine every two weeks for conjugal visits, and she spent most of the summer here with our children. We also plan to have her kids and mine in the Sandhills for the holidays. And I promised Jack to try and get him into the Donald Ross Junior Championship at the resort between Christmas and New Year's." That would conclude with a father-son one-day tournament. Bryan and Tom were already signed up to play and had invited us to join them. Jack seemed excited about this prospect.

"I see," my brother said. "That all sounds like a pretty complicated life."

"Life's pretty complicated," I agreed. "Just look at you and me."

He gave me a softly pained look. I knew it was a subject he would prefer to skip, but the wounded silence between us had gone on nearly five years, which was far too long. This unresolved matter—our suspended friendship—was one of the reasons I'd come back to my old stomping ground.

He shook his head, sipping his beer. "Yeah. I wish all that hadn't happened. I'm sorry it did."

"Me, too. Cruel is the strife that separates brothers," I said, quoting Aristotle. "But things worked out okay in the end. Come to think of it, I owe you a serious thanks."

Dick arched his eyebrows like a guy waiting for a mean punch line, but there was none. I explained what I meant.

"If Mom hadn't lost her house I would never have agreed to help design a golf course for the man who owned the assisted-living place she was living in." The nine-hole Scottish-style golf course I'd helped design for Highland Green Golf Club had earned nice comment in the New England press since its opening in early 2004. The project had been so successful, the owner had recently asked me about designing the concluding nine. But with two fine longtime golf clubs in our area, I'd convinced him what was really needed in the region was a comprehensive golf learning center—a place to help grow the game on the grass-roots level, and perhaps become a permanent home of the state's golf hall of fame. Highland Green's owner, a man named John Wasileski, had enthusiastically signed on to both ideas, and I'd agreed to design the new Highland Green Golf Learning Center and the hall-of-fame site, too.

"That's pretty cool," Dick said, visibly relieved that I wanted to bury the hatchet anywhere but his head. "Maybe I'll come up and take some lessons."

"You could use some."

My brother wasn't a very good golfer. But he was my only brother. Being back here had powerfully reminded me of that and made all the other stuff between us suddenly seem irrelevant.

"There's an expression in golf I like," I said. "It's what happens when two opponents have a three-foot putt that neither wants to try and make. You look at each other and say in desperation, 'Good, good?' That means, 'Let's call it a draw and move on to the next hole.'"

Dick smiled. "Sounds good to me," he agreed. "Let's do that."

"In that case," I proposed, lifting my stout to his light beer, "Good, good. Let's move on to the next hole in life."

"I agree." He touched his glass to mine. "Here's to the Royal and Ancient, too. Any club that would have you, little brother, must be honorable—or plain desperate."

Just then, Tom Stewart swung through the door of Dugan's and found his way to our table, waving to the waitress for his usual libation. Doc Morris trailed him by thirty seconds. I introduced these two noble Idle Knights to my brother, and in no time Tom was regaling Dick with a story about a famous golfer and a pair of enthusiastic female fans in the basement of Dugan's on Saturday night of U.S. Open week. Pretty soon he was telling the same jokes I'd recently told him.

At one point I glanced over at my big brother and smiled, pleased to see Dick at ease with my friends, thinking how happy our parents must have been at that moment, wherever they were watching from. The relief I felt was intense. The emotionally charged issue that had so divided us—what to do with our mother's house and remaining assets—was as old and commonplace as the parable of the prodigal son, and the deaths of our parents had devastated my brother and pitched me headlong into a midlife crisis. And yet, as our late philosopher dad was fond of reminding my brother and me as we were growing up, "A crisis is merely an opportunity waiting to be born." The Greek word for *crisis* means "decision." By deciding to return to the Sandhills, I had taken the first step toward reconciliation—the rebirth of a vital relationship we both needed and desired.

As we left Dugan's a while later, two women were arriving for supper. One of them stopped me.

"Are you Jim Dodson from *The Pilot?*" she asked.

"Yes, ma'am." It seemed pointless to deny it.

"I *love* reading your column in the Sunday paper. My husband and I fight over who gets the paper first. That one about pool moms was a stitch. I heard you speak at the Rotary last week. You were great. I hope you don't leave when you writer-in-residence job is up."

She blushed then, glancing at Tom, Dick, and Walter, who were silent but visibly amused by this exchange. "I'm sorry. I hope I haven't embarrassed you," she apologized.

"He's unembarrassable," Tom said. "You should see his golf swing."

"We're glad to hear he's popular around these parts," confirmed my brother, joining in the banter like old times. "We thought he'd end up in prison."

The women laughed. The other one spoke up. "Would you ever agree to come speak to our book group in Seven Lakes?"

"Of course," I said. "When do you want me?"

"Anytime I can have you," she said with enthusiasm, breaking everyone up again.

As we crossed the parking lot to his car, Dick touched my arm and said, "You've got quite a gig going here, little brother—speaking to the Rotary and exciting the ladies at the Seven Lakes book club, eh? Dad and Mom would love it. Do you always have women mobbing you in pubs?"

"It's the Old Spice. I remind them of their fathers."

"I can see why you came back. I hope you do stick around a while."

"Me, too. I have only one real regret." I told him what it was—failing to bring our mother back to North Carolina before she died. "She never stopped thinking about her garden and her life on Dogwood Drive," I confirmed.

Dick nodded. "Maybe *that's* why you're here."

"That thought has occurred to me. Jack suggested the same thing not long ago."

We shook hands and then, like old times, hugged and said goodbye, promising to meet again soon, maybe even play a little golf. I watched him get in his car, thinking how good it felt to have my brother back and hoping he felt the same way.

His window rolled down, and he leaned out. "Take care of yourself. Let's do this again soon, bubba."

"Will do. Go do good and don't look back," I said, suddenly thinking of Pat Robinson's Dutch blessing to Jack.

Dick smiled. "That sounds like something Dad would say."

I smiled back at him. "It does, doesn't it?"

IT WAS SUCH a beautiful evening I decided to walk home to Southern Pines and ask David Woronoff to bring me back for my car later.

Midland Road was the street that caddies from the early resort followed when walking home, and I decided there might be a Sunday column in retracing their steps. Moreover, David had cooked up the intriguing idea of a group of the usual suspects (Stewart, Morris, Dempsey, et al.) playing our way in an alternate-shot format across the countryside from Pinehurst No. 2 to Mid Pines Golf Club on New Year's Eve, a nutty golf marathon the boy publisher of the Sandhills had already begun affectionately calling the First Ross Cross-Country Championship. I thought it might be useful to scope out the terrain in case this crazy competition actually took place.

So I set off along the fringes of No. 2, thinking how this was exactly the sort of yeoman competition that would have appealed to another guy named Dick—that is, Richard Tufts, who has rightfully been called the father of amateur golf in America. No game had a more diligent champion than the grandson of Pinehurst's founder. No one provided more support to the evolving golf dreams of young Edward Harvie Ward, either. Or more heartbreak, as it later turned out.

As Leonard Tufts's health seriously declined in the 1930s, his charming Harvard-educated son Richard took over running the Pinehurst Resort and by all accounts steered it adroitly through the toughest years of the Great Depression—among other things overseeing the installation of the first grass greens and a rebirth of the amateur game following the First World War. The younger Tufts was determined to perpetuate the values of the golden amateur best symbolized by Bobby Jones, Glenna Collett Vare, and many other stars from that era when golf was played for glory rather than money.

"Nobody loved the amateur game more than Dick Tufts," Harvie told me emphatically one spring morning at the Pine Crest shortly before he headed out to give a promising youngster lessons at Forest Creek Golf Club. "Dick was certain that if the professionals ever took over this game completely, the big-money crowd would ruin golf in no time flat. It was thanks to him that Pinehurst really came into its own after the war, though he eventually had to pay a price for that. No good deed goes unpunished, as they say."

Pinehurst's North and South Championship, with its separate amateur and professional segments, had long been a popular stop on golf's late-winter circuit, a beloved event that attracted the cream of golf and lavishly treated players and their wives to a week of Old South splendor at the Holly Inn and Carolina Hotel. As an unapologetic promoter of golf's traditional amateur values, Tufts had no problem hosting the visiting professional players because they attracted the spotlight of the national media that underscored the legitimacy of Pinehurst's claim to be the nation's "home of golf," a place where both the golden amateur and the hard-boiled circuit rider could find common teeing ground.

In many ways, the stunning emergence of Harvie Ward in 1948 perfectly summarized Dick Tufts's best paternalistic hopes for the game of golf in America in general, and Pinehurst in particular. Ward, twenty-two, then a senior at the University of North Carolina, showed up as just another talented college golfer and, against all odds, used a hot putter to vault himself into the thirty-six-hole final against Frank Stranahan, the celebrated 1946 North and South winner and leading amateur player of the day.

The contrast between the two couldn't have been more striking, producing a script straight from the films of Frank Capra. Harvie, an easygoing, joke-cracking son of a small-town Southern pharmacist, learned his game primarily hacking around in a rural nine-hole, sand-green golf course in Tarboro, North Carolina. By his junior year, with a short game that was nothing shy of spectacular, frat boy Harvie Ward was the toast of his college campus. Stranahan was twenty-five and a world traveler, the handsome weight-lifting scion to the Champion spark-plug fortune, hardened and suntanned from weeks of competing against the leading pros on the professional winter circuit, a disciplined and muscle-bound playboy so confident of dispatching the affable, unknown college kid he actually booked the main ballroom of the Carolina in advance for a victory party for one hundred of his closest friends.

Stranahan's path to the final, over an impressive field that included the leading amateurs of the day, wasn't a surprise to anyone. He eliminated his opponents with mechanical precision. Ward's ascent, on the other hand, was a chaotic affair that saw him have to ask his college coach for permission to play at the last minute, then find a seven-dollar-per-night rooming house in Southern Pines after shooting seventy-four in the Monday qualifier, making it into the field of sixty-four players. After just five holes on Tuesday morning, in a match against Charles Mulcahy of New York, the likable collegian found himself already four down "and so goddamned nervous and out of sync," Harvie remembered, "I was pretty sure I'd be headed back to Chapel Hill real quick."

Somehow he relaxed and his putter warmed up. Harvie tied his opponent on the eighteenth hole and won the right to advance on their first playoff hole. "After that, I went back to Pope's Cottages in Southern Pines and phoned my coach to ask permission to stay another day, then washed out my clothes in the sink. I hadn't planned on staying long enough to need fresh clothes. This routine went on for days, as I advanced to the next stage of the competition. My clothes never got completely dry."

Ward needed to make a downhill fifteen-footer on Thursday afternoon to dispatch Dick Chapman of Pinehurst 2-and-1 and advance to the semifinals against another largely unknown golfer named Arnold Palmer, a sophomore from Wake Forest College.

"I'd heard about Harvie through the college grapevine, but I don't think he knew me from the bellhop at the Carolina Hotel," Arnold recalled. "The word on Harvie was that he could putt from anywhere, and when I heard he'd beaten Dick Chapman, hell, I knew I was probably in for a tough match."

Harvie beat Palmer in a romp, 5-and-4, and the two smiling collegians posed for a photograph after their match, which Harvie later asked Arnold to sign. Two weeks after their meeting, Arnold would shoot 145 to edge Ward by a stroke and capture the Southern Conference Championship.

When word filtered back to Harvie's Zeta Psi fraternity house in Chapel Hill that one of their own was playing for the second biggest prize in amateur golf after the U.S. Amateur, dozens of Zeta Psi brothers raced to Pinehurst to watch the drama unfold. A fraternity brother brought Harvie a change of clothes for his final match against the dapper Stranahan. Harvie's mom and dad and two sisters drove up from Tarboro, too.

Golf World magazine, which began publication in Pinehurst about that time, captured the mood of the scene when an estimated two thousand rowdy spectators turned out to follow the Ward-Stranahan duel: "A number of attractive coeds from Chapel Hill, some in bare feet with painted toes, were included in an exuberant gallery of collegians, wealthy tourists, town folks and Negro caddies on the championship course at Pinehurst Saturday." Harvie's father promised to discuss buying him a new car if he somehow managed to "beat that Adonis from Ohio."

Privately Harvie confided to Decatur Cunningham, a frat brother from Greensboro, that he simply hoped to "Make a good showing before the home crowd—and make my dad proud."

The match seesawed through the morning round with neither

player gaining more than a brief 1-up advantage. Stranahan's game was sharp, almost robotic, while Harvie missed several greens but managed to halve holes by making long putts. "Every time I would hit a shot," Harvie remembered, "the Zeta Psis would let out cheers and war whoops. Most of them had never watched a golf match before and had no idea how to behave. Dick Tufts tried his best to quiet them down, and I could tell the noise really irritated Frank, but he never said a word. Unfortunately, they even cheered when he hit a poor shot—which wasn't often."

Remarkably, over the first thirty-four holes of their match, Ward one-putted seventeen times to reach the penultimate hole with a one-hole advantage. On the par-three seventeenth hole, Ward put his ball in the bunker while Stranahan found the putting surface. Harvie blasted his ball to within three inches for a one-putt par; Frankie missed a short putt for par. The unlikely challenger made par on the final hole to secure the championship—and promptly got lofted to the shoulders of his fraternity brothers and carried off the course to receive his silver champion's tray from a beaming Richard Tufts.

According to Cunningham, a visibly irked Stranahan—never the easiest of losers—extended his hand to the jubilant winner and remarked, "If you couldn't putt, Harvie, why, you'd just be another good-looking guy on a golf course."

The next year, despite Ward's distinct home-field advantage, Stranahan returned to exact revenge by clipping Ward, 2-and-1. That same year, 1949, Harvie captured the NCAA championship—using a pitch-and-run technique he claimed to have developed around the infamously unforgiving crowned putting surfaces at Pinehurst's championship course. In 1952 he used the same skills to adroitly maneuver around the dangerous greens at Prestwick Golf Club in Scotland and beat Frank Stranahan once again, taking the British Amateur Championship.

When the adopted son of Pinehurst captured the U.S. Amateur Championship in 1955, two years after Ben Hogan returned from the dead to have his finest year ever in golf, thus beginning his own exodus from the game, the press began calling Harvie Ward the heir apparent to Hogan's reign. Some newspaper wags predicted he would turn professional any day. Rival Arnold Palmer did so that very year. Ken Venturi would follow a short time later.

Nothing, in fact, could have been further from the easygoing Carolinian's mind, much to the satisfaction of one Richard Tufts, the man *Sports Illustrated* had labeled "America's Mr. Golf," the unapologetic flamekeeper of America's gilded amateur values. In many ways, Harvie Ward had no closer friend or greater ally than Dick Tufts—which explains why what happened next proved so devastating to both Ward and amateur golf.

THE PROBLEM BEGAN when the lavish spending habits of Eddie Lowery, Harvie's West Coast employer, a successful San Francisco car dealer, attracted the interest of California's tax authorities, which in turn triggered a federal inquiry into Lowery's personal and business finances. Among other things, the Feds questioned the large tax deductions Lowery, a powerful and visible member of the USGA's executive committee, claimed for covering the expenses of his two amateur protégés, Ken Venturi and Harvie Ward, at the Masters and other high-profile golf tournaments around the country.

By 1956 none other than Richard Tufts himself had ascended to the powerful presidency of the USGA, the organization that sanctioned and monitored amateur golf in America. Among the important improvements Tufts undertook during his tenure was a simplification of the rules and an effort to end the cloudy sponsorship practices surrounding amateur play. Contributing to Tufts's sense of urgency, several well-publicized scandals involving wagering pools around popular big-money Calcutta events, such as the one held each spring at Seminole Golf Club in Florida, threatened to give amateur golf everywhere a black eye and a bad reputation.

Tufts felt, passionately and for good reason, that the influence of money was going to compromise amateur golf's reputation as the final refuge of the sporting gentleman, so he moved early to resist raising the purse of his own North and South Open after the PGA brazenly "suggested" that he increase it to ten thousand dollars. Tufts also came to loggerheads with the PGA over enforcing regulations, the latter permitting a distinctly liberal interpretation of certain rules (primarily concerning the marking and cleaning of balls on the green, repairing pitch marks, and the age-old stymie rule) that it felt might restrict the flow of play and, by extension, hurt the pro game's emerging popularity—meaning gate receipts and potential corporate sponsorships.

Propelled by a strong Yankee conscience and a passionate love of "pure amateur competition," golf's grand old man, as Pinehurst historian Richard Moss sums up, saw himself as a bulwark against the corruption of the game he had come to love from playing with and against his own father. "In the years between 1951 and 1962," Moss writes, "Richard Tufts became an active advocate of the 'old golf' as it confronted the 'new golf.' He fought on a number of fronts." Tufts even articulated his views in a famous Creed of the Amateur which goes in part: "In my mind an amateur is one who competes in a sport for the joy of playing, for the companionship it affords, for health-giving exercise, and for relaxation from more serious matters. As a part of this light-hearted approach to the game, he accepts cheerfully all adverse breaks, is considerate of his opponent, plays the game fairly and squarely in accordance with the rules, maintains self-control, and strives to do his best, not in order to win, but rather as a test of his own skill and ability."

When Eddie Lowery's tax troubles threatened to embroil the USGA in a broader scandal that could prove disastrous to its reputation, the executive committee moved to swiftly minimize the damage. One year after his appearance at the Masters in 1956, Ward was summoned to a closed-door meeting outside Chicago to answer charges that by accepting Lowery's travel largesse, he had, in fact, violated the conditions of his amateur status. This came as a big surprise to Harvie Ward — and many other leading amateur players, for that matter.

"The night before I went to meet the board," Harvie recalled "I got a phone call from a lawyer back East, Edward Bennett Williams, advising me to bring a good lawyer of my own to argue my case. This was a complete surprise to me. I thought the committee just wanted to make sure I wasn't getting paid money to *play* amateur golf. But it went much deeper than that. Williams told me they needed to make an example of somebody to prove they had their eye on the ball. They needed and wanted a scapegoat."

Harvie decided to face his tribunal without benefit of counsel.

"You see, I didn't feel I'd done anything wrong. For one thing, I could justify my expenses at the Masters and other places, because wherever I went I met with businesspeople and usually sold them a few cars. That was, after all, my job . . . and I did it well. Venturi, too. Looking back, I may have been naive, but that made the whole thing legitimate in my mind. I thought for sure I could go in there and have a friendly chat and straighten this whole mess out."

At least initially, Harvie's longtime mentor Richard Tufts felt the issue might be resolved with minimal sanction for what he thought was an honest mistake on young Harvie's part. Eddie Lowery, who resigned from the USGA Executive Committee to face his federal tax tribunal, repeatedly stated that he had taken Ward, Venturi, and others as "personal guests" to various golf championships in America and Britain, and that "if there is blame to be assigned in this matter, the blame is mine entirely for assuring Harvie that he was operating well within . . . existing amateur rules."

During the months leading up to the closed-door hearing at the USGA's Midwestern headquarters in Golf, Illinois, Tufts's Pinehurst mailbox had been flooded with dozens of letters from leading figures in business and politics, a veritable who's who of the American golfing establishment, weighing in to extoll Harvie Ward's exemplary qualities as an amateur golf champion and urging leniency. In a private letter dated May 27, 1957, U.S. Senator Prescott Bush, a former executive committeeman and father of a future president, reminded Dick Tufts that several prominent USGA officials — including himself — had "combined private business and official USGA duties" while traveling to championship venues.

On the same day, Tufts replied to his friend the senator, hoping to reassure him that the matter would soon be resolved in manner fair to both amateur golf and Harvie Ward.

> I have had some correspondence with members and feel sure they will be inclined to be liberal in interpreting the matter of expenses and also in the handling of Harvie's case. Perhaps Harvie's prominence would not be a factor but I am sure that his very excellent conduct would be. This whole amateur situation is certainly a difficult one because the standards are breaking down in nearly every sport. We have tried very hard to carry on the same ideals that you and tour associates had when you were on the committee.
>
> Finally, it may interest you to know that I have received quite a large number of letters about Harvie and have yet to receive one which does not urge that we be lenient in the consideration of his case.

In an announcement that stunned the sporting world and sent shock waves reverberating through all of golf, however, the USGA Executive Committee voted unanimously to suspend Harvie's amateur status for a year and thus prevented the reigning two-time amateur champion from competing for an unprecedented third consecutive national title.

This perfect storm of Tufts's personal quest to clean up amateur golf, combined with the growing financial ambitions of professional golf, had, in fact, dealt amateur golf what amounted to a death blow, as within two years virtually every promising college star jumped from the ranks of the golden amateur to the rolls of the paid professional. Likable Harvie Ward, meanwhile, went into a booze-fueled tailspin for the next thirty years of his life.

"Looking back, the hardest part for me," he quietly confided, "was being at that hearing and looking over at my old mentor, Dick Tufts, assuming he was going to speak up on my behalf and come to my rescue. But he didn't. I realize now that he *couldn't*. Dick knew I hadn't intentionally bent the rules. He also knew how much I loved amateur golf. Amateur golf was my whole life. I had no desire whatsoever to turn pro and play for money. But he refused to even meet my eye. I left that meeting room so devastated I was numb with disbelief. Later I got incredibly angry and decided to show them they needed me more than I needed golf."

Ward quit playing for a year. "I took up tennis," he said, "and started running with a different crowd. At first I didn't miss it because the booze and girls helped ease the pain—or so I told myself."

And yet, once his amateur status was officially reinstated, he made the Walker Cup for a third time and finished his playing career with an unblemished record—seventeen wins that stood until Tiger Woods eclipsed it. Ward never factored in any of the major championships he entered, however, and his attempt to turn professional some years later proved, by his own standards, an unqualified flop. Once, while playing in his friend Bing Crosby's annual winter clambake at Pebble Beach, a pint of liquor fell out of his windbreaker, and Harvie broke up the gallery by playfully marking his ball with it, a parody of his former self, the golden boy turned court jester, amusing crowds that were accustomed to the antics of tipsy golf celebrities.

One summer afternoon while we sat together on the Donald Ross porch over at the resort, Harvie admitted, "I think of those years as the lost years of my life, when nothing I touched seemed to work out right or give me any real happiness or peace of mind. I still joked around and played the role of a nice guy who didn't care what had been done to him. But inside, brother, I was one unholy mess."

In the 1970s Harvie returned to his old Pinehurst stomping ground to serve as head teaching professional and director of golf for the new Foxfire Golf Club, a post he held for eight years. "That's where I began to finally discover what I may have been put on this earth to do," he said with a thoughtful smile. "I was here to have fun playing golf with my buddies and teach others how to play this crazy game. I was here to pass the game along."

In 1977 he won the North Carolina Open and officially retired from playing competitive golf. "That was my big comeback," he joked. "That was enough for me." In 1983, Ward left the Sandhills for a similar teaching job at Jack Nicklaus's Grand Cypress Golf Club in Orlando, Florida. Two years later, someone introduced him to Payne Stewart, then almost thirty years old and searching for a replacement for the only teacher he'd ever had, his own father, William Lewis Stewart, who had died that year from bone cancer. "Payne was in grief, and I'd been in grief for decades—so we were a team made for each other," Harvie quipped.

"Payne and I had a productive but volatile relationship from the start. He was a spoiled rotten kid with a Rolls-Royce swing but as good as anybody I ever saw from one hundred yards in. He just needed to get his head on straight and learn how to win again. That's a father's role in life—and he'd lost his. So I sort of filled in. I think I helped Payne begin to realize something about patience and dedication—but also about getting your heart and head to work in the same direction.

"Maybe the most important thing in life is figuring out where you're supposed to be. I'd learned that the hard way. My job was to try and help Payne understand this before his time ran out."

During their years as pupil and mentor, Payne Stewart's career flourished. He jumped to the top ten on the money list and won several big tournaments. When Stewart came to Pinehurst in 1989 and informed his teacher that he wanted to learn how to work the ball like Seve Ballesteros, the darling of pro golf at that moment, famous for his daring recovery shots from anyplace on the golf course, Ward advised him not to tamper with his swing. A short time later, Ward found out that Stewart had acquired a new teacher. That same year, Payne won his first major, the 1989 PGA Championship. Two years after ditching Harvie, Stewart won his first U.S. Open at Hazeltine, in Minnesota.

"I was happy for him but it also hurt," Harvie admitted. "I gave Payne things nobody else had given him, and he never even bothered to call me up to say he wanted to try working with someone else. That would have been fine. We could have shaken hands and wished each other the best. But he did it behind my back. It was like Dick Tufts all over again, only this time I was in the father role."

This time, however, Harvie had a form of stability he hadn't known in decades. Prior to the split with Stewart, he'd met and married his fifth wife, Joanne, who among other things got him off booze for good and convinced Harvie to move home to Pinehurst. "It was the only place I ever heard him talk about with such unreserved pleasure," Joanne once told me. "Harvie Ward was not just a son of the game but a son of Pinehurst."

Settled comfortably into his new life on Blue Road with a house full of dogs and old friends, Harvie began teaching at Mid Pines and eventually out at the spectacular new Forest Creek Golf Club.

By the time the Open made its first trip to Pinehurst in the summer of 1999, Ward and his most famous protégé hadn't spoken for a decade. On the final morning of the championship, a balmy Father's Day, Harvie sat in his house on Blue Road trying to decide whether he should go find Stewart and wish him the best of British luck. Payne was in the hunt for his third major and second U.S. Open title.

"You need to go," Joanne told her husband.

So Harvie went. "I came up quietly behind him on the practice tee and watched him hit balls. At one point he hooked a ball, and I remarked, 'Well, you've still got that Rolls-Royce swing, but I sure as hell didn't teach you to do *that*,' or something along those lines. The words were hard to get out of my mouth, but he knew who said them, even before he looked around at me. It was emotional for both of us."

After years of inner turmoil, Payne Stewart had undergone his own spiritual rebirth. Their reunion was a brief but joyful one. "We hugged each other the way a father would hug a lost son, and I told him I was sure he could win the Open. A heavy weight was lifted from us both. I wished him good luck and told him to go out there and take that damn thing *home*."

These were the final words the two men ever exchanged. Later that day, an hour before dusk, Stewart won the 99th U.S. Open on a dramatic fifteen-foot putt, raising a triumphant fist

in the air, lifting himself onto his toes and stepping into im-
mortality as the ball toppled into the cup.

Weeks later, Harvie was busy teaching at Forest Creek when
Joanne phoned to give him the terrible news that Payne Stewart
had perished in a freak plane mishap over the Midwest. "That
was the final sadness, almost too much to bear," Harvie told me,
his famous blue eyes watering at the memory. "I thank God we
had our reunion and set things right before he was gone."

I WALKED INTO David Woronoff's office, hot, tired,
and flushed from my hike along the caddie trail from Pinehurst to Southern Pines. During much of the walk, I'd replayed
in my head these scenes of Harvie's glamorous rise and fall
and ultimate spiritual redemption. It served to remind me how
these ancient Sandhills had played a vital role in that process—
effectively becoming the cure that may have saved his life. By
returning to where his heart wanted to be, he'd discovered
what he was "put on this earth to do"—"to have a little fun
playing golf with my buddies and pass the game along." As I
walked the old caddie trail thinking about Harvie's unexpected
epiphany, it struck me that I was having more fun writing for
The Pilot than I'd had in thirty years—and that maybe I, too,
was passing something of value along to others, including my
son. The reconciliation with my brother seemed to confirm this
possibility. And I was having more fun playing golf with my
buddies than I'd had in years. Whatever it was exactly—the
first stirrings of my own Pinehurst cure or perhaps a spiritual
epiphany of some kind—I decided, it couldn't have come at a
better moment.

"*There* you are," David said, hopping up from behind his

desk. "I was about to come looking for you. Someone said they saw you walking from Pinehurst, and I wondered if you had car trouble."

"I just wanted to see if I could walk from there to here. I also wanted to get a sneak peak at the Ross Cross-Country course."

"That's going to be a blast," David said with his usual collegial enthusiasm. "Maybe it'll become an annual thing." He asked how I felt about playing as partners.

"Nothing would give me more pleasure," I assured him. "But I'll tell you what Arnold Palmer said to me the first time I got to play golf with him. It was in the daily "shootout" at Bay Hill, and we were partners. I was extremely nervous, as you might expect."

David grinned. "Oh, yeah? What'd he say—where'd you get such ugly green pants?"

"No. Palmer was the soul of courtesy. He whispered: 'Relax and have a great time, Shakespeare. Just don't screw up.'"

CHAPTER NINE

The Fairway Home

Okay. I've got it figured out how we can do it."

"Do what?" I asked, distractedly. I was preparing to chip from a few feet off the seventeenth green. Short chips are the poorest part of my game.

"Move here," Wendy said simply. She had a strange look on her pretty face, her lower lip protruding. I call this her "planning look."

Her third shot lay on the green, a few feet from the hole. She was putting for par, on the threshold of having perhaps her best score ever—just two holes from breaking ninety.

It was a glorious late Easter afternoon at Mid Pines Golf Club, the sky pale blue, the dogwoods at peak bloom, and by some thoughtful quirk in the universe we appeared to have my favorite golf course on the planet entirely to ourselves.

"But I haven't suggested that we move here," I pointed out to her.

She cupped her eyes against the low sun and smiled at me the way she sometimes smiles at her sons when they are being difficult or missing her point. "You didn't have to, babe. You talk about being here in your sleep."

"Oh. Sorry to keep you awake," I mumbled, aiming my Hogan wedge at the difficult pin at the back of the putting surface.

"Well I'm not," she declared. "You're like a different person down here. You're so productive and happy. What a great winter it's been, not the least of what being here has done for your golf game."

Moments after she said this, as if the gods wished to prove her correct, I holed a short chip to get to one over par on the back nine. My front nine had also been one over. Moments later, she rolled her par putt into the cup and beamed as she jotted four on the card, and we shouldered our bags and set off for the eigtheenth tee. I could see Wendy's growing ardor for the game when she looked offended that I proposed taking a riding cart.

"You have to admit you've been thinking about it," she prodded as we fell in side by side along the home fairway, our clubs clicking on our backs.

I admitted that I had. Since that revealing hike along the old caddie trail at New Year's, the thought had never strayed far from my mind. But our lives were deeply entrenched in Maine. There was the house, her job, the feelings of my teenage children and of her children too. Mine had grown up in that house, and Maggie, somewhere around age ten, forced me to make a "pinkie promise" that I'd never sell it. She said she planned to get married someday in the gardens I'd spent years and uncounted sums building.

"I didn't say it would be easy. But life changes, and I think the timing might be right. Maggie goes out the door to college before long, and Jack is just a year behind her. Besides, from what I can tell, Maggie enjoys being down here and so does Jack." She waited a beat and added, "Myrtis and Jean Morrison are onboard with the idea, too. They say you've done wonders for Max. Myrtis says he's come to think of you as the son he never had. I understand Jean even calls you Grumpy Junior."

I smiled at her, taking a slow practice swing with my driver. "He just likes me because I laugh at his jokes when no one else will. We have that in common."

"See?" Wendy declared. "You two are *perfect* for each other. Golf, gardening, grumpiness—even arguing about God and politics. By the way, Pat Robinson thinks we should do it, too. We'll need a plan, though."

"You've discussed it with her?"

"We had lunch at the Stephens House last week. She just moved there and seems happy. You won't believe this, but she's moved into the room your mom was going to move into. Is that an *amazing* coincidence or what?"

"The dame says there are no coincidences," I said, remembering how Pat's Episcopalian faith had been influenced and broadened by her fascination with Tibetan Buddhism.

"I think I agree with her."

I hit a decent drive that drew a little from right to left. Then, wordlessly, we picked up our bags and hiked to the final women's tee, where Wendy teed up her ball and began her preshot routine. Watching Wendy, I realized, not for the first time, how much I enjoyed playing golf with my wife. If she lived here, I thought, she would become a regular golf junkie in no time flat, living a Sandhills life Pat Robinson had once envisioned herself living. There was tender symmetry to that, underscored by the bittersweet law of circularity and a gravitational pull that seemed to describe my life these days.

"I really do want to be here for the Women's Open next summer," she announced, taking aim at the fairway. "You should see if Jack wants to be a standard-bearer or maybe work for *The Pilot*. I'll bet David could find him some fun job to do."

"I'm sure he could. I guess the only real question is if Jack would want to be here. I'm still not sure the golf bug has bitten him."

"You can only offer it. You've given him the tools. He has to do the rest. Now hush *up* while I hit."

She took a fierce cut and nailed her tee shot. It flew two hundred yards and landed right center of the fairway.

Girdled by flowering dogwoods and azaleas, the home hole at Mid Pines sweeps majestically downhill and up again to the feet of the lovely Georgian-style hotel, a simple but spectacular finisher. The only physical difference in the place from the summer afternoon I stood on the terrace with my dad and promised to reform was that the terrace was now the pro shop. Otherwise, little had appeared to change. Maybe *that* was part of the Pinehurst cure. Amidst a world in flux, nothing here appeared to change all that much.

As we approached the day's final green, Wendy sighed, hooked her arm through mine, and said: "This has been the nicest day I can remember."

"Better than that day at Chantilly?" I asked.

A few years before, during my final trip abroad as a travel correspondent, we'd found ourselves playing golf late in the afternoon on France's most celebrated private course at Chantilly, having strolled up straight from winning an unexpected nine hundred francs on the last race at the local steeplechase and blowing it on local cheese and wine, then suddenly finding the famous but empty golf course with scores of unseen cuckoos serenely calling our names in the surrounding forests. Afterward we met a trio of Frenchmen playing cards on the terrace, and they insisted we join them and their wives at a crowded bistro in the town. Five or so hours after that, we somehow found our way through the darkened countryside to the beautiful château where we were staying, vowing that there could never be a more perfect day.

She smiled. "France was great. This might be even better."

SHE WAS RIGHT, of course. It had been the busiest and most rewarding year I could recall in a long time.

During the Christmas holidays all our children had come to visit, and by all accounts had a good time becoming better acquainted with my old stomping ground. Though I failed in my efforts to get Jack late entry into the crowded field of the Donald Ross Junior Championship at the resort, he and I managed to play the intriguing Pit Golf Links in Aberdeen with its designer, Dan Maples, son of Frank Maples, Ross's longtime maintenance chief at Pinehurst. We were joined by Dan's son Brad, a recent N.C. State graduate who had entered his father's course-design business. After a two-month layoff from the game, Jack shot an eye-opening thirty-nine on the front side, only to blow up to a fifty-two on the back. But Dan softened the blow with interesting stories about the private Donald Ross and about a championship course he'd finished constructing in 2002 at Natanis Golf Course up in Maine.

"That's where the state high school championships are played every October," Jack piped up, clearly impressed. "It's supposed to be really hard."

Dan smiled. "You wouldn't like it half as much if it was a pushover, would you?"

"No sir," Jack responded, perhaps envisioning himself playing it for the state high school title.

A few days later we teed up with John Dempsey out at Forest Creek Golf Club where Harvie Ward spent his final days teaching, a spectacular layout that had cracked several top one hundred lists. The witty, golf-mad president of Sandhills Community College graciously invited young Jack back to play in the college's annual summer fund-raiser as his partner, and Jack enthusiastically agreed. So maybe the golf bug was beginning to sink its teeth in, I decided.

We had several lively father-son matches against the wily Stewarts, all of which we lost. By this point Jack had knocked the rust off his game and posted impressive scores in the low eighties and—music to my aging ears—inquired if I had indeed decided to stay at *The Pilot* during the approaching summer.

"It's possible," I replied as we drove home one afternoon from the Elk's Club. "Why?"

"I'd like to come down and work on my game," he said with simple conviction, repeating his hope to make the varsity and possibly win the state high school golf championship. "Don't you think I could do it?" he asked.

"Of course you can. It'll take a lot of hard work. You have a Rolls-Royce swing, Old Champ, but you rarely take it out of the garage for a spin. Look how good Bryan's game is getting. It's because he's working on it."

"I'm going to do that from now on," Jack inisted, then asked if we might play in the National Father and Son Team Classic down in Myrtle Beach that coming July. He remembered this from a conversation we'd had with a mother and her son in a restaurant at Sea Island.

"All things are possible," I heard myself say, pleased by this explosion of youthful determination—the fruits of which remained to be seen. "I'll look into it."

"That would be awesome."

THIS WAS THE SUBLIME portion of the holiday. The ridiculous part happened as winter darkness settled on New Year's Eve and David Woronoff and I approached our team ball lying in the front-facing bunker on that same final green at Mid Pines. Following a comic alternate-shot hike across five Sandhills golf courses stretching from Pinehurst to Southern Pines, the first (and probably final) Ross Cross-Country Golf Championship drew to a close with the other four teams waiting on the green. David and I were in a tie for last place.

"Look where you put us," I snapped with mock irritation, glaring at our plugged shot in the face of the bunker. "All you had to do was hit a simple wedge shot onto the green from a hundred yards. What a total choke job." I added every unflattering name I could think of, much to the amusement of our opponents.

David, grinning, took a sip of his beer and snapped back, "Shut up and hit our ball. It's getting dark and I want to get to the hors d'oeuvres."

I walked into the bunker, wiggled my feet into the sand, took an indifferent glance at the hole, then blasted. The ball flew twenty yards through the air, bounced once, and dropped into the cup for a birdie, proving once again it is infinitely better to be lucky than good at golf.

"Great shot," David cried as we circled the green in a send-up of Hale Irwin's high-fiving romp upon winning at Medinah in 1990. "At least I get the *assist*!" All our opponents could do was grumble and shake their heads at the blind injustice of golf.

Moments later, after Idle Knight Tom Stewart and our host Kelly Miller both uncharacteristically missed short birdie putts that would have given their respective teams the outright win, the first Ross Cross-Country finished in a highly unsatisfying three-team tie.

"I guess we'll have to carry it over to *next* New Year's Eve," President Dempsey observed as we climbed the hill to the terrace where a warm spread of food and drink had been thoughtfully provided by our host.

"Sounds good to me," David said enthusiastically. Then he glanced at me and added, "Guess that means our writer-in-residence will have to sign up for another year."

"I second that motion," Tom Stewart said.

"Let me get this straight," I responded. "After all the rotten names I called you in the bunker five minutes ago, you want me to stick around?"

David shrugged. "You redeemed yourself. Besides, if I let you leave, I'll be murdered by one of your adoring pool moms. The Women's Open is also coming up, and we'll have to defend our title at the next Ross Cross-Country. You'd better stick around."

It was nice to feel wanted. As I drove home to get ready for the New Year's Eve gathering Wendy had planned for the cabin,

I realized what uncomplicated fun I always had with these aging sons of the Sandhills game, these latter-day Idle Knights.

As a result of my Sunday pieces in *The Pilot*, almost every week I was invited to speak somewhere around the region, to a book or garden club or to a civic organization. Each outing seemed to deepen my appreciation of life here and nudge my roots deeper.

For example, I'd recently agreed to speak to the English Speaking Union at CCNC, a black-tie affair that had prompted Myrtis Morrison to put me in her Cadillac and drive me fifty miles to a tailor she knew in another town. On the way there and back, she told me about her childhood growing up as the daughter of the town's only doctor and about taking herself off to Duke University and meeting Grumpy, then a med student doing his residency at Chapel Hill. After he completed his navy service in Charleston, they'd moved to sleepy Southern Pines to take over the practice of the local ophthalmologist, who had recently died.

"Max jumped right in and never took a vacation for the next thirty years," she related. "He always wanted to play golf—his daddy gave him a left-handed set when he graduated from high school—but he never had the time. We had the three girls, and he worked every day but Sunday, poor thing, which he spent in the garden. It wasn't until he retired ten years ago that he finally took up playing. He couldn't live without it now."

She glanced over at me and said, "You're kind to play with him. I know his game is pretty bad, but he loves playing. You bring the best out in him. It's wonderful to see him so relaxed. After Elizabeth, I never thought I'd seem him like that again."

"I love playing Grumpy golf," I admitted. "Max has a swing

that looks as if he built it in his workshop. He makes *me* laugh. Besides, we're a winning team and have the ugly golf shirts to prove it."

The previous November, Max had invited me to play in the Dornocher, an annual event at CCNC named for a group of founding club members who made an annual pilgrimage to Donald Ross's birthplace in Scotland. That day Max's four-part swing and mail-order clubs performed brilliantly. He shot eighty-three — twelve strokes below his handicap — and I shot seventy-six on the Dogwood Course, leaving us tied with two other teams for first place, which we subsequently lost in a coin flip. Even so, we were awarded expensive CCNC golf shirts. Grumpy's was tangerine. Mine was even greener than the hideous Open pants I'd never had the courage to wear a second time. So I gave it to David Woronoff, who was not only a hound for free shirts but had no discernable taste in golf attire.

During the trip to fetch the tux, Myrtis gave me what amounted to a social history of Pinehurst and Southern Pines, including a detailed account of how the Tufts family ran out of money and Richard Tufts, on the brink of bankruptcy, was forced in 1970 to sell the resort to the Diamondhead Corporation for a paltry ten million dollars, roughly a third of what it was believed to be worth. About that same time, she pointed out, private residential clubs like CCNC, Harvie Ward's Foxfire, and Pinewild opened up, attracting droves of wealthy retirees and second-home owners to the Sandhills.

"Max says that selling Pinehurst broke Dick Tufts's heart, because nothing was ever the same again," she observed quietly, confirming a story Herb Wind had once told me during one of our final spring lunch conversations.

Not long after Diamondhead purchased Pinehurst and began constructing condos and revamping Pinehurst No. 2 in ways that ultimately horrified traditionalists and longtime loyalists, Wind dropped his bag at Peggy Bell's smaller and quieter Pine Needles Lodge and drove down Midland Road to visit his old friend Dick Tufts at his cottage by the third fairway of No. 2. "We had our usual toddy," Wind told me, "and talked about the big changes the new owners were making, few of which pleased Dick, including the hall of fame and large professional tournament they were mounting. He felt that everything his father and grandfather had worked to create at Pinehurst was being systematically destroyed before his eyes." Dick Tufts died a short time later, not long before the golf world's first hall of fame opened its doors just off the slopes of Pinehurst No. 2's fifth fairway.

Despite a gala opening in 1974 that managed to attract Nicklaus, Palmer, and even the reclusive Ben Hogan back to the "Home of American Golf" — as the resort's literature began to unapologetically call itself about that time — neither the hall of fame nor the over-the-top two-week professional golf tournament designed specifically to exploit the hall's opening survived more than a handful of years. By the early 1980s, Diamondhead was in bankruptcy, and Pinehurst was saved from a possibly darker fate by Dallas developer Robert Dedman Jr. and his ClubCorp group of upscale resort properties. In a nutshell, Dedman, a student of the game and fanatical golfer, updated the aging resort's inns and hotels, built a new championship layout, and restored Pinehurst No. 2 to its traditional glory. He also lured the USGA back to the Sandhills for the U.S. Women's Amateur Championship in 1989, which in turn led to a pair of Tour championships in 1991 and 1992, followed by the

U.S. Senior Open in 1994. Five years later, Pinehurst came full circle when it hosted its first U.S. Open. Following in his dad's footsteps, after the senior Dedman died in 2002, son Bob took over Pinehurst and vowed to keep it the shrine to the game it had always been.

"Now you'll have something to *really* talk about when you speak to the English Speaking Union," Myrtis Morrison declared after our illuminating trek to secure a tux. "And you'll look handsome doing it." Whereupon she glanced at my feet. I hadn't worn socks since I'd arrived back in the Sandhills. Few sons of Carolina ever do.

"Wear dark socks," she added with a no-nonsense maternal tone. "Harvie Ward might like that look, but I'm not sure the Union would be happy."

"Yes, ma'am," I said. "Thanks, Mom."

DAME PAT ROBINSON was delighted to hear of Myrtis's stories when I drove up a few weeks later in the winter to see Jack off on an exchange program to Ecuador and bring her the first finished copy of *Beautiful Madness,* the account of my year of living horticulturally. By coincidence the book appeared in bookshops the day before Pat's eighty-eighth birthday. Naturally, I dedicated the book to the crusty old literary dame who didn't believe in such things.

"This is the nicest birthday gift I could have," Pat declared as we sat in the parlor of the sunny Stephens House in Maine. Indeed, I discovered, Pat had moved into the same cheerful upstairs bedroom my mom and I had looked at shortly before my mom passed away.

I patted the dame's pale hand and told her she meant more

to me than she could know. Following my mom's death in 1999, Pat had not only ably filled in as my surrogate mom—dispensing valuable wisdom and advice on any number of questions ranging from the state of modern letters to the baffling behavior of my teenagers—but she had also midwifed seven of my books into print, serving as first reader and critical advisor to all of them.

"I have something for you." She opened a bag and withdrew a yellowing document of some kind. It turned out to be her copy of the program from the 1953 Ryder Cup at Wentworth, in England, an event she helped organize as a U.S. Navy officer's wife.

"I want you to have this. It's from the year you were born."

"I couldn't possibly keep this," I said, deeply touched by her gift.

"Of course you can." Pat dismissed my halfhearted protest. "It's not what we keep in life that matters, dear boy. It's what we pass along. You know that by now. So you take this with you—and you can give it to Jack someday. How *is* our young world explorer?"

"He's fine, last I heard from him, somewhere in the jungles of Ecuador." I was carefully turning the pages of the program, which the captains and players from both teams had signed. Most players today, I thought, with their private jets and investment counselors waiting, would never take the time.

I explained that Jack's mom and I had finally heard from the boy we'd nervously sent off to the high Andes. He'd been out of touch for several days, exploring ruins and swimming in a river that was said to be the headwaters of the Amazon and probably full of man-eating fish.

"Bravo for Jack," Pat declared. "He'll be fine. Better than fine!

This is just the start of his big adventures. That's the Ryder Cup, by the way, where our friend Ben Hogan decided not to show up. The press, I must tell you, was not pleased about Ben's decision. They considered it a snub. But you know that wasn't true. Personally, I forgave Ben for not showing up."

Dame Pat spoke of Ben Hogan as if they'd been chums. Perhaps, in a way, they had been. She'd once had a private golf lesson from Hogan during the war. She was clearly Ben Hogan's kind of gal, beautiful and no-nonsense.

Later, in her cheerful room overlooking a massive, spreading birch tree, Pat made me a cup of herbal tea before I hit the road to Boston to start my book tour for *Beautiful Madness*. With scholarly seriousness, Pat asked me how being the Louis D. Rubin Jr. Writer-in-Residence at Hollins University was working out. I'd started that job on my birthday a few weeks after the holiday break.

I told her I enjoyed it more than most things I'd done. I loved my students and felt honored to be teaching at such a marvelous school. Granted, in order to do it I was piling more miles on my new Subaru Outback than a trucker working double shifts, but I'd never had such satisfaction in my working life—along with writing my Sunday essay for *The Pilot*. Teaching was a rich icing on that cake.

"You've found what you were meant to do," she said emphatically. "I think you're finally ready for what's coming next."

"So what is coming next, Madam Oracle?" I asked with amusement.

"I think it's time for you to go home," she said simply, "or maybe I should say to take the fairway *home*."

I smiled, wondering exactly what she meant. "Where is anyone's home?" I asked, not expecting an answer.

"You tell me." She was looking at me with her tired, soulful eyes.

"I've loved my life in Maine," I said a bit defensively.

"And well you should. Maine is a garden spot of the world — even if you can't see the garden for half the year. For Ray and me this was home. I'm not so sure about *you*."

"I've come to love being down in the Sandhills," I admitted. Outside Pat's window the bare limbs of the birch were radiant against a purple winter dusk.

"You have performed your obligations here. I was hoping you might reach that conclusion."

I sipped my herbal tea. Part of me hated to think she was right. A larger part knew she was.

"I feel guilty about that," I admitted. "I thought my children would someday put my bones in the the rocky soil of Maine, in my garden or the golf course I helped design. I never saw this coming."

She gave me a faint smile. "We seldom do. I think it was that remarkable Mary Oliver who said we need only three things to live in this world — to love what is mortal, to hold it against your bones knowing your life depends on it, and when the time comes to let it go. To let it *go*."

"You think so?"

"Absolutely certain, dear boy. It's time to let go." Her smile increased. "Besides, maybe Maggie and Jack can spread some of your ashes on the golf course and your garden down there when it's your turn."

Some weeks later, a few days after I finished my book tour, Tom Dugan phoned me from his winter home in Florida. I was delighted to hear from Tom because it meant he was soon coming to the Sandhills for a spring visit. Thomas "Bunny" Dugan — no direct relation to my favorite pub in Pinehurst — was my oldest golf pal from the north. Not long after I moved to Maine in 1985, Tom became my regular partner and closest friend at Brunswick Golf Club. After my father's death in 1995, Tom and I played for the next decade in a regular foursome that included the legendary athletic director of Bowdoin College, Sid Watson, and the school's hockey coach, Terry Meagher.

But after Sid died of a heart attack the winter I turned fifty, the three of us got together only a handful of times, and the year after that we didn't play at all. Tom dropped out of the club, and I rarely showed up. It was never the same: something essential was missing.

On New Year's Eve, following the comic ending to our silly Ross Cross-Country Championship, I had phoned Tom in Florida to wish him and his wife a happy New Year and invite them to stop off in the Sandhills on their way north in the spring. I'd filled him in on my work for *The Pilot* and how a cast of local characters and Idle Knights had resuscitated my game. Tom said he would love to come visit if only to officially approve my new pals. I assured him he would fit right in. If ever a man was worthy of Idle Knight status, it was Bunny Dugan.

"Hey," he said, after we caught up on other topics, including Wendy's first-ever sub-ninety round of golf at Mid Pines, "how's Jack doing? Did he play hockey this year?"

Schoolboy hockey was close to Tom's heart, and I told him Jack had indeed played hockey, though he'd had to cut the season short in order to go poke around the rain forests of Ecuador.

"He's a born traveler like you," Tom said. "So how's his golf coming along?"

"Bit of a mystery," I replied. "Whenever he's here in the Sand-hills, he plays very well. But back in Maine he can't seem to find his game. Between you and me, it's driving us both a little crazy."

Tom chuckled. "He just needs time and seasoning. Maybe you and he should enter a tournament or two. That would toughen him up."

"Actually, I signed us up for the National Father and Son Championship in Myrtle Beach," I explained. "He's looking forward to the golf. I'm looking forward to the topless pancake houses."

"They have topless pancake houses in Myrtle Beach?" Tom seemed amazed.

"They have everything in the Vegas of the East." Half the golfers we knew from New England took their annual spring pilgrimages to Myrtle Beach to escape their wives and wake up their hibernating games. "So when are you coming to Pine-hurst?" I demanded. "I can't wait to show you the old Elks Club course three blocks from our cabin."

There was a pause at his end. "Right," Tom said. "About that."

He cleared his throat. "The other day, I came home after golf and felt a sharp pain in my right shoulder. I thought it was the usual aches, no big deal. Jane made me go to the doctor a few days later." He chuckled. "I am, after all, pushing eighty-three."

"So what happened?" I tried to sound unconcerned.

"They found a large tumor growing under the shoulder blade. I guess it's spread to other places. They want to do some more tests. Some kind of treatment."

"When?"

"Starting tomorrow."

We talked for a few minutes longer. Tom apologized for being unable to come to Pinehurst and meet the Idle Knights. I told him not to worry, but to do his treatment and we'd reschedule for another time when this problem was behind him. Like Pat Robinson's ailing heart, I took Tom's cancer personally.

"Sounds good," he said quietly. "I'd love nothing better. I have one favor to ask—you being our group's resident writer and all."

"Name it," I said.

"I'd like you to write my obituary for the paper and maybe say a few kind words about my golf swing when it comes . . . time. Jane is taking this very hard," he admitted. "Knowing you'd do that would make it a little easier for her."

"I'd be honored," I managed to say.

We talked for another half hour, changing the subject, for a few moments ignoring the gravity of what we shared, reminiscing about some of the unforgettable times we'd had playing golf over the years in Maine.

"Please give Nibs my best," Tom said finally, as we wound things up. "I predict he'll be a great player—and an even better man." I'd never heard anyone but Tom use my own nickname for Jack. Tom had three grown sons of his own.

"I will certainly do that." I stuggled to control my emotions. Unable to stop myself, however, I sighed and said: "This is so *damned* unfair, you know?"

Tom was calm. "I know. If I was your age, Jim, I'd be mad as hell about it. But I'm not. I'm eighty-three, and I've had one hell of a great life, not to mention the best golf partners a guy could ever have."

For a moment I didn't know what to say. My eyes were filled with tears. "Thank you," I said, rubbing them. "I feel the same way about you."

TOM DUGAN DIED three weeks later. Jane phoned me only hours after I finished writing his obituary in my office at Hollins for newspapers in Boston and Saint Louis, where Tom's children lived, and prepared my remarks for his memorial service, which Jane scheduled for a weekend in late June. She wanted a summer date so most of their friends and fellow snowbirds would have returned to Maine.

That next Sunday morning, I was tying on my bow tie for a walk to the Presbyterian church when the phone rang. It was John Dempsey wanting to know if I might be interested in skipping church to meet him and the Stewarts at Pine Needles for a late-morning round. He proposed that Tom and I play himself and young Bryan, whose game was growing sharper every week. Bryan had just fired his first round of even par to beat his old man for the first time ever, a true red-letter day. Tom was still buzzing from this momentous turning in the road.

"You know," I told President Dempsey, already loosening my bow tie, "I'd love nothing better. Tell you what, Tom and I will give you and Bryan a stroke per side."

"God loves a cheerful giver," Dempsey laughed. "We'll take two strokes and see you boys on the first tee in half an hour."

Several hours later, I came back into the cabin as the phone was ringing. Golf with Dempsey and the Stewarts had been the lift I needed. Pine Needles was in the early preparation stages for hosting the 2007 U.S. Women's Open—a second opportunity, as I viewed it, for Jack to work at a National Open and maybe take away some nice memories.

I'd planned to spend a quiet evening reviewing my lecture notes and to catch an early start up the road to Roanoke in the morning. It was final-exam week at Hollins. My tenure as the Rubin Writer-in-Residence was drawing to a close, and I was already missing the place and my students.

"Sweetie," said Wendy gently, "I have some sad news. Pat Robinson died on Friday morning."

I sat down in my reading chair, stunned and—once again— bereft of speech.

Wendy said she'd waited until Sunday afternoon to tell me because she knew I would have immediately jumped in the car and raced up the road to Maine. But she knew I had final exams to deliver on Monday and Tuesday, recommendations to write for students applying for jobs or graduate school, and a report to file with the school's trustees before a farewell dinner that Friday evening.

"Pat wouldn't have stood for your missing any of those things," she accurately pointed out.

Jane Robinson, I learned, had phoned Wendy on Friday to let her know Pat had passed away. Jane had asked if Wendy would mind sitting with Dame Pat's body while the final arrangements were made. In the Tibetan Buddhist tradition that both Jane and Pat observed, the living must sit with the departed for several days so the soul can say a proper goodbye and move along to the afterlife.

"I knew you would want to sit with her," Wendy said. "So I went and sat for both of us. She looked very peaceful. I told her how much we loved her."

A while later, I walked down to Max and Myrtis's house in the twilight for supper. Max made my usual double bourbon with crushed ice, and I sat and told them stories about Tom Dugan and Pat Robinson — how Tom had survived twenty-six bombing missions over Germany and come home to star on the first Olympic hockey team; how Pat had been given jonquils by Virginia Woolf, a golf lesson by Ben Hogan, and had kept up a lively correspondence for decades with the reclusive William Saroyan.

"They sound like such lovely people," Myrtis said. "You were fortunate to have them in your life when you did. I don't think these things are accidental."

"Neither did Pat. She and Tom loved the stories I told them about you and Grumpy."

Myrtis wiped her eyes, and Max showed me his scorecard from a round with his regular group at Foxfire that afternoon. He'd shot an impressive eighty-five — a round that included his first hole in one.

"You're on a roll," I told him. "Not bad for a beginner."

After supper they walked me to the door. The evening train was rumbling through the heart of Southern Pines. I'd come to find that sound pleasing, oddly comforting. It was headed north, the same as me.

WHILE ON MY WAY to speak at Bunny Dugan's memorial service and bring Jack south for a few weeks of intense golf therapy, I stopped off in Latrobe to see Arnold Palmer's new house.

The visit was long overdue. I hadn't been back to Latrobe since Winnie Palmer's funeral in 1999. Owing to the cherished memories I'd accumulated from being there at a significant period in their lives—Winnie had been diagnosed with cancer, and Arnold decided to stick close to home during the three years I helped him write his memoirs—the desire to return hadn't been terribly keen.

But Arnold was making a new start in life, and he invited me to come see the new house he'd built for his bride, Kit, and to have dinner at the club where he grew up. He suggested that we watch the Saturday round of the 106th U.S. Open together.

The new house, sitting directly across the cul-de-sac from Arnold and Winnie's cozy ranch house, was stunning—a large, open sporting lodge made from pink and gray Pennsylvania fieldstone. On the afternoon I rolled into town, Arnold and his longtime assistant, Doc Giffin, were already having cocktails and watching Phil Mickelson charge to the lead over Winged Foot's fabled West Course.

Afterward Arnold and I went alone to supper at the Latrobe Country Club.

"So how is Pinehurst working out, Shakespeare," he asked as we waited for our steaks and sipped our Ketel Ones. We'd grown close during the three years I'd worked with him on his autobiography. My book about my dad and his father had brought Arnold and me together. *Final Rounds* had been Winnie's favorite book—the primary reason Arnold invited me to help him write his long-awaited memoirs. His relationship with his dad,

Deacon Palmer, was the key to understanding Arnold Palmer, Winnie pointed out.

"It's worked out better than I could have hoped for," I said, and confided how Wendy and I were discussing the possibility of pulling up stakes and moving to the Sandhills. The only thing holding us back was the question of timing—when and how to break the news to my kids. I had no idea if they would accept the notion of my returning permanently to my roots. But I feared it wouldn't be easy.

"They'll be fine with it if they know you're doing it for the right reasons," Arnold insisted. "Kids adapt. That's why I never gave up Latrobe. This is where I feel most at home. That's important when you get up in years." He sipped his drink and smiled wryly. "And even *you* are finally getting up there, Shakespeare."

The conversation shifted to his old friend and nemesis, Harvie Ward. I asked him if there was any truth to a story I'd heard that Harvie started two under par in one of their fabled college matches but found himself three down after just four holes because Arnold made two birdies, an eagle, and an ace.

Arnold chuckled. "It's true. It was a Southern Conference match during my sophomore year, I think. That was about the only time I ever managed to beat ole Harv in those days. He was unbelievable. Luckily I beat him to Winnie, though."

"Harvie was one of a kind," I agreed, explaining how Ward and Tom Stewart had joined forces to convince me it was time to move back to North Carolina. I told him how, the last time I'd seen Harvie, he'd given me a putter to give to Jack. I told Arnold about the Pinehurst cure, Harvie's name for whatever mystical quality made the Sandhills such a healing place.

"That sounds like Harvie. I think what he means is that everyone who goes there becomes a son or daughter of the game. It makes us all feel as if we belong to something larger than what we achieve on any scorecard. It's not about making money or even winning tournaments. It's really about playing the game for fun."

"You sound like Dick Tufts."

"Dick was a great fellow. *He* sure loved the game. We could use a few more like him these days. Harvie, too"

Over coffee and a nightcap, Arnold dropped a couple bombshells on me. The first news was that he was changing his Bay Hill tournament's name to the Arnold Palmer Invitational, bucking the trend toward naming events for their primary commercial sponsors. I was pleased to hear this.

His other decision — reached a few hours before, it turned out — was to withdraw from the Senior Open field in Kansas and announce that his days of playing golf in public were over. I pointed out how sad this news would make golfers everywhere feel, beginning with me. With Nicklaus having played his final round at St. Andrews, it was now the official end of professional golf's golden age.

On a brighter note, I asked if he still intended to go to the Ryder Cup in Ireland that fall. The event was being played on a golf course he'd designed at the K Club. Arnold smiled and nodded his head. "Of course I'm going. But I'm afraid the Americans are going to get their caps handed to them by the Europeans."

"Why is that?" But I already knew what the King was going to say. We'd had this conversation half a dozen times over the years that we'd been collaborators and friends.

Arnold shook his large gray head. "They've forgotten where they came from. They don't play for the pleasure of the game anymore. Some do but most don't. Money's important, but so is tradition. That's obvious when you see how we've fared in Ryder Cups lately. That used to be the most fun thing in golf. The players and their wives all socialized and had a great time. Now it's strictly business—at least on our side." He looked at me and smiled. "Maybe they should go back to Pinehurst and get the cure, too."

I tried another tack, hoping to find a happier middle ground, asking about his grandson, Sam Saunders, who would be playing golf on scholarship at Clemson in the fall. I told him about my Jack, who Arnold had last seen when he was knee-high to a ball washer. The King was pleased when I told him Jack had completed his JV campaign with no losses and hoped to make the varsity golf team at summer's end.

"He's grown and improved so much," I said, "I'm going to have to get him new clubs. What would you recommend?"

"Give Corey his specs, and I'll have a set of Tour irons sent to him," Arnold said.

"Oh, no," I protested. "I couldn't do that."

The King of Golf gave me what I'd come to regard as "the Look," a stare that said he didn't wish to be trifled with.

"They're not for *you*," he genially barked. "They're for Jack. He'll grow into them."

Several hours later, I let myself out of Arnold and Winnie's old house, where, as usual, I slept in the familiar guest bedroom under a wall of family pictures, and drove past the golf course where Arnold Palmer grew up, passing the big red barn where I saw Winnie alive for the final time. As I drove past the lighted barn and headed for a darkened country road over the hills to the Pennsylvania Turnpike, I wondered if Arnold had placed his big blacksmith's finger on why Pinehurst and Southern Pines had such a magical effect on people who came there seeking relief or a new start.

It wasn't just the unique pine-scented air or the lovely stillness that envelopes a player on a golf course anywhere in the Sandhills. It was indeed the fact that anyone who loved the game felt at home there, part of something larger than a score on a card. There was no other reason for Pinehurst to exist except for golf. As my father had once described the place, it was where one went to learn the "higher" game—or maybe simply to fall in love with the game all over again.

Over dessert a few hours earlier, I had told my childhood hero about buying the ugliest green pants imaginable a few days before the Open at Pinehurst, an impulse inspired by him, explaining how they were nearly identical to the bright green pants he was wearing when I watched him blow the Greater Greensboro Open.

"I think I should send them to you in exchange for Jack's golf clubs," I proposed. "They'd probably go over big in Ireland."

Palmer laughed hard, then gave me his famously stern look. "You can *keep* those pants. I threw mine out right after that tournament."

CHAPTER TEN

The Vegas of the East

U ncertain how the news would be received, I waited
for the right time to tell Jack about my big decision to
move home to North Carolina.

The evening that followed the first day of competition at the
National Father and Son Team Classic turned out to be the
moment, the summit of mighty Mount Atlanticus the place. In
ancient days, after all, tribal elders often took their sons to the
summit of the tallest mountain around, believing the height
and isolation assured a closeness to the gods that invested them
with a greater capacity for conveying wisdom and insight. In our
case, alas, the only mountain available to us along the coastal
plain of South Carolina's famed Grand Strand was a tacky wonder of the modern world, a miniature golf complex rising like
a plastic Vesuvius two hundred feet over the sprawling neon
excess of the greater Myrtle Beach carnival midway and the glittering commercial sprawl of the Vegas of the East, as some call
the booming golf and entertainment capital.

We'd had a promising opening day at the Father and Son

Classic, playing a beautiful but unforgiving Tournament Players
Club course with a salty, oddly endearing father and son-in-law
duo from suburban Boston, Burt and Bill, who kept us loose
and relaxed with their off-color jokes and constant needling of
each other. More importantly, their encouragement of Jack had
a buoyant effect on his mood and game. Showing poise and the
best focus I'd seen him display—even the beginnings of an
actual preshot routine I'd been suggesting for years—Jack fired
an impressive seventy-nine that could have been seventy-six if
a putt here or there had dropped. I, meanwhile, cobbled out a
workmanlike seventy-eight. By the end of the first day's competition, we found ourselves in a tie for third place in the Davis
Love flight, definitely in contention to win our flight.

Jack was glowing as we left the grounds of the TPC and
headed for an early supper on Ocean Boulevard. After chicken
wings at Hooters—a first for us both—we went to blow our
two-hundred-dollar tournament gift card at the sponsoring golf
superstore. Jack bought several golf shirts, a Titleist cap, and
two dozen Pro-V1 balls. I splurged on a new three ball putter,
adding it to my vast collection of costly flat sticks that had lost
their putter magic years ago.

After that, as darkness settled over the Vegas of the East, in
search of clean fun and honest amusement before returning to
our beachside motel, we grabbed ice cream sundaes and passed
a succession of tacky miniature golf complexes and wound up
choosing the most dramatic of the lot—a mythological mountain rising above the gaudy vacation boomtown that many for a
time feared Pinehurst might become after the founding family
lost control of the resort. For a variety of reasons, owing mostly
to the absence of a nearby ocean, that fate never befell Pinehurst.

The lighted miles of strip bars and all-night pancake houses, the ranks of cheesy theme motels and wacky golf complexes had migrated to a living ocean rather than the dried-up seabed of a long-departed one.

As we played our way to the top of Mount Atlanticus, where we paused to take in a fine evening breeze and watch the lights of the Grand Strand blink on, I recalled how playing golf until dark with my dad was one of the sustaining pleasures of my life. For the moment at least, my new putter appeared to have magic, though they all do just off the showroom floor. It's when I take them into the heat of competition that they let me down, and wind up joining the harem or swimming for their lives.

"Jack," I said as we leaned side by side on a railing, permitting two young dudes and their cute dates to play through, "I need to tell you something important. I'd like your honest opinion."

"Sure, Pappy." He was, for good reason, in an upbeat frame of mind, discreetly eyeing one of the girls—a petite blond with a cute bow mouth and green eyes. She kept glancing at Jack. "What's up?"

"What would you say if I told you I want to move back to North Carolina?"

He gave an easy shrug. "That's cool. When?"

"I don't know. Not right away. Maybe not till you're out the door to college. It'll take time and planning. We'll play it by ear."

Perplexed by his equanimity, I explained that no details had been worked out, that this was something that had gradually come to me during my year at *The Pilot*. I told Jack that being here had helped me avert a midlife career crisis and shown me the path of life that was opening up.

I also told him what Tom Stewart and the other Idle Knights had come to mean to me, and how my desire to play the game had been rekindled. Finally, on the heels of losing both Pat Robinson and Tom Dugan, I said that Myrtis and Grumpy Morrison had grown to be like the parents I greatly missed and that Jean Morrison had even taken to referring to me as her "brother from another mother."

"They're very nice people," Jack agreed. "Mrs. Morrison kind of reminds me of Gammy. You do seem happier down here, Dad. Even Mom can tell that." He was silent for a moment, still watching the girl. "Will you, like, ever write golf again?" His tone said he couldn't believe I'd walk away from a career that had carried me around the world.

"Probably not the Tour." I pointed out that I'd begun my journalism career in North Carolina as a general-interest reporter, and that's how I expected to wind it up somewhere down the road.

Jack glanced at the scattered lights from the summit of Mount Atlanticus.

"What about our house. Would we, like, keep it or sell it?"

"That's the big question."

I knew the house, for good reason, was likely to be a contentious point for Jack, and maybe even a larger one for his sister. I wasn't sure yet how I felt about parting with it.

"Have you told Maggie?" Jack seemed to be reading my thoughts.

"Wanted to float the idea by you first, Old Champ. The house is one of those details we'll have to figure out. Part of me can't bear the thought of selling it—too much of our history is there. Another part of me, though, says it's just a house. Some days I think we should find a way to keep it. Other days I think we should sell it and move on. Any bright ideas?"

A faint nod as if he understood. Followed by a brief shake of the head as if he had no suggestion. "Not really."

"We'll figure it out. In the meantime, I'll continue to go back and forth so I don't miss any of your school activities. How does that sound?"

"Don't you get tired of driving so far?"

"Sometimes. But it's better than having to strip down just to fly on an airplane. I feel the same way about commercial flying as I do professional golf—it ain't nearly as exciting as it used to be. Besides, I use the time to catch up on my sleep and make notes for my *Pilot* pieces."

He nodded, missing my attempt at humor. The joke had fallen flat with Grumpy Morrison, too. Maybe it was time to take it out of service.

"Could I drive it, too, sometime—from Maine to North Carolina?"

"Nothing would please me more, Junior. That way Pappy could actually sleep."

Jack had his driver's permit and could legally operate a vehicle with his mom or me riding shotgun. In a handful of days, however, he would be sixteen and eligible to apply for a full license. The freedom of the open road beckoned. After Maggie moved on to college, I'd promised him that my aging Volvo would be his. His sister appeared to be headed to the University of Vermont. I hoped that, when it was time, Jack might choose to come south for his higher education—so Pappy and Junior could convene for a little golf therapy the way my dad and I had during my college days. Those were some of my most cherished memories.

Jack studied the slowly turning Ferris wheel across the lighted midway. Teenage shrieks and hurdy-gurdy music floated on the moist, salty breeze from the direction of the midway and the beach. You could hear the whispering thunder of the surf.

"Dad," he said quietly after a moment or two, "what if I told you I want to go to school down here—in Pinehurst, I mean?"

I glanced at his handsome profile again. So *this* explained why he hadn't shown much surprise or resistance to my big announcement. The little rascal, who was now nearly as tall as I, was thinking along the same lines.

"You mean finish high school in Southern Pines?"

"Yes, sir. At Pinecrest High."

He looked directly at me, the evening air ruffling his light brown hair. "Bryan and I were talking about it. He's probably going to play on the Pinecrest golf team next spring. If I lived here I'm sure I could make the team, too. College coaches are already looking at Patrick Barrett and some of the other guys on the team. I'll bet I could get good enough for them to be interested in me, too. You know?"

I glanced out at the Ferris wheel, pondering this unexpected twist. His big announcement had trumped mine. So much for the wise elder on the ancient mountaintop. The bug evidently had bitten hard. It was almost like *Pappy* had been set up by those ancient mirthful gods.

"I bet you could, too, Jack. But are you willing to make the sacrifice it would take to get that kind of notice?"

"You *know* I am," he said with the first real show of emotion. I got the impression he was shocked that I wasn't jumping up and down with joy.

I knew that my son was a terrific young man with a good

heart, strong values, decent morals, and a world of interests and natural abilities, any of which qualities could take him wherever he wished to go in *his* life—not mine. However, golf had merely been one of a half dozen primary passions that attracted, and sometimes distracted, his critical attention. My Jack, like both his grandfathers before him, was a true jack-of-all-trades, a Renaissance kid who could slide by with minimal effort.

That had both good and bad implications. Things came relatively easily to him. But what he was talking about would require a major reconfiguring of his priorities as well as the unstinting support of everyone around him, including—and maybe most of all—his mom. That would be no small selling job.

"In that case," I said, leaning on my elbows and lacing my fingers, "let me put it another way. I don't know if everyone else would be willing to make the sacrifice it would take to make it work."

"Like who?"

"What about your buddies back in Maine? I How could you leave them?"

Jack shrugged again. "Austin's going to private school in New Hampshire this year, and Andy's deep into tennis these days. Drew's talking about going to college down here, maybe to Elon. I might apply there, too. Even if I don't get a scholarship anywhere, you said yourself that I could probably walk onto the school team somewhere."

"I did," I said, remembering the conversation. This was the first I'd heard about Elon University, though. I had recently lectured there in some journalism classes, and been blown away by what I'd seen. Elon was anything but the sleepy college of "Fighting Christians" it had been when I was growing up twenty miles from its front gate. The school was now a university, scaling the rankings of the best private institutions in the nation. Even if Jack failed to walk onto the golf team, he could do far worse than attending Elon.

"What about your mom? Have you mentioned this to her?"

Something in him softened. "Not yet. I thought maybe you could talk to her."

I nodded and glanced out at the glittering lights, picturing how the news that Jack wanted to go south would go over. A heat wave in a winter ski resort might be greeted with more enthusiasm. Truthfully, I wasn't crazy about the prospect of his finishing high school in Pinehurst. Maine was his home the way North Carolina was mine. He had a wonderful history there.

"It's an intriguing idea," I said, mustering as much encouragement as possible given such short notice. "But your mom would have to be onboard with this idea for it to work. Between you and me, I'm not sure she's ready to let you go. We *have* to keep her feelings in mind. So don't get your hopes up too high."

Jack nodded, still watching the two couples. I could tell my guarded response wasn't the one he'd hoped for. The cute blond had thumped her hot pink ball so hard it missed the target—the open mouth of a mythic sea monster—and flew past the railing into the Myrtle Beach night. The others were laughing and she was blushing and saying, "Cut it out, y'all. That's not *funny.*"

"There is an orientation meeting at Pinecrest High next week," Jack related matter-of-factly. "I want to attend that. They have great AP courses and an International Baccalaureate program that really interests me."

"Fair enough." I said. "No harm in getting the facts."

We followed the couples through the gaping mouth of the beast. I stroked my ball and watched it bounce off the creature's lip and fall into a murky pool, costing me a two-shot penalty and the lead.

Jack concentrated on his putt. I could almost see the wheels in his brain turning with newly found confidence. He smoothly stroked his Titleist, and it rolled up the tongue of the beast and dropped to a lower tier where it went into the hole for an ace.

"Nice shot," I said. "You've got ole Harv's White Hot putter working well this week. Save some of that for tomorrow, though."

"I will."

Our putting match on mighty Mount Atlanticus ended in a draw. So we played a second eighteen holes. This time Junior beat Pappy, 4-and-3.

THE NEXT DAY, at Wild Wing's Avocet Course, during the alternate-shot format aptly called a Modified Pinehurst Scotch, Team Dodson came apart like a cheap beach chair in a riptide. Both of us struggled all day to find fairways and greens, growing more and more frustrated as the heat rose and the day wound along. In the end, we scraped out a dismal best-ball eighty-three that dropped us twenty positions on the Davis Love flight leader board.

That evening, after dinner and a movie at a lively commercial district called Broadway on the Beach, we got ice cream sundaes for a second time and made a farewell cruise through the tacky Grand Strand, listening to the music of Jackson Browne and Guster. Jack was noticeably downcast. Long silences filled the car as we turned and headed back in the direction of our seaside motel. I asked him if he'd had a good time at the Father and Son Classic.

"Yeah," he rallied. "It's been great. But I guess we're pretty well out of it now."

"On the contrary," I said, invoking the wisdom of my fellow Idle Knight, Tom Stewart. "Golf and life are both games subject to change without notice. With luck and good focus, why, we could play ourselves right back into the hunt tomorrow."

"You think so? We were awful today," he accurately pointed out. "That doesn't make sense. We've both been playing so well. Your game has been great."

I smiled and shrugged. "Some days everything goes in the hole, Jack. Some days nothing does. Golf is the hardest game on earth to play consistently well—which is why so few people do it. For what it's worth, I also think match play is easier than medal play—at least for me."

"Yeah," he agreed lifelessly.

I remembered some lines from a poem by Edgar Guest. Guest was a regular patron of Pinehurst and one of Opti the Mystic's favorite poets. The poem had been given to me by Dr. Leon Buck, a hall-of-fame golfer from Bath, Maine, who'd won scores of Pine State amateur championships and had even played in the North and South with Harvie Ward.

"Golf is like the game of living," I said. "It will show up what you are. / If you take your troubles badly, you will never play to par. / You may be a fine performer when your skies are bright and blue / But disaster is the acid that shall prove the worth of you. / So just meet your disappointments with a cheery sort of grin, / For the man who keeps his temper is the man that's sure to win."

Jack glanced over and allowed a tolerant smile. At least he hadn't rolled his eyes the way many teenagers would have.

"Cornball, I know, but your granddad worshipped Edgar Guest—the patron saint of American admen. Still, it's true what Guest says. Keep your faith and your temper, and just try to have fun. You might be surprised how well we'll do tomorrow."

With that, I gave him a playing tip that a tournament-savvy friend from Seminole had recently given me for competing in big events. "Whenever he's trying to shoot a good medal score against the field, he plays a mental match against his partners on every hole. He says that if you do this, your focus remains right where it ought to be and you don't get ahead of yourself worrying about the outcome."

"Does it work?"

"He currently holds both the Seminole and Pine Valley club championship titles. I don't know anyone else who's done that."

"Are you talking about Mr. Miller?"

"That's right." A few days before heading to Myrtle Beach for the Father and Son Classic, Jack and I had tuned up with a round at Mid Pines with Kelly Miller and his son Blair, who attended Ole Miss on a golf scholarship. This was Jack's first exposure to Mid Pines, and I was pleased that he'd played well, shooting eighty-one. Even better, he seemed to get a kick out of playing with Blair.

"Let's go have fun tomorrow," I said. "There's no pressure on us. Here's an idea—why don't we play a silent match against each other? Who knows, you might actually beat the old man."

"Sounds good." I heard a tiny note of optimism in his voice. But then Jack glanced out the window at the lights and fell silent again. A few moments later, he asked: "So, Dad. Do you still *like* Maine?"

It was an absurd question, but I knew why he was asking it. The conversation on top of Mount Atlanticus was weighing on his mind. He needed to be sure how I felt about where he came from.

"No, Nibs," I allowed quietly. "I love Maine."

I reminded my son that I'd lived in Maine nearly half of my life—the place over the horizon where I'd gone and found my destiny. The Pine State was where I'd put down roots and made my family; where I'd designed and built the only house I'd probably ever build with my own hands. It was also where I'd had the only regular golf group I'd ever known and the only place I had helped design a golf course—the golf course that was now home to the varsity golf squad he was determined to make in a few weeks, assuming he decided to finish high school in Maine.

"You really think I should do that, don't you?" Disappointment was apparent in his voice.

"Short answer—yes, I do. For your mom if not for you. But for you, too, Old Champ. That's where *your* history lies, the place you'll always look back on with unqualified affection, even if you someday leave it."

What he didn't know was that I'd slipped out of our motel room while he was showering that morning and phoned his mom to give her a heads-up about this unexpected development down south. Unfortunately, the conversation hadn't gone as well as I'd hoped it might. She'd jumped to the conclusion that I'd cooked up a plot to take her only son away from Maine. Fair or not, I could understand how she'd reached that conclusion.

"I really think it would be impossible for your mom not to see you for weeks at a time," I explained. "There's also your sister to think about. If I was forced to stay here all the time, I wouldn't be able to see Maggie during her final year of high school. She wouldn't be happy about that. It wouldn't be fair to her, buddy."

He nodded, but then became agitated.

"But *why?*" he said, angrily. "Maggie doesn't care where we are! Besides, if mom cared about my feelings, she would want me to go to school where *I* want to go."

"You don't know anything about the school down here," I responded, sharper than I'd intended to. "This is your junior year coming up—the most important year of high school. Let's face it, son. You need to make up ground for last year's adventures with Miss Shoe."

Ah, *Miss Shoe.* For a moment at least, this silenced him.

Entering into his sophomore year, Jack had achieved an outstanding grade-point average. But after getting it into his head that his young and inexperienced AP English teacher, owing to her strong political opinions and unconventional views about life in general and writing in particular, was unsuited for the task of inspiring young people to write—a judgment that turned out to be accurate—he made no effort to disguise his dislike of her teaching methods.

It was another case of the fruit falling close to the tree. When I had been a junior in high school, a short story I wrote won a citywide writing contest called the O. Henry Award and landed me in an advanced creative writing course where a young and inexperienced teacher named Miss Wiggins, fresh from graduate school and full of antiestablishment views, concluded my writing was "too conventional." She'd made it clear I didn't belong in a class where the favored scholars were writing elegiac poems to broken Coke bottles and first impressions of life on LSD.

After a succession of poor marks on stories I knew were decently written, I brazenly submitted my O. Henry Award short story and earned a D. When Miss Wiggins discovered what I'd done, she threatened to have me booted from her class, and I wound up receiving the only poor grade I ever earned in an English class.

My story had a touching O. Henry ending, however. A decade after this costly run-in, which may or may not have doomed my admission to the northern college I had my eye on at the time, while working in Atlanta as the senior writer for the oldest Sunday magazine in the nation, I received a phone call from none other than the former Miss Wiggins, now married and teaching at a private school in suburban Atlanta. "I'd love to buy you lunch sometime," she said a bit sheepishly, "and offer you an apology." A short time later we met at her new school and she did just that. She also invited me to speak to her advanced writing classes, and wryly introduced me to them as "the best student writer I ever had—though neither of us *knew* it at the time."

Jack's English teacher punished him with a D on several of his key writing submissions, including one that later wound up being the lead piece in the school's literary magazine. Their war of attrition continued to the end of the term, at which point Jack's mother and I finally stepped in to find out how a kid who'd always been at the top of his class and was clearly a promising young writer could suddenly detest writing and be one notch above failing. During our meeting, Miss Shoe informed us she was heading back to graduate school, feeling she wasn't a "good match for high school." Jack, it seemed, had paid the price for helping refine her career plans.

After such a disappointing day on the golf course, Miss Shoe was the last thing he wished to hear about.

"You don't understand," he said as we rolled back to our motel in Myrtle Beach. "I *want* to go to school in Pinehurst. It will help my grades *and* my golf."

I smiled at the neon-lit darkness ahead. We were passing a garish pancake house whose parking lot was full of cars. Packs of middle-aged guys in golf caps were heading inside.

"Stop laughing," he insisted. "I'm serious about this!"

"I am, too, son. I'm laughing at the pancake house, not you."

Jack glanced at the pancake house. I used the opportunity to take a deep breath. "Listen, buddy, a minute ago you asked me if I still liked Maine. I told you I love Maine. That's no lie, Jack. One reason I love Maine so much, in fact—maybe *the* reason I love it so much—is because you and Maggie are from there. In my opinion, you need to go home in two weeks, try out for the varsity golf team, and finish high school *there.* Maine is your home the way North Carolina is mine. If you don't do that, I think you'll look back and regret it someday."

An angry silence filled the car. Guster was singing about some girl named Ramona, a catchy little tune.

Jack said no more, staring out the passenger window. I took another deep breath, since the first one hadn't seemed to help much.

"Let's talk about this when we get back to Southern Pines and can discuss it with your mom in a more civilized manner. I promise we'll check out the Pinecrest orientation and give her a full and objective report. No harm in getting the facts, right?"

"Yep," he allowed tersely, still refusing to look at me.

FOR THE THIRD and final round of the Father and Son Classic, which called for a two-man Captain's Choice format, we got paired with a friendly father and son team from Virginia Beach who sprayed the ball all over the place on a tight and demanding Wachesaw Plantation East course. Jack violently hooked his opening drive, and I feared a long day looming ahead of us, until something rather nice happened.

After making a double bogey to open, Jack chipped in for birdie on the second hole. After that, he settled into a beautiful rhythm and struck his ball to the heart of almost every fairway, chipping and putting extremely well. On the final hole, facing a tough headwind and sharp dogleg to the right that brought a dangerous series of fairway bunkers and a black water canal into play, Jack crushed a mammoth drive over both the dogleg and canal to a narrow throat on the fairway, then wedged his ball to within three feet of the cup, and sank his final putt for his third birdie of the day, to finish with a round of seventy-eight, his best score ever.

Although I fared one stroke better, in our unofficial side match play, he beat me two-and-one. So, in a way, the son had finally beaten the old man at his own game. I wished my fellow knight Tom Stewart was handy to celebrate. At the very least, I'd have made Sri Tommy buy me a consoling beer or two.

Jack and I slapped hands, shook hands with our playing partners, then drove back to the Avocet Course to check our final standings in the tournament flight. The concluding steak dinner was already going on by the time we arrived. As we were searching for our names on the final leader board, Bill and Burt spotted us and strolled over.

"How'd you boys wind up?" demanded Burt. He was drinking a Miller Lite and listing to starboard.

"Fifth place." We had climbed back over twenty teams to end up more or less where we'd finished after day one. The flight's winning team had beaten us by only three strokes. In my book, that was a huge moral victory for the good guys.

"Good for you boys," Bill chortled, offering a vigorous high-five to Jack. Tubby white guys giving high-fives look silly except perhaps at a Myrtle Beach golf outing. Jack blushed but politely slapped hands with him.

"You've got a nice game, kid," Burt told him. "Keep it up." He winked at me. "Your old man will soon be history."

"With any luck," I chipped in.

As we drove back to the Sandhills, Tom Stewart phoned from Pebble Beach, where he'd taken Bryan to play for the first time. It was early afternoon in California. They'd just finished their morning round on that famous Monterey Peninsula landmark—the only course that can rival Pinehurst No. 2's standing as a public shrine to the American game.

"I just had some really bad news," Tom said. "My kid sister, Murphy, is in a hospital in Michigan. She's dying. We're leaving here today. Ilana's bringing Bryan back, and I'm going to be with Murphy."

I told him how sorry I was to learn this news. I knew how close Tom was to his three sisters. He asked how we'd done in the Father and Son Classic.

"We ended up in fifth place out of thirty teams in our flight.

Jack played extremely well. He carried us. We made a big come-back, and he came within a stroke of beating me."

"No *kidding?*" Tom sounded pleasantly surprised, though I could almost feel his sadness across a continent. "If I get back to Pinehurst before he leaves for Maine, why don't the four of us have our own father-son match on No. 2—so I'll have some-thing to lord over you all winter."

"Are you sure you'd be up for that?" I asked.

"I couldn't think of anything that would make me feel better. Murphy would want that."

CHAPTER ELEVEN

Playing Till Dark

The new Callaway Tour irons arrived two days before Jack's golf-team tryouts commenced in Maine. To be on the safe side, I suggested he use his familiar Taylor-Made irons to play his qualifying rounds, but he would have none of that.

He went out and shot several decent nine-hole scores and did indeed make the varsity squad, but once again his scores were nothing like the ones he'd posted down in Pinehurst and Myrtle Beach and Sea Island.

Maybe the apple really *didn't* fall far from the tree. The explanation might simply have been that he was more comfortable playing with his old man and buddies for fun than against a tournament opponent or Old Man Par, which, if true, was a trait he shared with *both* Bobby Jones and me. He also seemed to have my tendency to play better on tougher golf courses, which I'd long ago concluded had something to do with my wandering attention.

Whatever it was, I feared the problem was exacerbated by my reluctance to champion his cause to spend his final two years of high school in North Carolina. Not long after his mom and I decided Pinehurst was a nonstarter for high school, Jack and I had an argument that thoroughly rattled us both.

It began, as most parent-child disagreements seem to, over something entirely unrelated to the issue—my objections to the manner in which he came whipping so swiftly into the driveway in the Volvo he'd borrowed from his sister that he nearly struck our lumbering golden retriever. I'd been coming out of my barn office at that moment and witnessed his recklessness. I confronted him, reminding him how all it would take was a single moving violation for a rookie driver like himself to have his brand-new license yanked.

"What the *fuck* do you care?" he snapped at me, pausing on the steps of the house. "You're not even *here* anymore."

My hackles immediately flew up at the usage of the f-word—not to mention the stinging accusation. Jack had never used such language in addressing his mom or me. Struggling to keep my anger in check, I told him in that his attitude was completely unacceptable.

He laughed as if mocking me. He seemed to be in a hurry, impatiently jingling his keys, my former Volvo keys. "Oh, *please,* Dad. You talk that way all the time. Ask anybody."

Before I could respond to this, he added angrily. "Let's face it, Dad, everything has changed. You want to be down there and *hate* being up here. That much is pretty obvious."

"That's bullshit, Jack," I replied, finally losing my own cool.

"No it's not. You love being there. You hate being here. I heard you say so just yesterday."

I paused and took a deep breath, recalling how the day before, while we were driving into town together through a tangle of new construction projects that had transformed our once-quaint Yankee village into a suburban commercial district seemingly overnight, I'd remarked with regret that I "hated" what had happened to our beautiful town in just a handful of years. Suddenly commercial development was everywhere you turned, streets were under construction, and half a dozen of our closest neighbors had actually moved away. To me, it no longer felt like the place that had been my happy home for almost twenty-one years. "I hate to think what Topsham is going to look like a decade from now," I grumbled without pausing to think how Jack might perceive my complaint—a convenient rejection of his hometown.

"Listen, Jack. I understand your anger," I said, forcing myself to calm down and try to explain things better to him.

"The fuck you do," he shouted at me, jolting me by his second use of the word.

"If that's the way you feel," I snarled, "maybe you should go to your mom's house and think it over!"

"*Fine,*" he fired back, tossed his car keys to me, and began stalking off down the driveway. It was nearly dark. It was also five miles through the country to his mom's house.

I stomped into the house and discovered my wife standing quietly at the kitchen counter, holding a cup of tea she'd obviously just made but hadn't touched. She was giving me her version of Arnold Palmer's look of disapproval.

"You should be ashamed of yourself," Wendy said quietly.

"What?" I bellowed with exasperation. "He was the one who used the f-word, not me!"

"I'm not talking about the f-word. All teenagers talk that way these days. I'm talking about telling your son to go to his mom's house. This is Jack's house, his home. I've heard you say that so many times. But you effectively told your son that he's no longer welcome in his own home."

She paused, stirring her tea, looking down at the cup. Then she looked at me again. Her voice was calm but serious.

"If you're smart, you'll go after him and get this sorted out. You may have been saying one thing, but he obviously heard something else. He's still processing all of this change. Teenagers think they're the only ones whose lives change—not their parents'."

I grumbled around the kitchen, opening the refrigerator door and shutting it, yanking open a drawer and closing it, finally walking over and taking my own car keys off the peg. By the time I caught up with Jack, he was halfway down our darkened road to the main state road that leads into town. I rolled down the passenger window.

"Hey, Ace," I said calmly, "hop in. Let's talk."

"I don't want to talk," he said, refusing to look at me.

"Really, Jack. *Stop*. I'm sorry I told you to go to your mom's. I was frustrated at—well, it doesn't matter. I got the impression that's where you wanted to be. Could we please just talk this over?"

He walked on, unnervingly, for several more seconds before he drew up, still staring down the road.

"Let's go get coffee at the new Starbucks," I proposed.

"I thought you hated going into town."

"Not really. For the record, all the big changes make me miss the way our town *used* to be when you were small. But I like Starbucks coffee."

After a moment or two more, he opened the door and got in. He was still staring at the road ahead. Lights were coming on. We always seemed to have these discussions at dusk.

Apropos of nothing related to this moment save perhaps the hour, I remarked, "This used to be my favorite time of day to be on the golf course with your granddad. We often finished up just as darkness fell. It was like we were the last guys on the golf course anywhere in the world." I depressed the gas pedal and we started toward Starbucks. "Sentimental memory, I guess," I said, suddenly missing my own dad.

"*No,* it's not," he said with surprising vigor.

I reached over and patted his knee. The left knee of his jeans had an artful tear. "Son, listen, I'm sorry. Maybe the timing is off for this whole moving thing. If the job down south is meant to be, it'll still be there in a couple years. I'll tell David Woronoff that this isn't the time . . ."

He cut me off. "I don't *want* you to do that," he said, once again flaring. "I completely *get* why you're there. It makes complete sense, Dad! You just need to understand that even though you're here for two weeks every month, same as always, everything is different now. That's not good or bad. But it *is* different. Even when you're here, I know you really want to be there. In some ways, you've already moved."

"Point conceded," I reluctantly agreed. We eased into the Starbucks parking lot, and I switched off the car. "Between you and me, I'd love to have you with me down in North Carolina, but that isn't in the cards. In my experience, life rarely works out the way you think it should. There's no blueprint, no formula, and the timing is rarely what you might prefer. You have to follow your best instincts and pay attention to your heart. In another year or so, you'll be leaving this place behind—maybe forever. I don't want you to look back and regret having left too soon." I gave his knee another pat. "Besides, maybe you're going to win the state schoolboy championship, after all."

He gave me a stormy look. "That's not very funny."

"Who's laughing? I'm dead serious. It could happen."

And with this, I leaned over and kissed his once-downy cheek. That cheek now had a manly stubble on it. He was physically changing faster than the town of Topsham.

"Listen to me," I said. "You're a far better golfer than I was at your age. You've traveled farther and seen a hell of a lot more than I ever saw at your age. How many kids have played the Old Course *and* swum in the headwaters of the Amazon with killer piranha fish?"

"I didn't actually get to play the Old Course with you. I wasn't *old* enough, remember?"

"Fair enough," I said, fondly recalling that unforgettable afternoon six years before. "But you did a heck of a job as my caddie. And that day is coming." I used this moment to casually mention that I'd been officially invited to join the Royal and Ancient Golf Club of St. Andrews.

He looked at me with surprise. "Are you kidding?"

"Nope. It happened last fall. I forgot to tell you. Someday soon I get to kiss the captain's balls. We'll have a place to go have a nice beer the next time we play the Old Course and you kick my butt."

"That is *so* cool," he said, nodding.

"I'm glad you think so. I do, too."

We sat silently for a moment, watching a group of laughing

high school kids go into the Starbucks. They looked familiar, though I couldn't call up their names.

"Jack," I said quietly, "I'm incredibly proud of you—whatever you do from this point on. It doesn't matter to me if you win the state golf championship or earn a scholarship offer to college. What matters to me is that you follow your heart wherever it wants to take you." I added, "I'm sorry about what happened. I guess I'm not used to hearing the f-word like that. Do I really use it, too?"

He gave a fractional smile. "Mostly on the golf course when you're doing your Irish thing with Mr. Stewart."

"I should be ashamed. I'm a terrible role model. Please don't tell the R and A. They'll boot me out before I even get to have a beer at the clubhouse bar."

"I won't." He paused, glanced at me, and added, "Dad, almost everything I ever learned I learned from you."

I didn't know what to say. My throat was suddenly tightening. I was deeply, unexpectedly touched.

"That's a pretty *feckin'* scary thought, Nibs," I finally said, clearing my throat and putting on a poor brogue.

Nibs smiled and slapped my knee. "Let's go get coffee. And by the way, there are no piranhas in the upper Amazon."

ON A WARM, fragrant Indian-summer afternoon in early September, the Mt. Ararat Eagles opened their fall golf season against cross-river rivals Brunswick High on the Highland Green golf course.

Curiously, though hardly surprisingly, when once more I asked Jack how he would feel if I tagged along to watch him play, he again admitted that he would prefer I didn't because my presence would make him too nervous. So I merely watched him tee off and asked some kindly guardian angel to help the lad rediscover his missing Pinehurst game.

He didn't—he shot a poor forty-eight for the nine-hole match—but still somehow managed to win his first varsity game. Unfortunately, his team didn't fare well either, dropping a close decision to their rivals.

Six weeks later, in mid-October, I was back in North Carolina passing through Greensboro and heading for the Sandhills at dusk, the tail end of a trip home to watch Jack play the final hole of his first varsity golf season, when I made a detour to find a familiar figure on a park bench.

I parked and walked over to where Eddie Snow sat beneath the crab apple tree. Most of the tree's leaves were already gone. The forecast was for a cold autumn night. I'd brought a jacket I seldom wore anymore, a lined L. L. Bean coat. Eddie was wearing a thin sweater. He glanced up as I approached.

"Hey," I said casually. "I'm looking for my old friend Eddie Snow. Seen him around lately?"

The man shook his head faintly and looked down at his open road atlas.

"I wanted to say hello and give him this jacket," I explained. But Eddie remained silent.

"If I left this with you," I persisted gently, "do you think you could make sure he gets it?"

He gave an almost imperceptible nod, still looking at his atlas. It was still open to the Keystone State.

"I just drove through there," I said. Eddie glanced up at me with his ice blue eyes. They were clear, but he appeared confused.

"I came down through Pennsylvania this afternoon," I elaborated. "I was up in Maine watching my son Jack finish up his junior golf season, waiting at the final green with the other parents when he came off. He doesn't feel comfortable having me follow him around the course yet. I'm hopeful that by next season he may, though."

I was talking too much, almost babbling.

Eddie who wasn't Eddie looked down at his atlas again. So I stood for an awkward moment more and then gave up, laid the jacket across the back of the bench, said goodbye, and started back for my car. I needed to move along. I'd promised to have a drink with my landlady, Mrs. Cutler, at seven and was then going to have supper with Max and Myrtis.

"So how'd he do?" A voice stopped me as I walked away. I paused and turned around. Eddie who wasn't Eddie looked at me the way a skittish animal looks at a human stranger.

"He did great," I said with a smile. "He didn't play the way he always seems to play down in Pinehurst. But he won eight out of nine matches this year. His team finished fifth in the state."

Eddie nodded. His voice was soft, as if it were an instrument rarely used. "What's it like now in Maine?"

"Pretty cold," I said. "There will be snow soon. We're lucky to be down here."

"Do you live here now?"

"Yes. In Southern Pines."

"So you still play golf?" he asked, almost staring at me in the twlight. I took heart from the word *still*. Maybe he remembered me after all.

"Yes. I play with some guys down in Pinehurst. We're not very good, but we have a lot of laughs."

Eddie's gaze held mine for a moment more. "Do you like being a father?" he asked.

This question by a lost Idle Knight caught me off guard, but at least I didn't have to think about it.

"It's more satisfying than anything I can think of—even golf with your buddies," I replied.

Eddie who wasn't Eddie offered no more. He looked down at his atlas again, turning a page. As I was driving away, though, I thought I saw him pulling on the jacket.

THE WAY WE LEAD our days, wrote Hollins graduate Annie Dillard, is the way we lead our lives. The northern golf season was history, and sudden endings and unexpected paths seemed to be everywhere I turned that week.

One bracingly cold Sunday morning after a vigorous hike around the reservoir, Tom Stewart and I walked into the Short Stop only to hear that Brent Hackney had passed away in his sleep. I was saddened to learn this—having never taken Brent up on his offer to grab a beer and learn more about the new arts monthly he was editing, *PineStraw* magazine.

The next morning, Andi Hofmann, Patrick Barrett's mom, phoned me at *The Pilot* to let me know Marmalade the cat had gone missing from the porch of the Pine Crest. She'd gone out for an evening stroll and never returned.

"She was so old, we think she may have wandered off and died. Everyone around here is really sad. I wanted to let you know she was gone before you heard it from someone else. I know how close you two were."

"That's true," I said. "Though I don't think she really knew me from Nick Faldo's valet." I thanked Andi for letting me know an era had passed and asked how Patrick was spending his winter.

"He's playing in a lot of weekend tournaments, traveling everywhere it seems. A number of schools are interested in him. How about Jack?"

I told her Jack was starting his ice hockey season. His golf game was on ice until he came for the New Year holiday and maybe played with the rest of us in the second annual Ross Cross-Country. I also hoped we might be able to finish playing No. 2, I added, because last summer he, Bryan, Tom, and I had completed only thirteen holes when a thunderstorm chased us off the course. Jack and I had been two holes down to the Stewarts, but he'd just made a birdie when lightning struck.

"The rumor going around town is you've decided to stay permanently," Andi said. "I hope that's true. I can't help but think how pleased Harvie would be if he knew."

"I'm glad you think so," I said, hoping there was no truth to the folk wisdom that death always comes in threes, as my Southern Baptist grandmother used to say. I hated to think of losing another friend that week.

In mid-February, Tom Stewart turned sixty. Ilana threw him a huge surprise birthday bash at the Pinehurst Fair Barn. I got him there under the ruse of speaking to a group of corporate fat cats who wanted to pick his brain about fine golf art and would probably open up their checkbooks in simple gratitude for his expertise.

At one point, after he'd recovered from the shock of half the town gathered to wish him well, I collared my Idle Knight and thanked him for helping convince me it was time to return to my boyhood stomping ground. I also demanded to know how he intended to reinvent himself for the next ten years of his life. The off-year political elections were fast approaching, I pointed out.

"Maybe you should toss your golf cap into the ring and make another bid for Congress," I proposed over the din of the party band. "This time, the golfers of the Pines will put you over the top."

"It's tempting," Tom admitted with a laugh. "I can almost feel Mother Teresa urging me to do it. Or maybe that's just my boxer shorts riding up."

"I'll be your unofficial free media consultant," I proposed. "As your spin doctor, I feel obliged to ask if there are any compromising skeletons in your closet I should know about. We don't want a nasty October surprise."

He pretended to give it thought. "Only my membership in a secret society called the Idle Knights Adventure and Philosophy Club. They're so selective they make the Tin Whistles look like a bunch of Shriners in cheap fez hats."

"I hear they're so secret they don't even have a blazer patch yet."

"Hey, speaking of Tin Whistles," Tom continued, ignoring my jibe, "mark your calendar for the week after the Masters. The members of Augusta are honoring Dirty Derr with a lifetime achievement award. He covered sixty-two straight Masters, as you know. John was the Voice of the Masters."

"More importantly, he slow danced with Grace Kelly," I reminded him, pointing to the *other* man of the hour. At that moment, Derr was squiring my wife around the dance floor.

"Dirty Derr is something," Tom said admiringly, shaking his head. "You know, he turns ninety in October. I want to have a surprise party for *him*. I'm helping him pick out a new Masters blazer this week."

"We should immediately declare him our Idle Knight emeritus," I proposed. "That way you could buy him *two* blazers—one for the Master, another for his new Idle Knights blazer patch."

"Look at that," Tom said seriously, cutting short our banter. He was pointing over to a corner of the barn where Jack and Bryan were animatedly talking and doing something with their arms. After a few seconds I realized what it was. They were swinging invisible golf clubs.

"*There's* the next ten years for us both," Tom observed, placing his arm around my shoulders. "We're passing the torch to them, Brother Jim." He offered me his half-empty pint of stout, and I tapped the glass with my just-filled pint of Sam Adams.

"And not a minute too soon," I said. "By the way, how *is* our official Idle Knights blazer patch coming along? The official blazer committee asked me to officially ask you."

"It's coming. Get off my back about it, or I'll have the sergeant at arms throw you out of the club—or at least out of my birthday party."

"*I'm* the sergeant at arms."

"In that case, you'll have to throw yourself out." He grinned and winked. "But at least have some of the lovely birthday cake your wife made before you go."

Across the crowded, noisy room, David Woronoff was also thinking of his next ten years, as I learned after I wandered up on him a while later. "What would you say," he asked, "if I told you I think we should buy *PineStraw* magazine and you should become its editor?"

"I'd say I'm either very fortunate or the bar should cut you off. But either way, I'd probably say yes."

"It can't happen until after the Women's Open," David cautioned, displaying uncharacteristic reserve, "but it never hurts to think about the future. I'll bet our readers might love it."

"I'd love it, too," I admitted, thinking of the sweet irony of this unexpected turn in the road. Once again, I'd never seen this coming.

"You'd like the magazine's art director. Her name is Andie Rose. She and Brent Hackney started *PineStraw*. It's really her baby."

"I hope Brent would find it amusing," I said. "The former wire boy of his old newspaper taking over his magazine."

"It makes perfect sense," said David, the former paper-route kid turned newspaper publisher, the unexpected star of the venerable Daniels family media empire, suddenly sounding a great deal like Opti the Mystic. "I think that might actually make Brent happy."

A FEW NIGHTS AFTER the birthday party, I tagged along with Doc Morris on his evening rounds at Moore County Regional Hospital. When Grumpy Morrison had begun working there in the early 1960s, there were fewer than twenty physicians at Moore County Regional. Now there were more than two hundred. At one point during Walt's rounds, naturally enough, the subject of Harvie Ward came up.

"I remember the day we discovered his cancer," Walt said. "After I'd phoned UNC to get him into an advanced treatment program up there, Harvie proposed that we go out and play golf. That was how Harvie processed everything that happened to him—on the golf course, with a buddy."

"So how'd you play?"

Walt smiled. "To tell you the truth, I can't remember. I don't think we kept score. Just hit shots and talked. Harvie felt such peace on the golf course. In that way he was probably a lot like Hogan. The difference was, Harvie loved to be with his buddies, shooting the breeze and hitting great shots. He lived for that."

Not long after I called on the Last Amateur to say goodbye, Harvie invited Walt to accompany him on a final trip out west to Cypress Point and the San Francisco Golf Club where Harvie still holds the record for shooting sixty-three—twice. "He held up unbelievably well," Walt remembered. "He knew this was probably his last time on a golf course, and he played almost every shot along the way. It took all the strength he had, but it made him very happy. At one point, I'll never forget, he took my arm and thanked me for agreeing to go along with him—not because I was his physician, but because I was from here. Some things, he said, were just understood between sons of the Old North State."

The Last Amateur's final nine holes came out at Forest Creek, where he found such peace and happiness teaching young people to play the game. According to one member, Harvie played nine holes, shot even par, then called it a day. He never returned to the golf course.

He passed away peacefully in his sleep, with Joanne by his side, on September 4, 2004.

Two days before his death, as it transpired, I'd taken off with a group of foundation members from my alma mater to play a series of Ryder Cup–style matches at my golf club in North Devon, England. Several guys in the group were from the Pinehurst area and friends of Ward's, too.

We had no idea Harvie had died until Tom Stewart tracked me down at a hotel outside London a few days after the fact to tell me about Harvie's memorial service, held at the Members Club at Pinehurst.

"There wasn't a dry eye in the house—mostly from the funny stories everybody told about ole Harv," Tom explained. "We were all laughing and crying. I wish you could have been there. But I bet Harvie would rather have been with *you* guys."

LATE ON SUNDAY afternoon at the 62nd U.S Women's Open Championship at Pine Needles Lodge and Golf Club, I filed my final column for *The Pilot*'s *Open Daily* and went searching for my son.

David Woronoff had put him to work as a photographer's assistant to Joann Dost, Pebble Beach's official photographer, the Ansel Adams of golf, as she's been called. Joann and I had just completed our collaboration on Seminole's club history, and she had jumped at the chance to return to her roots as a working photojournalist at the National Women's Open, an assignment I helped engineer.

True to form, Joann hit the ground running in the Sandhills, stalking the world's best women players from dawn till dusk each day of the action. I'd caught only fleeting glimpses of her and her young assistant, a lanky kid in a reversed Titleist cap who lugged her gear and ferried her photo disks back to the championship's busy pressroom.

Every night that week, Jack seemed dangerously close to exhaustion but couldn't stop talking about Joann's work ethic and brilliant skills with a camera. The cover shots she and her teenaged assistant achieved for the front page of *The Pilot*'s daily tournament newspaper were outstanding.

Once again, however, I felt out of my element, or simply behind the times, snooping around the crowded championship site, more at home with the spectators than the professional players, almost none of whom I knew anything about. For one thing, nearly a third of the field hailed from Korea. But it was thanks to them that something unexpected and downright extraordinary happened.

On day four, after veteran Juli Inkster blew up her score and blew off our scheduled interview, desperate for a subject for the Saturday edition of the paper, I decided to go find a Korean print journalist to explain the phenomenon of what some wags in the press center were already calling the "Asian Invasion" and "the coming of the Seoul Sisters."

There were scores of Korean TV and Japanese print journalists on hand, it turned out, but only one Korean print journalist assigned to cover the American women's Tour full-time. His name was Min Suhk Choi.

I found Min standing beside the first tee where a Korean teenager named Ji-Yai Shin was teeing off. Shin was only a few shots out of the lead. As we tagged along after her, I asked Min to explain the explosive growth of golf in his country, and he did so, eloquently giving me a comprehensive rundown of how Se Ri Pak's breakthrough in 2001 had unleashed nothing less than a cultural tsunami of interest in golf back in his country, particularly among young women hungry to establish a name for themselves in such a traditional male-dominated society. It was a brilliant thumbnail analysis that gave me insight and a fine column on young Ji-Yai Shin.

Somewhere near the end of our walk together around the wonderful Ross-designed course, I asked Min how he'd come to be a golf journalist. Every writer's path to the game was different.

Mine, I'd come to realize, or simply finally to acknowledge, happened purely through my father's influence—a love of the game and the people who played it that had been passed along to me here in this same prehistoric seabed.

"I read a book," Min explained in his rudimentary but perfectly clear English. "This book made me wish to become a golf journalist."

"That's interesting," I said without thinking much about it—remembering my own love affair with the golf writing of Henry Longhurst, Charlie Price, and others of the trade who'd made Pinehurst either a temporary or permanent home.

"It was written by an American," Min volunteered. "It is about a man who took his father to England and Scotland to play golf. His father was dying." He paused, looking at me. I suddenly saw the emotion gathering in his eyes. He quietly explained, "My father gave me this book, you see. He died a short time later." He paused and added. "I became a golf journalist because of that book. It was my father's favorite book, too."

I didn't know what to say. Just then, a woman touched my arm.

"Excuse me," she said. "Aren't you Jim Dodson, *The Pilot* columnist?"

"Yes, ma'am," I managed, glancing at her, but mentally shaken by the revelation that had come from Min Suhk Choi.

"I know how you loved Marmalade, the cat at the Pine Crest," she said brightly. "Well, guess what? She's back." The woman was late middle-aged and blond. She was beaming. "Actually, it's not *the* Marmalade, but it is a small orange cat that could be her younger sister. And she's pregnant! I thought you might want to go over and see her—maybe write a column on the second coming of Marmalade."

"Yes, ma'am," I agreed, feeling light-headed. "I'll check it out. Thanks for the tip."

She waved and walked away. Min glanced at my press badge, which had been upside down during our stroll together through the pines. I turned it over and his face went pale.

"Are you the same James Dodson who wrote *Final Rounds*?" he asked me quietly, frowning.

"Apparently. I mean—yes, I think I must be. My friends call me Jim, though—and some worse than that," I said, attempting an Idle Knight jest.

Slowly, elegantly, gravely, Min bowed from the waist and extended his hand to me, a gesture of respect that left me speechless and flustered as we stood together on the busy tournament footpath. People in golf caps were glancing at us as they passed on each side, smiling and chatting, perhaps wondering what kind of peculiar Far Eastern ceremony was taking place.

"This is a great honor," Min said. "You are the reason I am here."

"No," I managed to get out, "my father's the reason we're *both* here. And my son, Jack, too." I explained that Jack was working inside the ropes of the tournament and loving every minute of it.

"Your father gave the game to you," said Min as we walked back to the clubhouse together. "And you now give the game to your son. Someday I would love to have a son, too."

A little later, still in a bit of a daze from this remarkable moment, I was standing with David Woronoff and Andie Rose at *The Pilot*'s place in the crowded pressroom when Min reappeared. He was holding a copy of *Final Rounds*. He asked if I would mind signing it. The book appeared to be well worn.

I introduced him to my boss and my new partner at *PineStraw.*

"So you liked that book, did you?" the cheerful boy publisher of the Sandhills asked Min.

Min nodded. Then he smiled without a trace of embarrassment. "I sleep with it by my pillow at night. Because of that book, I became a golf journalist. It makes me think about my father."

David, clearly as surprised as I'd been by this revelation, shook his head as we watched Min head back out to the golf course to catch up with the hard-charging Seoul Sisters, several of whom were in the hunt for the 62nd Open trophy.

"There's a sign from heaven that you were meant to come back here," David pleasantly observed. He waited a beat and wryly added, "Even so, I can't imagine sleeping with you anywhere *near* my pillow."

BY THE TIME I got down to the final green to try to find my son, the 62nd U.S. Women's Open was history.

Cristie Kerr had come from behind to win. Kerr was perhaps the LPGA's most remarkable comeback story in years. Following a brilliant junior golf career in Miami, the former Curtis Cupper and low amateur at the U.S Women's Open at Pine Needles in 1996 decided to forgo college and turn professional at age eighteen. With a world of high expectation riding on her slim shoulders, one major daily labeled her the "female Tiger Woods." Another simply tagged her "Can't Miss Kerr."

But miss she did. Almost overnight, everything began to go wrong for Kerr. Her parents split up, and her family—having sacrificed everything to pay for her golf dreams—was forced to file for bankruptcy. Kerr fell into depression and medicated herself with food, saw her weight balloon to 190 pounds, producing back spasms that restricted her once-free-flowing golf swing. By 1999, she was on a downward spiral and forced to return to the Tour Qualifying School.

Her epiphany came when she reached rock bottom, and she began working with a nutritionist and a fitness coach, rebuilding her game by "going back to the basics," as I heard her say to another reporter that week at Pine Needles. One year later and sixty pounds lighter, sporting contact lenses and a stylish new hairdo, Kerr found her game and jumped to number twelve on the Tour money list. The next season, in 2002, she finally won her first LPGA event. Now, five years beyond that and just twenty-nine years old—the same age as Ben Hogan when he arrived in the Pines and had his life and career suddenly reborn —Kerr finally had a major championship title to her name.

From a spot on the hill near the pro shop, I had watched "Comeback Kerr" drop her winning putt into the cup, bow her head, burst into tears, then scoop her ball from the cup and toss it to the wildly cheering gallery. With two quick steps, she then leapt ecstatically into the arms of her caddie-husband, Erik Stevens.

That's when I spotted Jack.

He was kneeling inside the ropes a few paces from the new U.S. Open champion while Joann Dost calmly recorded the tearful, historic moment. I walked down the hill to watch the presentation of the championship trophy and was pleased to see Jack still kneeling in the front row of the huge photo corps assembled on the green. With his Titleist golf cap reversed and three cameras slung around his neck, he looked for all the world like a wily veteran of the photojournalism game.

For the second time that day, I had to blink back tears.

THE DAY BEFORE he went home to qualify for his final high school golf season, we went to finish our business on No. 2, to play another father-son match with the Stewarts. But the boys had another plan in mind.

"Jack and I want to play you two," Bryan explained, grinning slyly.

"Dads against sons," Jack jauntily added. "No strokes given or accepted."

"There's not a chance on earth you guys can beat us," I said with a laugh, glancing at Tom.

"Got to love their ambition," Tom said, surprised, but also grinning. "It's nature's way. But can you lads spell ten-and-eight?"

Jack played poorly on the outward nine. But on the home nine he shot one over par to finish with an 82, making a pair of birdies on closing holes. Bryan brilliantly shot 76. Tom shot 79. I shot 78.

The sons beat the fathers on the final hole to win the match, one-up.

Tom was visibly moved. "The torch has been passed," he whispered to me after we all shook hands and left the green to go get a farewell supper at Dugan's Pub. "He'll be beating you any day now, pal. Wait and see."

BEFORE I GOT UP at speak to the seventy-fifth anniversary dinner of the Maine Seniors' Golf Association many weeks later, a sportswriter from the Portland newspaper leaned over and whispered, "Tell me something. What's wrong with Mt. Ararat's golf team? I picked them to be first or second in the state. I thought your son might be tearing up the golf course by now."

I smiled, unsure what to say. Once again Jack had come home from the Carolina Sandhills brimming with confidence and a game clicking on all cylinders. Once again after a promising start, he faltered badly in competition, always finding a creative way to blow up his score with one or two bad holes—playing most of the season stuck in the fourth or fifth slot, frustrating both himself and his coach.

On the plus side, he'd managed to win every match he'd played, but his scoring average was at least seven or eight strokes higher than it had been on much more difficult courses down south. With each passing week, he grew more and more frustrated—talking with me sometimes for upward of an hour on the telephone about the mistakes he was making. Each time, I counseled patience and a concentration on the basics, urging him to trust his swing, stay loose, and try to have fun. Someday soon, I promised, it would all come together.

So, naturally, I had no answers for the reporter. Instead, I smiled and remembered something I'd personally learned from my time in the Sandhills.

"Golf and life are both subject to change without notice," I said to the reporter.

Another summer had come and gone. Another autumn was rapidly drawing the curtain down on the golf season in Maine. Jack's official high school golf career had one match to go, a home match scheduled for the next afternoon against a strong team from Augusta.

An hour before dusk, I went out to watch the team finish its season. Several parents and the coach were clustered around the final green, a difficult par-three. A chilly evening was descending when the final group, Jack's group, appeared on the tee.

I could see Jack had the honors, a good sign. But he hit a poor shot, missing the green and landing his ball in the edge of the woods. Moments later, from an impossible lie, he chipped short of the green. A few moments after that, he nearly holed the chip, tapping in for a bogey four.

He walked toward us, shaking his head. His body English said how disappointed he was with his play. He signed his card and handed it to his coach. His coach looked at it, then suddenly grinned. "I've been waiting for this moment for two years," he declared.

"So how'd it go, Old Champ?" I asked my son, as surprised as I was pleased to have misjudged his body English.

"If I'd just made that damn par," he allowed, "I'd have shot even par."

As it was, Jack's score established both a team low score for the year, and—for the moment at least—the high school record for his old man's golf course. The team win, a romp as it turned out, put the Eagles in their conference championship game, scheduled for the next afternoon against Messalonskee over at Martindale Country Club in Auburn.

As we left the club, an exultant Jack asked if he could borrow my car that night to go have pizza and celebrate with the golf team. The old Volvo was in the shop. I told him that would be fine—for once skipping the automotive safety speech.

"Dad," he said suddenly, jauntily slapping my arm, "I need to say something to you. Okay?"

"I'm all ears, Junior."

"Thanks for making me come back here to finish school. I'm *so* glad you and Mom did. Otherwise, this never would have happened."

"I'm glad you feel that way," I said, once again touched by his candor. "Golf is full of nice surprises," I added, leaving the rest of it for him to someday discover.

The next afternoon in Auburn, for the first—and last—time ever, Jack invited me to follow the match with the parents from Messalonskee. This time I gave him no advice. He hardly needed it anymore. It was perhaps the most enjoyable walk of my life.

Jack played brilliantly, his best round ever in my estimation, driving the ball long and straight and calmly pulling off at least two miraculous escapes for pars from impossible lies. I noticed that he'd developed a nice preshot routine and a precise but measured putting stroke. Jack was no longer using Harvie Ward's old White Hot. That had migrated back to me. He was now using a new PING putter of his own choosing.

He won his match two-and-one against a fine and determined young player. A couple of his pals on the team were cheering "D-One! D-One!" as he came off the final hole, after nearly holing out from a hundred yards—a cheeky nickname, I learned, derived from his unfulfilled ambition to earn a golf scholarship. That clearly wasn't going to happen now, but he handled the ribbing with grace. Better yet, his Eagles were the new conference champs and headed to the state championship roundup at Natanis Golf Course, in Augusta.

THAT NEXT SUNDAY AFTERNOON, he and I drove up to play the new Natanis Tomahawk Course designed by my friend Dan Maples. It was a rugged beast carved through a dense evergreen forest and around bogs.

We played the first nine holes with a local physician and his older brother, who gave Jack useful pointers around the narrow and unforgiving track. After they left us, we walked along playing and talking in a manner that reminded me of the late afternoon rounds with my dad. The sun was almost behind the trees when we reached the final tee, a long downhill par-four to a green tucked behind a mirror-still pond.

"You know, Dad," Jack said after we'd hit our tee shots and started after them, "I really like playing with you at this time of day."

"I do, too," I said. "Your grandfather and I had some great talks and a hell of lot of close matches playing till dark, just like this."

"Who won most of the time?"

"After high school, I did. Before that, he won. It wasn't even close."

"I hope I do at least this well on Tuesday. They say eighty-two or eighty-three will get you into the individual finals."

"I hope you do, too. But whatever happens, you've had a great high school career. I'm very proud of you, Jack." For the record, his varsity was an impressive 16-4-2. This from a young man who'd played nowhere near his abilities.

I reminded him that his mom and I planned to pay for his college—but reiterated that there was nothing to stop him from playing his way onto a Division I golf squad if his game matured a little more. I also told him an interesting story John Derr had told me during the Hickory Open Championship at Mid Pines, where we'd played as partners a few weeks before.

One late autumn evening when the Voice of the Masters was at Princeton to broadcast the Ivy League football championship, he and a companion slipped off to play the Princeton golf course and saw an odd-looking figure approaching them in the dusk.

"His hair was wild and white. He was dressed in the long great coat for which he was famous. It was Albert Einstein. We stopped and chatted with the great man, and at one point I asked Einstein if he played golf. He looked at me, a little wild-eyed, I thought, and shook his head. 'No, I do not. I tried golf once and found it was *much* too difficult.'" Derr gave me one of his roguish smiles. "Every time I play badly, I remind myself that not even *Einstein* could figure out this damned game."

I wedged up and two-putted for an eighty-two on Dan Maples's fine Yankee golf course. My son wedged up and two-putted for an eighty-one.

"Congratulations," I told him. "You just beat your old man. Life as we know it will never be the same."

"I'm not so sure," Jack said, examining the card as we walked toward the empty parking lot where only my blue Subaru sat waiting to take us home. "We were so busy talking, I'm not sure if I got all the scores right."

I slipped my arm around his broad shoulders.

"Doesn't matter," I said. "I'll never forget today."

"Me either," he said. Moments later the math was double checked. He had, in fact, beaten me by a stroke.

IT WAS EVENING when I reached the porch of the Pine Crest Inn. The final hymn of the day had finished playing in the village chapel bell tower, and a lively Friday-night crowd was on hand, attacking the Chipping Board and noisily reliving their golf adventures over cocktails.

I bought a beer, opened my notebook, and sat down in a rocker near the front steps to jot down some ideas for the upcoming issues of *PineStraw*. I took a swallow of beer and breathed in the spicy evening air. It smelled—and felt—like home. This time I even knew the name of the hymn.

Naturally I found myself thinking about Jack. Earlier that week he'd gone back to Natanis and shot his worst competitive score of the year, a round that started with an ugly nine on the opening par-five he'd birdied just days before. By the time he'd recovered his game on the back side, even making a pair of birdies, the cause was lost. The state high school championship was history and so were his high school golf days. His teammates fared only slightly better; the Eagles once more finished fifth in the state.

On the positive side of the situation, he informed me that the college he was most interested in attending was an hour or so away from Pinehurst and Southern Pines. Elon had jumped to the top of his list. With luck, I was thrilled to think, he might wind up attending school, and playing a little golf, in the Old North State after all.

Just then, a small orange cat appeared from beneath the Pine Crest's steps and hopped up on the bench beside me. I reached over and let her sniff my hand. After a wary moment or two, she permitted me to scratch her tiny head. She did look a lot like the late, great Marmalade.

"You from around here?" a man's voice pleasantly asked.

He was an older guy, sitting in a wooden chair, obviously waiting for someone to arrive. He was holding a golf magazine and a glass of whiskey.

"I am," I said. "You?"

"Down from Wisconsin with my business partners. This is one hell of a place, isn't it? I could move here tomorrow."

"I know what you mean," I agreed.

As I said this, I was thinking about how Dick Tufts had passed something wonderful along to Harvie Ward and how Harvie had passed it along to a fatherless Payne Stewart. Arnie's dad, Deacon, had passed it along to him, just as my dad had passed it along to me. Tom Stewart was passing it to Bryan, and perhaps I'd even passed it along to Jack. Truthfully, I still wasn't certain what *it* was, though I knew it was very real.

"That cat wouldn't let me near her. But she seems to like you," the man pointed out, smiling.

The new Marmalade was softly purring. Her babies, I knew, had all been given away. But she'd found a new home, too.

"That's nice to think," I said. "But we're really just getting acquainted."

Someone approached the hotel's steps in the dark. I realized it was Tom Stewart, having closed up his shop around the corner. He was coming to have a beer with me and get the lowdown on the end of Jack's high school golf career.

He handed me something in a brown envelope.

"Open it up," he said, suppressing a good Irish grin. "I've got an idea about convincing the Pine Crest to turn their bar into a golf writers hall of fame. Who know, you might eventually get your own official barstool between Henry Longhurst and Bob Drum or Dick Taylor."

I opened the envelope and took out a blazer patch for the Idle Knights Adventure and Philosophy Club. It was a thing of beauty.

"So what do you think?" Tom demanded. "Worth the wait?"

"It's beautiful," I said, genuinely impressed.

"Good," he said, slapping me on the back. "Welcome home. You can buy the beer."

Over our beers, Tom had another big surprise for me.

"I've finally figured out what I'm going to do with the rest of my life," he said.

"Let me guess. Start a spiritual retreat for aging, burned-out golfers—Findhorn in the Pines," I said.

"Nope. I'm going to open a book store," he revealed. "That's always been a major dream of mine—to have a place where readers and visiting writers and assorted Idle Knights can gather to swap tales and shoot the breeze."

He said he hoped to have the Pinehurst Village Book Shop open within a year.

"That's wonderful news," I said. "I'll be your best customer. I'll actually *pay* to read your books."

"Great. But your first book is on me," Tom said, presenting me the copy of Sweet Sandy Herd's *My Golfing Life* that I'd been reading on the sly in his shop for well over a year.

"Oh, I couldn't accept this," I said, deeply touched by his continuing generosity. "This thing is a classic—and an expensive one at that."

"Fair enough," Tom said with a grin, taking back the rare book. "But at least let me buy the next round of beer."

ACKNOWLEDGMENTS

Thirty-five years ago, as a cub reporter for the *Greensboro Daily News,* I paid a call on Richard Petty, the so-called King of NASCAR, at his rural home south of the city. Near the end of our interview, as we leaned together on the hood of his famous sky blue number 43 stock car, I asked Petty, who was rapidly approaching the end of his reign as his sport's leading figure, if he had any advice for a young and ambitious driver starting out. Perhaps I had the unknown journalistic highway ahead of me in mind.

The King of NASCAR didn't even have to think about it.

"Never forget your raisins."

"I'm sorry," I said, thrown off by his strong Southern accent, "never forget *what*?"

Petty looked at me and smiled almost tenderly. "Never forget where you *come* from, son — the important values and people who raised you up. Those are your *raisins*."

This unexpected homecoming simply wouldn't have happened without the strong influence of several lovely folks who "raised me up" and to whom I feel the deepest gratitude.

To begin, I must thank Tom Stewart for introducing me a decade ago to Harvie Ward, one of the classiest acts golf ever produced, and for gently pestering me to finally wise up and come home to stay. Ditto young David Woronoff, the publisher of *The Pilot*, an award-winning and innovative newspaper that has twice been named the top community newspaper in America for a very good reason: they love what they do. Many thanks to the staff and employees of *The Pilot*, and to editor Steve Bouser especially, an endlessly patient and creative bloke, who has the unenviable task of editing my weekly Sunday essay for the paper.

I'd also like to extend warmest affections to president Nancy Gray and the English department at Hollins University, a marvelous institution that was kind or foolish enough to invite me to serve as its writer-in-residence for an unforgettable winter of my life.

Finally, I must thank my wife, Wendy, who had the good sense to hand me my car keys and shove me out the door to go say a proper goodbye to a dying friend; and my son, Jack, who capped off this journey home by helping his old man rediscover what is most valuable and precious about life's most enduring and revealing game: the relationships we make along the way.